AIR FRYER COOKBOC

for beginners and advanced users

400 all unique and healty recipes to fry, bake, roast & grill.
With pictures and nutritional information

BY

Linda S. Jones

COPYRIGHT 2020

1. ROASTED BROCCOLI AND CAULIFLOWER 16

2. APPLE FRITTERS 17

3. BEIGNETS 18

4. ROSEMARY GARLIC POTATOES 19

5. BABY BACK RIBS 20

6. SHRIMP 21

7. ASPARAGUS FRIES 22

8. SALT AND VINEGAR CHICKPEAS 23

9. BUFFALO RANCH CHICKPEAS 24

10. ACTIFRIED ORANGE SESAME CAULIFLOWER 25

11. RANCH PORK CHOPS 27

12. BROWN SUGAR AND PECAN ROASTED APPLES 28

13. MINI PEPPERS STUFFED WITH CHEESE AND SAUSAGE 29

14. PERUVIAN CHICKEN DRUMSTICKS WITH GREEN CREMA 30

15. TATER TOTS 32

16. BBQ BABY BACK RIBS 33

17. MAC AND CHEESE BALLS 34

18. SOY GINGER SHISHITO PEPPERS 35

19. ROASTED BRUSSELS SPROUTS WITH MAPLE-MUSTARD MAYO 36

20. ROASTED SWEET PEPPERS AND ONIONS 37

21. CARROTS WITH BALSAMIC GLAZE 38

22. CAULIFLOWER TOTS 39

23. TAJIN APPLE CHIPS 40

24. SHRIMP BOIL 41

25. GREEN BEANS WITH SPICY DIPPING SAUCE 42

26. EGG ROLLS 43

27. ROASTED RAINBOW VEGETABLES 44

28. PURPLE YAM FRIES WITH SOUR CREAM SRIRACHA SAUCE 45

29. APPLE PIES 46

30. POPCORN CHICKEN 47

31. TOSTONES 48

32. ROASTED BANANAS 49

33. STEAK TIPS AND PORTOBELLO MUSHROOMS 50

34. HONEY-CAJUN CHICKEN THIGHS 51

35. BLACKENED CHICKEN BREAST 53

36. CRISPY RANCH AIR FRYER NUGGETS 54

37. TARTAR SAUCE-BATTERED FISH STICKS 55

38. HONEY-SRIRACHA AIR FRYER WINGS 56

39. TEMPURA VEGGIES 57

40. PULL-APART PEPPERONI-CHEESE BREAD 58

41. PUMPKIN SEEDS 59

42. OLIVE-BRINED TURKEY BREAST 60

43. CHINESE FIVE-SPICE AIR FRYER BUTTERNUT SQUASH FRIES 61

44. PAKORAS 62

45. BANG-BANG CHICKEN 63

46. KOREAN CHICKEN WINGS 64

47. CRISPY KETO FRIED CHICKEN 66

48. STUFFED MUSHROOMS WITH SOUR CREAM 67

49. EASY SPRING ROLLS 68

50. STUFFED AIR FRYER POTATOES 69

51. CELERY ROOT FRIES 70

52. TEX MEX HASH BROWNS 72

53. RATATOUILLE, ITALIAN-STYLE 73

54. STUFFING-FILLED PUMPKIN 74

55. GUILT-FREE RANCH ZUCCHINI CHIPS 75

56. VEGETARIAN CHICKEN TENDERS 76

57. CHINESE PINEAPPLE PORK 78

58. POTATO-SKIN WEDGES 79

59. FALAFEL 80

60. SEXY MEATLOAF 81

61. TRIPLE-CHOCOLATE OATMEAL COOKIES 83

62. SHRIMP 84

63. PEANUT BUTTER & JELLY S'MORES 85

64. JERK PORK SKEWERS WITH BLACK BEAN AND MANGO SALSA 86

65. LOBSTER TAILS WITH LEMON-GARLIC BUTTER 87

66. MEDITERRANEAN VEGETABLE MEDLEY 88

67. CAULIFLOWER WITH ALMONDS AND PARMESAN 89

68. CHOCOLATE CHIP COOKIE BITES 90

69. CRISPY FISH PO' BOYS WITH CHIPOTLE SLAW 92

70. DONUT STICKS 93

71. DOUBLE CHERRY MINI EGG ROLLS 94

72. SESAME-CRUSTED COD WITH SNAP PEAS 95

73. SHORTBREAD COOKIE FRIES 96

74. TATER TOTS WITH GOCHUJANG CHEESE SAUCE 97

75. EASY BAKED POTATOES 98

76. TURKEY BREAST 99

77. COCONUT CHICKEN 100

78. OLD BAY CHICKEN WINGS 101

79. BRATWURST BITES WITH SPICY BEER MUSTARD 102

80. ZUCCHINI CURLY FRIES 103

81. PORK MEATBALLS 104

82. FRIED GREEN TOMATOES IN THE AIR FRYER 105

83. MUSHROOMS 106

84. VEGETARIAN CAULIFLOWER AND CHICKPEA TACOS 107

85. FINGERLING POTATOES WITH DIP 108

86. FINGERLING POTATOES 109

87. BLACKENED FISH TACOS 110

88. LATKES 111

89. SAUSAGE PATTIES 112

90. CRISPY BREADED PORK CHOPS 113

91. BALSAMIC GLAZED CHICKEN WINGS 114

92. CHOCOLATE CAKE IN AN AIR FRYER 116

93. KOREAN FRIED CHICKEN WINGS 117

94. SPICY ROASTED PEANUTS 118

95. ONION BHAJI 119

96. LUMPIA 120

97. MINI SCOTCH EGGS 121

98. KETO THUMBPRINT COOKIES 122

99. BUTTERNUT SQUASH HOME FRIES 123

100. VEGAN CHILI CHEESE FRIES 124

101. PAO DE QUEIJO 125

102. OVEN PORK JERKY 127

103. DRY RUB CHICKEN WINGS 128

104. BBQ CHICKEN TENDERS 129

105. BUTTERMILK FRIED CHICKEN 130

106. GOLDEN FRIEDCHICKEN TENDERS 131

107. MAPLE CHICKEN THIGHS 132

108. CHICKEN THIGH SCHNITZEL 134

109. SESAME CHICKEN THIGHS 135

110. BBQ CHEDDAR-STUFFED CHICKEN BREASTS 136

111. KOREAN FRIED CHICKEN 137

112. HEALTHIER BANG BANG CHICKEN IN THE AIR FRYER 138

113. CORNFLAKE CRUSTED CHICKEN TENDERS 139

114. POPCORN-CRUSTED POPCORN CHICKEN 140

115. GLUTEN FREE FRESH CHERRY CRUMBLE 142

116. CRISPY NACHOS PRAWNS 143

117. CHEESY GARLIC BREAD 144

118. VEGAN STUFFED BELL PEPPERS 145

119. APPLE DUMPLINGS 146

120. TACO DOGS 147

121. AIR FRYER PORK CHOPS (NO BREADING) 147

122. STUFFING BALLS 149

123. OKRA FRIES 150

124. HASSELBACK POTATOES 151

125. SALMON NUGGETS 152

126. CRISPY COD 153

127. CORN DOGS 154

128. TORI'S PUMPKIN BAGELS 155

129. STEAK AND CHEESE MELTS 156

130. STEAK FOR FAJITAS 157

131. PORK RIBS WITH GINGER GLAZE 158

132. TAJIN SWEET POTATO FRIES 160

133. INDIAN OKRA IN THE AIR FRYER (KURKURI BHINDI) 161

134. TURKEY BREAKFAST SAUSAGE LINKS 162

135. SALMON PATTIES 163

136. COCONUT CHICKEN IN THE AIR FRYER 164

137. BURGERS 165

138. FRIED GREEN TOMATOES 166

139. KETO CHICKEN WINGS 167

140. VEGAN BUFFALO TOFU BITES 167

141. ZUCCHINI FRIES 169

142. MEATBALLS 170

143. BACON-CHORIZO TATER TOT DRESSING 171

144. CRISPY RANCH MAC AND CHEESE BALLS IN THE AIR FRYER 172

145. KETO SALMON CAKES WITH SRIRACHA MAYO 173

146. ROOT VEGETABLES WITH VEGAN AIOLI 174

147. HUSH PUPPIES 176

148. CRUMBED CHICKEN TENDERLOINS (AIR FRIED) 177

149. OREOS 178

150. CRUMBED FISH 179

151. BREAKFAST FRITTATA 179

152. LEMON PEPPER SHRIMP 180

153. CORN ON THE COB 181

154. FRENCH TOAST STICKS 182

155. KETO GARLIC CHEESE BREAD 183

156. SWEET POTATO HASH 184

157. CINNAMON AND SUGAR DOUGHNUTS 185

158. BREAKFAST TOAD-IN-THE-HOLE TARTS 186

159. CHURROS 187

160. ONION RINGS 188

161. ROASTED ASIAN BROCCOLI 189

162. PARMESAN POTATOES RECIPE 190

163. PALEO FISH STICKS 191

164. THAI SALMON PATTIES 193

165. TANDOORI PANEER NAAN PIZZA 194

166. CAULIFLOWER CHICKPEA TACOS (VEGAN) 196

167. PERFECT SALMON 197

168. VEGAN BUFFALO CAULIFLOWER 198

169. STEAK AND ASPARAGUS BUNDLES 199

170. LOW CARB TANDOORI CHICKEN 200

171. SWEET POTATO TOTS 202

172. BANANA BREAD 203

173. AVOCADO FRIES 204

174. SOUTHERN STYLE CATFISH WITH GREEN BEANS 205

175. MAKES DELICIOUS ROASTED BROCCOLI WITH CHEESE SAUCE 206

176. STRAWBERRY POP TARTS 207

177. LIGHTEN UP EMPANADAS 208

178. PEACH HAND PIES 209

179. AIR-FRIED CALZONES 210

180. WHOLE-WHEAT PIZZAS 211

181. DOUBLE-GLAZED CINNAMON BISCUIT BITES 212

182. SPANAKOPITA BITES 213

183. SWEET POTATO CHIPS 214

184. CRISPY TOASTED SESAME TOFU 215

185. FLAX SEED FRENCH TOAST STICKS WITH BERRIES 217

186. CRISPY, SWEET BEET CHIPS 218

187. CRISPY VEGGIE QUESADILLAS 219

188. LOADED GREEK FETA FRIES 220

189. BREAKFAST BOMBS 221

190. PORK DUMPLINGS WITH DIPPING SAUCE 222

191. CURRY CHICKPEAS 223

192. BAGEL KALE CHIPS 224

193. SHRIMP SPRING ROLLS WITH SWEET CHILI SAUCE 225

194. FISH AND CHIPS 226

195. BACON AVOCADO FRIES 228

196. ANTIPASTO EGG ROLLS 229

197. CHEESY BEEF EMPANADAS 230

198. HOMEMADE CANNOLI 232

199. BROWNIES 234

200. BRUSSELS SPROUTS CHIPS 235

201. CHEESE BURGER 236

202. BLOOMING ONION 237

203. MOZZARELLA STICKS 238

204. GARLIC HERB TURKEY BREAST 239

205. CINNAMON ROLLS 240

206. PARMESAN FRIED TORTELLINI 242

207. FRIED PICKLES 243

208. S'MORES 244

209. MOLTEN LAVA CAKE 245

210. CRUSTLESS CHEESECAKE 246

211. VEGAN BEIGNETS 247

212. BLUEBERRY HAND PIES 249

213. SPICED APPLES 250

214. FLOURLESS KEY LIME CUPCAKES 251

215. BANANA S'MORES 253

216. CHURROS WITH MEXICAN CHOCOLATE 254

217. BRAZILIAN GRILLED PINEAPPLE 255

218. FRUIT CRUMBLE MUG CAKES 256

219. SOFT CHOCOLATE BROWNIES 258

220. OVEN APPLE PIE 259

221. CHOCOLATE ECLAIRS 261

222. PINEAPPLE CAKE 263

223. BRITISH LEMON TARTS 264

224. BAKED OATMEAL 265

225. WONTONS APPETIZER 267

226. TOASTED RAVIOLI 269

227. BREADED MUSHROOMS 270

228. CARROTS WITH HONEY 271

229. CHUNKY CRAB CAKE 272

230. COUNTRY FRIED STEAK 273

231. MONTE CRISTO SANDWICH 274

232. BLUEBERRY LEMON MUFFIN 275

233. MEXICAN-STYLE STUFFED CHICKEN BREASTS 276

234. MEATLOAF 277

235. SHRIMP A LA BANG BANG 278

236. SHRIMP A LA BANG BANG 279

237. ROSEMARY POTATO WEDGES 280

238. POTATO HAY 281

239. ROASTED CAULIFLOWER 282

240. DONUTS 283

241. SWEET AND SPICY BRUSSELS SPROUTS 284

242. TURKEY BREASTS 285

243. SWEET POTATO DESSERT FRIES 286

244. ZESTY RANCH FISH FILLETS 287

245. CHURRO BITES 288

246. CRISPY BREADED PORK CHOPS 290

247. COCONUT SHRIMP WITH PIÑA COLADA DIP 291

248. ZUCCHINI CORN FRITTERS 292

249. FRENCH FRIES 294

250. KOREAN FRIED CAULIFLOWER 295

251. TOASTED COCONUT FRENCH TOAST 296

252. SALMON 297

253. ZUCCHINI ENCHILADAS 298

254. EGG AND CORN SALAD 299

255. PARMESAN SHRIMP 301

256. HONEY CHIPOTLE BACON WRAPPED TATER TOT BOMBS 302

257. HOT DOGS 303

258. JALAPENO POPPERS 304

259. BAKED THAI PEANUT CHICKEN EGG ROLLS 305

260. GARLIC MUSHROOMS 306

261. PERSONAL PIZZA 307

262. GARLIC PARMESAN ZUCCHINI 308

263. HAMBURGERS 309

264. CHEESY TACO CRESCENTS 310

265. SAUSAGE BALLS 311

266. WHOLE WHEAT CHICKEN NUGGETS 312

267. CAJUN BREAKFAST SAUSAGE 313

268. WHOLE SALMON CAKES 314

269. TWICE AIR FRIED POTATOES 316

270. TEX MEX CAULIFLOWER RICE 317

271. CRISPY AVOCADO TACOS 319

272. TORTILLA CHISP 320

273. CRUMBLE WITH BLUEBERRIES AND APPLE 321

274. MADAGASCAN BEAN STEW 322

275. EGGPLANT BACON 323

KETO RECIPES 325

276. RIBEYE WITH COFFEE AND SPICE 325

277. BULGOGI BURGERS 326

278. BOURBON BACON BURGER 328

279. , EGG, SAUSAGE AND CHEESE, BREAKFAST BURRITO 329

280. CARNE ASADA 330

281. LOW-CARB KETO BEEF SATAY 331

282. PALEO KETO CHICKEN COCONUT MEATBALLS 332

283. CRUNCHY AVOCADO FRIES 333

284. CORNISH HEN 334

285. BRUSSEL SPROUTS 335

286. AIR-FRIED OKRA 336

287. EASY COCONUT PIE 337

288. GLUTEN-FREE LOW-CARB CHOCOLATE LAVA CAKE 338

289. EASY OMELETTE 339

290. PARMESAN DILL FRIED PICKLE CHIPS 340

291. FRIED CATFISH 341

292. GREEK SPANAKOPITA PIE 342

293. CRUNCHY BASIL CROUTONS 343

294. FRIED RAVIOLI 344

295. ROSEMARY GARLIC GRILLED PRAWNS 345

296. BEEF SCHNITZEL 346

297. VEGAN PECAN CRUSTED EGGPLANT 347

298. SPINACH FRITTATA 348

299. BROWNIES AFTER DARK 349

300. BANANA BREAD 350

301. BANANA MUFFINS 351

302. CHEESY GARLIC BREAD IN 353

303. PINEAPPLE STICKS WITH YOGHURT DIP 354

DESSERT RECIPES 355

304. NUTELLA-BANANA SANDWICHES 355

305. STRAWBERRY LEMONADE VEGAN POP TARTS 356

306. MOZZARELLA STICKS 358

307. SUGARED DOUGH DIPPERS WITH CHOCOLATE AMARETTO SAUCE 359

308. CHURRO DOUGHNUT HOLES 360

309. ZEBRA BUTTER CAKE 361

310. EASY CHOCOLATE SOUFFLE 362

311. THAI-STYLE FRIED BANANAS 363

VEGAN RECIPES 365

312. CHEESE SAMBOOSA 365

313. LEMON TOFU 366

314. CLASSIC FALAFEL 367

315. VEGAN CORN FRITTERS 369

316. LOW CARB CRISPY SEASONED JICAMA FRIES 370

317. CRISPY BAKED ARTICHOKE FRIES 371

318. BOW TIE PASTA CHIPS 373

319. PORTOBELLO MUSHROOM PIZZAS WITH HUMMUS 374

320. RADISH HASH BROWNS 375

321. SWEET SOUR PORK 376

322. COPYCAT TACO BELL CRUNCH WRAPS 377

323. RANCH STYLE CHICK PEAS 378

324. GLUTEN FREE ONION RINGS 379

325. ZUCCHINI PARMESAN CHIPS 380

326. AIR FRYER VEGETABLES 381

327. PORK TAQUITOS 382

328. PORTABELLO MUSHROOM PIZZAS 383

329. SHRIMP SCAMPI 384

330. JUICY BEEF KEBABS 385

331. SHRIMP EGGROLLS 386

332. STEAK WITH HERB BUTTER 388

333. HONEY ROASTED CARROTS 389

334. VEGAN SUSHI BURRITO WITH TOFU 390

335. TOFU AND VEGETABLES 391

336. ORANGE TOFU 393

337. CAULIFLOWER ARANCHINI BALLS 394

338. BABA GANOUSH 396

339. PEANUT BUTTER AND JELLY DONUTS 397

340. COCONUT FRENCH TOAST 399

341. CASHEWS BACON BIT 400

342. VEGETARIAN SOUTHWEST EGGROLLS 401

343. SWEET POTATO CAULIFLOWER PATTIES 403

344. SWEET POTATO HASH BROWNS 404

345. POTATO SKINS 405

346. SOUTHERN YELLOW SQUASH 406

347. MEDITERRANEAN VEGETABLES 407

348. ZUCCHINI, YELLOW SQUASH, AND CARROTS 408

349. CAULIFLOWER WINGS 409

350. AVOCADO FRIES WITH LIME DIPPING SAUCE 410

351. BEEF KABOBS 411

352. CAJUN SHRIMP DINNER 412

353. MAPLE SOY GLAZED SALMON 413

354. FISH FINGER SANDWICHES 414

355. KETO JICAMA FRIES 415

356. RASPBERRY BALSAMIC SMOKED PORK CHOPS 417

357. HAM AND CHEESE TURNOVERS 418

358. WASABI CRAB CAKES 419

359. SWEET AND SOUR PINEAPPLE PORK 420

360. BOURBON BACON CINNAMON ROLLS 422

361. FIESTA CHICKEN FINGERS 423

362. CHOCOLATE CHIP OATMEAL COOKIES 424

363. GREEN TOMATO 425

364. REUBEN CALZONES 427

365. LEMON SLICE SUGAR COOKIES 428

366. PEPPERMINT LAVA CAKES 429

367. QUENTIN'S PEACH-BOURBON WINGS 430

368. CORN NUTS 431

369. SMOKY CHICKPEAS 432

370. NUTTY FRENCH TOAST 433

371. BAKED APPLE WITH WALNUTS 434

372. VEGGIE WONTONS 435

373. BACON WRAPPED FILET MIGNON 436

374. SALTY PISTACHIO SMALL BATCH BROWNIES 438

375. PLANTAIN CHIPS 439

376. PALEO SALMON CAKES 440

377. TUNA PATTIES 441

378. PALEO PARSNIP FRENCH FRIES 442

NUTRITIONAL INFORMATION 442

379. PALEO CAULIFLOWER TATER TOTS 443

380. FLOURLESS CHOCOLATE ALMOND CUPCAKES 444

381. GLUTEN-FREE EASY COCONUT PIE 445

382. CHEESECAKE BITES 446

383. PALEO APPLE CIDER VINEGAR DONUTS 447

384. COCONUT-ENCRUSTED CINNAMON BANANAS 448

385. JUICY TURKEY BURGERS WITH ZUCCHINI 449

386. CRISPY CHEESY VEGAN QUESARITO 450

387. CHIPOTLE QUESADILLAS WITH MINTY MANGO SALSA 452

388. WHISKEY GARLIC TOFU OVER VEGETABLE QUINOA 453

389. VEGAN GOAT CHEESE BACON WRAPPED DATES 454

390. BLACK BEAN TOTCHOS WITH GARLIC LEMON SAUCE 455

391. BEETROOT CHIPS 456

392. COCONUT SHRIMP WITH SPICY MARMALADE SAUCE 457

393. EGGLESS CHOCOLATE CHIP MUFFINS 458

394. KETO RADISH CHIPS 459

395. CHERRY PIE 460

396. MOZZARELLA CHEESE STICKS 461

397. CHOCOLATE ZUCCHINI BREAD 462

398. APPLE PIE 463

399. BLACKBERRY HAND PIES 464

400. CRUSTY ARTISAN BREAD 466

1. ROASTED BROCCOLI AND CAULIFLOWER

INGREDIENTS

- 3 cups broccoli florets
- 3 cups cauliflower florets
- 2 tablespoons olive oil
- ½ teaspoon garlic powder
- ¼ teaspoon sea salt
- ¼ teaspoon paprika
- teaspoon ground black pepper

INSTRUCTIONS

Warm-up an air fryer to 400 degrees F (200 degrees C) as advised by the manufacturer.

Put broccoli florets in a large bowl, secure for microwaves. Cook over high power for 3 minutes in the microwave. Drain any liquid that has built up.

Throw the broccoli into the bowl with cauliflower, olive oil, garlic powder, sea salt, paprika, and black pepper. Put together well. Pour the mixture into the container for the air fryer. Cook for 12 minutes, and toss vegetables for even browning halfway through cooking time.

2. APPLE FRITTERS

INGREDIENTS

- cooking spray
- 1 cup all-purpose flour
- 1/4 cup white sugar
- 1/4 cup milk1 egg
- 1 1/2 teaspoons baking powder
- 1 pinch salt
- 2 tablespoons white sugar
- 1/2 teaspoon ground cinnamon
- 1 apple - peeled, cored, and chopped
- Glaze:
- 1/2 cup confectioners' sugar
- 1 tablespoon milk
- 1/2 teaspoon caramel extract
- 1/4 teaspoon ground cinnamon

INSTRUCTIONS

Preheat an air fryer to 350 F (175 C). Place a round parchment paper into the air fryer frame. Spray cooking spray with nonstick.

In a small bowl, bring together the flour, 1/4 cup sugar, milk, egg, baking powder, and salt. Stir before all together.

In another cup, blend 2 tablespoons of sugar and cinnamon, and scatter over apples until covered. Mix apples once mixed into a flour mixture.

Drop the fritters onto the bottom of the air fryer tub, using a cookie scoop.

Air-fry 5 minutes in the preheated fryer. Flip the fritters and cook for about 5 minutes, until golden.

Alternatively, combine the sugar, butter, caramel extract, and cinnamon from the confectioners together in a container. Move fritters with glaze to a cooling rack and drizzle over.

NUTRITIONAL INFORMATION

Per Serving: 297 calories; 2.1 g fat; 64.9 g carbohydrates; 5.5 g protein; 48 mg cholesterol; 248 mg sodium.

3. BEIGNETS

INGREDIENTS

- 1 1/2 teaspoons melted butter
- 1/2 teaspoon baking powder
- 1/2 teaspoon vanilla extract1 pinch salt2 tablespoons confectioners' sugar, or to taste cooking spray
- 1/2 cup all-purpose flour
- 1/4 cup white sugar
- 1/8 cup water1 large egg, separated

INSTRUCTIONS

Preheat air fryer to 370 ° F (185 ° C). Spray nonstick cooking spray on a silicone egg-bite container.

In a large bowl, whisk together the flour, sugar, water, egg yolk, butter, baking powder, vanilla extract and salt. Stir to combine.

In a small bowl, beat the egg white with an electric hand mixer at medium speed until soft peaks form. Fold the batter in. Use a small hinged ice cream scoop to add batter to the prepared mold.

Place the silicone mold filled into the air-fryer bowl.

Fry 10 minutes in the preheated air fryer. Carefully remove the mold from the basket; pop out the beignets and turn over onto a round of parchment paper.

Place the parchment round in the air fryer basket with beignets back in. Cook for another 4 minutes. Remove the beignets from the basket of the air fryer and sprinkle with the sugar of the pastries.

NUTRITIONAL INFORMATION

Per Serving: 88 calories; 1.7 g fat; 16.2 g carbohydrates; 1.8 g protein; 29 mg cholesterol; 74 mg sodium

4. ROSEMARY GARLIC POTATOES

INGREDIENTS

- 1 1/2 pounds multi-colored new potatoes, halved
- 2 tablespoons olive oil
- 2 cloves garlic, minced
- 1 teaspoon finely chopped fresh rosemary
- 1/2 teaspoon kosher salt
- 1/2 teaspoon lemon zest

INSTRUCTIONS

The air fryer is preheated to 400 degrees F (200 degrees C).

In a large bowl, add the potatoes, garlic, rosemary, and salt. Arrange potatoes without overcrowding in a single layer of air fryer basket; operate in batches, if appropriate. Cook for about 20 minutes, until the potatoes are brown and tender. Upon eating, brush on lemon zest.

NUTRITIONAL INFORMATION

Per Serving: 97 calories; 3.5 g fat; 15.2 g carbohydrates; 1.8 g protein; 0 mg cholesterol; 125 mg sodium.

5. BABY BACK RIBS

INGREDIENTS

- 1 rack baby back ribs
- 1 tablespoon olive oil
- 1 tablespoon liquid smoke flavoring
- 1 tablespoon brown sugar
- 1/2 teaspoon salt
- 1/2 teaspoon ground black pepper
- 1/2 teaspoon garlic powder
- 1/2 teaspoon onion powder
- 1/2 teaspoon chili powder1 cup BBQ sauce

INSTRUCTIONS

Remove membrane with a paper towel from the back of ribs, and rinse ribs. Cut the rack into four pieces. In a small bowl, blend olive oil and liquid smoke and fry on both sides of the ribs.

In a cup, mix brown sugar, salt, pepper, garlic, onion powder, and chili powder. Spice generously on both sides of the ribs with seasoning mix. Let the ribs rest for 30 minutes to improve the flavour.

Preheat an air fryer to 375 F (190 C).

Place bone-side down ribs in the air fryer tub, making sure they do not touch; if possible, cook them in batches.

Cook for another 15 minutes.

Flip the ribs over (meat-side down) and cook for another 10 minutes. Pull ribs from the air fryer with half cup BBQ sauce and clean bone-side ribs.

Put the basket into the air fryer and cook for 5 minutes. Flip the ribs over, spray the side of the beef with the remaining half cup BBQ sauce; cook for another 5 minutes or until you hit the desired char.

NUTRITIONAL INFORMATION

Per Serving: 445 calories; 29 g fat; 26.8 g carbohydrates; 18.2 g protein; 88 mg cholesterol; 1070 mg sodium.

6. SHRIMP

INGREDIENTS

- 2 eggs
- 1/2 cup fish fry breading mix
- 1 pound large shrimp, peeled and deveined cooking spray

INSTRUCTIONS

The air fryer is preheated to 390 degrees F (200 degrees C).

Beat the eggs gently in a shallow platter. Pour the mixture into a separate shallow plate.

Dip the shrimp into the egg, letting the excess drip away. Toss the shrimp in the breading fried fish and put on a tray. Let them rest for ten minutes.

Spray the air fryer basket with cooking spray and put the shrimp inside, to ensure that the shrimp does not overlap. Depending on the size of your air fryer, you might need to do two batches. Mist shrimp with spray to cook.

Cook them for 3 minutes. Flip the shrimp and mist with the cooking spray again so that no dry or powdery areas are present. Cook for 2 to 3 minutes. Repeat with shrimp leftover.

NUTRITIONAL INFORMATION

Per Serving: 161 calories; 4.4 g fat; 6.4 g carbohydrates; 22.7 g protein; 271 mg cholesterol; 238 mg sodium.

7. ASPARAGUS FRIES

INGREDIENTS

- 1 large egg
- 1 teaspoon honey
- 1 cup panko bread crumbs
- 1/2 cup grated Parmesan cheese
- 12 asparagus spears, trimmed
- 1/4 cup stone-ground mustard
- 1/4 cup Greek yogurt
- 1 pinch cayenne pepper (optional)

INSTRUCTIONS

Preheat an air fryer to 400 F (200 C).

In a long, narrow dish mix egg and honey, and beat together. In a separate plate, add the panko and the Parmesan cheese. Coat each stalk of asparagus in egg mixture and roll into panko mix to coat.

Put 6 spears in the air fryer and cook for 4 to 6 minutes to desired brownness. Repeat with spears left over.

In a small bowl, mix mustard, yoghurt, and cayenne pepper. Serve asparagus spears with dipping sauce.

NUTRITIONAL INFORMATION

Per Serving: 127 calories; 4.3 g fat; 18 g carbohydrates; 7.5 g protein; 39 mg cholesterol; 365 mg sodium.

8. SALT AND VINEGAR CHICKPEAS

INGREDIENTS

- 1 (15 ounce) can chickpeas, drained and rinsed
- 1 cup white vinegar
- 1 tablespoon olive oil
- 1/2 teaspoon sea salt

INSTRUCTIONS

In a small saucepan, mix chickpeas and vinegar, and bring to a simmer. Take off fire. Let it stand 30 minutes.

Drain some chickpeas and cut any loose skins.

Preheat an air fryer to 390 F (198 C). Spread chickpeas uniformly through the bowl. Cook for about 4 minutes, until dried out.

Switch chickpeas to a heat-resistant bowl and sprinkle with oil and sea salt. Toss to shirk. Return chickpeas to air fryer and cook for about 8 minutes, shaking basket every 2 to 3 minutes, until lightly browned. Serve straightaway.

NUTRITIONAL INFORMATION

Per Serving: 229 calories; 8.3 g fat; 31.7 g carbohydrates; 6.9 g protein; 0 mg cholesterol; 859 mg sodium.

9. BUFFALO RANCH CHICKPEAS

INGREDIENTS

- 1 (15 ounce) can chickpeas, drained and rinsed
- 2 tablespoons Buffalo wing sauce
- 1 tablespoon dry ranch dressing mix

INSTRUCTIONS

Preheat an air fryer to 350 F (175 C).

Line a sheet of baking paper towels. Spread chickpeas over towels made from paper. Place a sheet of paper towels over the chickpeas and press gently to remove excess humidity.

Layer chickpeas in a saucepan. Attach the wing sauce and mix to toss. Apply powder to ranch dressing and blend well.

Place chickpeas into an even layer in the air fryer bowl.

Cook on for eight minutes. Shake and cook for another 5 minutes. Shake for another 5 minutes, and cook. Shake for the final 2 minutes, and cook. Let cool for 5 minutes, and immediately serve.

NUTRITIONAL INFORMATION

Per Serving: 177 calories; 1.6 g fat; 33.6 g carbohydrates; 7 g protein; 0 mg cholesterol; 1033 mg sodium.

10.   ACTIFRIED ORANGE SESAME CAULIFLOWER

INGREDIENTS

- 2/3 cup water
- 1/3 cup cornstarch
- 1/3 cup all-purpose flour
- 1/2 teaspoon salt
- 1/2 teaspoon ground black pepper
- 1 medium head cauliflower, cut into florets
- 2 ActiFry spoons vegetable oil
- 1 orange
- 2 tablespoons soy sauce
- 2 tablespoons rice vinegar
- 2 tablespoons ketchup
- 2 tablespoons brown sugar
- 1 tablespoon toasted sesame oil
- 2 cloves garlic, minced
- 1 teaspoon corn starch
- Sliced green onion
- Toasted sesame seeds

INSTRUCTIONS

In a large bowl, whisk together the cornstarch, water, flour, pepper, and salt, until smooth.

Remove florets of cauliflower and mix until they are powdered.

Move the cauliflower to a baking sheet lined with parchment paper. Chill yourself for 30 minutes.

Bring your ActiFry cauliflower in. Drizzle with vegetable oil and cook tenderly for 22 minutes or until browned.

Alternatively, weigh 1 teaspoon of orange zest, and set aside. To weigh 1/4 cup orange juice.

25

In a saucepan, add orange juice, soy sauce, rice vinegar, ketchup, brown sugar, sesame oil, and garlic; over medium heat, bring to a simmer.

Stir 1 teaspoon of water to the cornstarch until dissolved.

NUTRITIONAL   INFORMATION

Per Serving: 250 calories; 10.9 g fat; 35.2 g carbohydrates; 4.3 g protein; 0 mg cholesterol; 864 mg sodium.

11.   RANCH PORK CHOPS

INGREDIENTS

- 4 boneless, center-cut pork chops, 1-inch thick
- cooking spray
- 2 teaspoons dry ranch salad dressing mix aluminum foil

INSTRUCTIONS

Place the pork chops on a plate and spray both sides lightly with spray for cooking. Sprinkle with ranch seasoning mix on both sides, and let sit for 10 minutes at room temperature.

Spray an air fryer basket with a cooking spray and preheat the fryer to 390 degrees F (200 degrees C).

Place chops in the preheated air fryer to ensure that the fryer is not overcrowded, operating in batches where possible.

Cook for five minutes. Flip chops, and cook for another 5 minutes. Let rest for 5 minutes on a foil-covered plate before serving.

Note:

When you need to air fry in batches, keep the cooked chops warm in an oven at the lowest setting while the other chops are frying. Add an extra minute to the cook-time for thicker chops. Cook 1 minute less for thinner chops.

NUTRITIONAL INFORMATION

Per Serving: 260 calories; 9.1 g fat; 0.6 g carbohydrates; 40.8 g protein; 107 mg cholesterol; 148 mg sodium.

12. BROWN SUGAR AND PECAN ROASTED APPLES

INGREDIENTS

- 2 tablespoons coarsely chopped pecans
- 1 tablespoon brown sugar
- 1 teaspoon all-purpose flour
- 1/4 teaspoon apple pie spice
- 2 medium apples, cored and cut into wedges
- 1 tablespoon butter, melted

INSTRUCTIONS

Preheat the air fryer to 360 ° F (180 ° C).

In a small bowl, mix pecans, brown sugar, flour, and spice apple pie. In a medium bowl, put the apple wedges; drizzle with butter, and toss to coat. In the air-fryer tub, arrange apples in a single layer and sprinkle with pecan mixture.

Cook in the preheated air fryer for 10 to 15 minutes, until apples are tender.

Note:

you can also use Cinnamon in place of apple pie spice.

NUTRITIONAL INFORMATION

Per Serving: 204 calories; 11.3 g fat; 27.9 g carbohydrates; 1.2 g protein; 15 mg cholesterol; 44 mg sodium.

13. MINI PEPPERS STUFFED WITH CHEESE AND SAUSAGE

INGREDIENTS

- 8 ounces bulk Italian sausage
- 1 (16 ounce) package miniature multi-colored sweet peppers
- 2 tablespoons olive oil, divided
- 1 (8 ounce) package cream cheese, softened
- 1/2 cup shredded Cheddar cheese
- 2 tablespoons crumbled blue cheese (optional)
- 1 tablespoon finely chopped fresh chives
- 1 clove garlic, minced
- 1/4 teaspoon ground black pepper
- 2 tablespoons panko bread crumbs

INSTRUCTIONS

preheat a large skillet over medium-high steam, without sticking. Cook in the hot skillet and stir sausage until browned and crumbly, 5 to 7 minutes. Drain grease and discard; set aside.

Preheat an air fryer to 350 F (175 C).

Lengthwise cut a slit from stem to tip in one side of each sweet pepper. Brush the peppers with 1 spoonful of olive oil and put them in the basket of the air fryer.

Cook for 3 minutes in the preheated air fryer. Shake the basket and cook, about 3 minutes longer, until the peppers start to brown and soften. Cut the peppers and let them stand until they are cool enough to handle; leave on the air fryer.

While the peppers cool, stir in a medium bowl sausage, cream cheese, cheddar cheese, blue cheese, chives, garlic, and black pepper until well mixed. In a small bowl, mix the bread crumbs with the remaining 1 spoonful of olive oil.

In each pepper, spoon the cheese and sprinkle with a mixture of bread crumbs. Place stuffed peppers in the air fryer bowl, work in lots if necessary and cook for 4 to 5 minutes until the filling is heated through and the bread crumbs are toasted. Slightly cool; serves dry.

NUTRITIONAL INFORMATION

Per Serving: 101 calories; 8.6 g fat; 2.6 g carbohydrates; 3.6 g protein; 20 mg cholesterol; 159 mg sodium

14. PERUVIAN CHICKEN DRUMSTICKS WITH GREEN CREMA

INGREDIENTS

- olive oil for brushing
- 2 cloves garlic, grated
- 1 tablespoon honey
- 1 tablespoon olive oil
- 1 teaspoon salt
- 1 teaspoon ground cumin
- 1/2 teaspoon smoked paprika
- 1/2 teaspoon dried oregano
- 1/4 teaspoon ground black pepper
- 6 (4 ounce) chicken drumsticks
- Crema Sauce:
- 1 cup baby spinach leaves, stems removed
- 3/4 cup sour cream
- 1/4 cup cilantro leaves
- 2 tablespoons fresh lime juice
- 1 clove garlic, smashed
- 1/2 jalapeno pepper, seeded
- 1/4 teaspoon salt
- 1/4 teaspoon ground black pepper

INSTRUCTIONS

Brush the olive oil in an air fryer jar.

In a large bowl, add the garlic, sugar, 1 tablespoon of olive oil, cinnamon, cumin, paprika, oregano, and pepper. Add drumsticks; coat toss. Arrange drumsticks upright in the prepared basket, leaning against and against the basket wall.

Cook in the air fryer at 400 degrees F (200 degrees C) until 175 degrees F (80 degrees C) reads a thermometer inserted in the thickest part of the drumstick, 15 to 20 minutes. Rearrange drumsticks for even cooking with kitchen pliers halfway through cooking. Meanwhile, in a food processor's bowl, add spinach, sour cream, cilantro, lime juice, garlic, jalapeno pepper, salt, and pepper; process until crema is smooth. Drizzle over the drumsticks with some crema sauce and serve with remaining crema.

Note: Any excess sauce can be processed and refrigerated in an airtight container for up to 5 days. Use as a salad dressing, topper on baked potatoes or on tacos.

NUTRITIONAL INFORMATION

Per Serving: 271 calories; 17.7 g fat; 5.8 g carbohydrates; 21.9 g protein; 82 mg cholesterol; 574 mg sodium.

15. TATER TOTS

INGREDIENTS

36 frozen bite-size potato nuggets (such as Tater Tots)

INSTRUCTIONS

Preheat an air fryer for 4 minutes, at 350 degrees F (175 degrees C).

Place the desired amount of potato nuggets in a single layer in the air fryer bowl, and operate in batches if appropriate.

Cook for 6 minutes in a preheated air fryer. The bucket is shaking. Cook for about 4 more minutes until crispy, or to the desired doneness.

NUTRITIONAL INFORMATION

Per Serving: 110 calories; 6.1 g fat; 15.9 g carbohydrates; 1.5 g protein; 0 mg cholesterol; 258 mg sodium.

16. BBQ BABY BACK RIBS

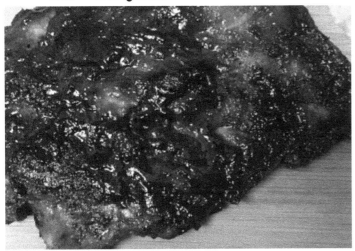

INGREDIENTS

- 3 pounds baby back pork ribs
- 1 tablespoon brown sugar
- 1 tablespoon white sugar
- 1 teaspoon sweet paprika
- 1 teaspoon smoked paprika
- 1 teaspoon granulated garlic
- 1/2 teaspoon ground black pepper
- 1/2 teaspoon ground cumin
- 1/2 teaspoon granulated onion
- 1/4 teaspoon Greek seasoning (optional)
- 1/3 cup barbeque sauce

INSTRUCTIONS

Preheat the air fryer to 350 F (175 C).

Strip the membrane from the ribs back, split the ribs into four equal portions.

In a small bowl, add brown sugar, white sugar, sweet pepper, smoked paprika, granulated garlic, pepper, cumin, onion and Greek seasoning. Rub spice mixture over the entire ribs and put it in the basket of the air fryer.

Cook the ribs 30 minutes in the air fryer and transform after 15 minutes. Brush for another 5 minutes with barbecue sauce and air fry.

NUTRITIONAL INFORMATION

Per Serving: 615 calories; 44.3 g fat; 15.6 g carbohydrates; 36.5 g protein; 176 mg cholesterol; 415 mg sodium.

17.   MAC AND CHEESE BALLS

INGREDIENTS

- 6 cups water
- 1 (7.25 ounce) package macaroni and cheese dinner mix
- 1/4 cup milk4 tablespoons margarine
- 3/4 cup shredded sharp Cheddar cheese nonstick cooking spray
- 1/2 cup panko bread crumbs
- 1/2 cup seasoned bread crumbs
- 1/2 teaspoon salt
- 1/2 teaspoon garlic powder
- 2 eggs, beaten

INSTRUCTIONS

Pour water into a bowl over high heat, and bring to a boil. Stir macaroni pasta from the box for dinner. Cook for 7 to 8 minutes, stirring occasionally, until tender. Drain; Rinse not. Return to the pot and stir in cheese sauce, butter, and margarine included. Remove the cheddar cheese and stir until the cheese is melted and well mixed.

Refrigerate the macaroni and cheese, 2 hours to overnight, until solid.

Macaroni and cheese scoop into 1 1/2 inch balls and put on a paper-lined cookie sheet with parchment. Freeze 1 hour.

Preheat an air fryer to 350 degrees F (175 degrees C), as directed by the manufacturer. Spray nonstick cooking spray to the tub. In a medium bowl, bring together the panko, bread crumbs, salt, and garlic powder. Dip each ball into beaten eggs, and then combine with the panko.

Place mac and cheese balls in a single layer in the air fryer tub, make sure they are not touching; if possible, cook in batches.

Cook for 6 to 8 minutes in the preheated air-fryer. Turn over and cook, for 3 to 4 minutes, until golden brown.

Note: Make the macaroni and cheese mix according to individual instructions for packaging.

NUTRITIONAL INFORMATION

Per Serving: 87 calories; 4.2 g fat; 9.3 g carbohydrates; 3.7 g protein; 21 mg cholesterol; 227 mg sodium.

18. SOY GINGER SHISHITO PEPPERS

INGREDIENTS

- 6 ounces shishito peppers
- 1 teaspoon vegetable oil
- 1 tablespoon reduced-sodium soy sauce
- 1 tablespoon fresh lime juice
- 1 teaspoon honey
- 1/2 teaspoon grated fresh ginger

INSTRUCTIONS

Preheat an air fryer to 390 F (199 C).

In a medium bowl, stir peppers with oil to coat. Place peppers in the basket of the air-fryer. Cook for 6 to 7 minutes, shaking the basket halfway through, until blistered and soft.

Alternatively, in the same medium bowl, add the soy sauce, lime juice, honey, and ginger. Attach the cooked peppers, then toss them to cover. Serving hot.

Note: For a grilled steak these roasted peppers make a great side. Whether you prefer serving as an appetizer, you should rely on 8 portions of the appetizer.

NUTRITIONAL INFORMATION

Per Serving: 36 calories; 1.2 g fat; 6.2 g carbohydrates; 1.1 g protein; 0 mg cholesterol; 136 mg sodium.

19. ROASTED BRUSSELS SPROUTS WITH MAPLE-MUSTARD MAYO

INGREDIENTS

- 2 tablespoons maple syrup, divided
- 1 tablespoon olive oil
- 1/4 teaspoon kosher salt
- 1/4 teaspoon ground black pepper
- 1 pound Brussels sprouts, trimmed and halved
- 1/3 cup mayonnaise
- 1 tablespoon stone ground mustard

INSTRUCTIONS

The air fryer is preheated to 400 degrees F (200 degrees C).

In a large bowl, whisk 1 tablespoon of maple syrup, olive oil, salt, and pepper together. Sprinkle with Brussels and toss to coat. Arrange Brussels sprouts in a single layer without overcrowding in the air fryer basket; operate in batches, if necessary. Cook for four minutes. Shake basket and cook for 4 to 6 minutes more, until the sprouts are dark brown and tender.

Whisk the mayonnaise together, remaining 1 tablespoon of maple syrup, and mustard in a small bowl. Toss sprouts in some combination of the sauce and/or serve as a sauce to dip in.

NUTRITIONAL   INFORMATION

Per Serving: 240 calories; 18.3 g fat; 18.3 g carbohydrates; 4 g protein; 7 mg cholesterol; 298 mg sodium.

20.   ROASTED SWEET PEPPERS AND ONIONS

INGREDIENTS

- 1 cup sliced green bell pepper
- 1 cup sliced red bell pepper
- 1 cup sliced red onion1 tablespoon olive oil
- 1/2 teaspoon kosher salt
- 2 tablespoons chopped fresh cilantro
- 1 tablespoon fresh lime juice

INSTRUCTIONS

Preheat an air fryer to 350 F (175 C).

In a large bowl, add the pepper, onion, olive oil and salt. Move mixture to basket with the air fryer. Cook, stirring once, for 7 to 9 minutes, until peppers and onion are tender and start brown. Turn into a bowl for serving. Add lime juice and cilantro; toss to coat.

Note: Use whatever mix you like of red, green, and/or yellow sweet peppers.

NUTRITIONAL   INFORMATION

Per Serving: 55 calories; 3.5 g fat; 5.6 g carbohydrates; 0.8 g protein; 0 mg cholesterol; 244 mg sodium.

21. CARROTS WITH BALSAMIC GLAZE

INGREDIENTS

- olive oil for brushing
- 1 tablespoon olive oil
- 1 teaspoon honey
- 1/4 teaspoon kosher salt
- 1/4 teaspoon ground black pepper
- 1 pound tri-colored baby carrots
- 1 tablespoon balsamic glaze
- 1 tablespoon butter
- 2 teaspoons chopped fresh chives

INSTRUCTIONS

Brush the olive oil in an air fryer jar.

In a large bowl, whisk together 1 spoonful of olive oil, butter, salt, and pepper. Remove carrots and paint with a toss. Place the carrots in a single layer of the air fryer basket, in lots, if necessary.

Cook 390 degrees F (200 degrees C) in the air fryer, stirring once, for about 10 minutes until tender. Switch moist, cooked carrots to a large bowl, add butter and balsamic glaze and toss to coat. Sprinkle, and top with chives.

Note: When you substitute baby carrots with full-size carrots, just halve any big pieces lengthwise and cut them into 2-inch sections.

NUTRITIONAL INFORMATION

Per Serving: 117 calories; 7.7 g fat; 11.9 g carbohydrates; 0.8 g protein; 8 mg cholesterol; 228 mg sodium.

22.   CAULIFLOWER TOTS

INGREDIENTS

- 1 serving nonstick cooking spray
- 1 (16 ounce) package frozen cauliflower tots

INSTRUCTIONS

Air fryer preheats to 400 degrees F (200 degrees C). Spray nonstick cooking spray to the air fryer pot.

Place as many cauliflower tots as you can in the tub, make sure they don't strike, and cook in batches if necessary.

Cook for 6 minutes in a preheated air fryer. Take the basket out, turn the tots over, and cook for about 3 minutes until browned and cooked through.

NUTRITIONAL   INFORMATION

Per Serving: 147 calories; 6.1 g fat; 20 g carbohydrates; 2.7 g protein; 0 mg cholesterol; 494 mg sodium.

23. TAJIN APPLE CHIPS

INGREDIENTS

- 1 apple, cored
- 1/2 tablespoon chile-lime seasoning, or more to taste

INSTRUCTIONS

Preheat the air fryer to 180 ° F (82 ° C).

Apple with thin slice and mandolin.

Place as many apple slices as you can in the air fryer basket to ensure they don't strike.

Cook for 12 minutes in the air fryer, and operate in lots if necessary. Take the basket out, turn the apple slices over, and cook for 8 to 12 minutes more until lightly browned on the other side. Sprinkle immediately with chile-lime seasoning.

NUTRITIONAL INFORMATION

Per Serving: 36 calories; 0.1 g fat; 9.5 g carbohydrates; 0.2 g protein; 0 mg cholesterol; 300 mg sodium.

24. SHRIMP BOIL

INGREDIENTS

- 1 pound baby red potatoes
- 1/4 cup water
- 8 ounces Cajun-style andouille sausage, sliced1 ear corn, sliced in half lengthwise and cut into 2-inch pieces
- 1 medium onion, sliced into petals
- 4 tablespoons olive oil, divided
- 3 teaspoons seafood seasoning, divided
- 1 pound raw large shrimp, peeled and deveined
- 1 lemon, cut into wedges

INSTRUCTIONS

The air fryer is preheated to 400 degrees F (200 degrees C).

Put the potatoes in a healthy bowl for microwave use. Stir in water and microwave for 5 minutes on high. Place the bowl under cold water until cool enough to touch potatoes.

Slice the potatoes lengthwise in half and put them in a large bowl. Add chopped bacon, corn, and onion. Mix the olive oil and 2 teaspoons of seafood seasoning in 3 tablespoons; swirl to paint.

In a separate bowl, put the shrimp and add the remaining 1 tablespoon of olive oil and 1 teaspoon of seafood seasoning; stir to coat.

In the air fryer bowl, put 1/2 of the potato mixture, and cook for 10 minutes. Remove and boil for another 5 minutes. Remove 1/2 of the shrimp and cook until the potatoes are tender, the sausage is cooked through and the shrimp on the outside is bright pink and the meat is opaque, about 5 minutes more. Move to a serving platter and repeat with other mixture of potatoes and shrimps. Serve with wedges of Lemon.

NUTRITIONAL INFORMATION

Per Serving: 505 calories; 31.2 g fat; 29.7 g carbohydrates; 28.9 g protein; 205 mg cholesterol; 1130 mg sodium.

25. GREEN BEANS WITH SPICY DIPPING SAUCE

INGREDIENTS

- 1 cup beer
- 1 cup all-purpose flour
- 2 teaspoons salt
- 1/2 teaspoon ground black pepper
- 1 (12 ounce) package fresh green beans, trimmed
- parchment paper cut to the size of the air fryer basket
- Dipping Sauce:
- 1 cup ranch dressing
- 2 teaspoons sriracha sauce
- 1 teaspoon prepared horseradish, or to taste

INSTRUCTIONS

In a cup, add the malt, flour, salt, and pepper. Coat beans in small batches with the batter, and shake off the waste.

Preheat air fryer to 400 degrees F (200 degrees C), as directed by the manufacturers.

Place the parchment paper at the bottom of the basket with the air fryer. Place the battered beans on a single layer in the air fryer. Cook outside, for 8 to 10 minutes, until turn golden brown and crispy. Repeat with any battered beans leftover.

Mix the ranch dressing in a tub, sriracha sauce, and horseradish. Serve along with the green beans

NUTRITIONAL INFORMATION

Per Serving: 466 calories; 31.6 g fat; 35.4 g carbohydrates; 5.9 g protein; 16 mg cholesterol; 1863 mg sodium.

26.   EGG ROLLS

INGREDIENTS

- 2 cups frozen corn, thawed
- 1 (15 ounce) can black beans, drained and rinsed
- 1 (13.5 ounce) can spinach, drained
- 1 1/2 cups shredded jalapeno Jack cheese
- 1 cup sharp Cheddar cheese, shredded
- 1 (4 ounce) can diced green chiles, drained
- 4 green onions, sliced
- 1 teaspoon salt
- 1 teaspoon ground cumin
- 1 teaspoon chili powder
- 1 (16 ounce) package egg roll wrapperscooking spray

INSTRUCTIONS

Mix together corn, beans, spinach, jalapeno cheese, cheddar cheese, green chilies, green onions, cinnamon, cumin, and chili powder in a large bowl to fill.

Place the wrapping of an egg roll in an angle. Use your finger to moisten water gently on all 4 sides. Place the filling in the center of the wrapper around 1/4 cup. Fold 1 corner over filling, and tuck to form a roll in the sides. Continue with the remaining wrappers and mist with a cooking spray on each egg roll.

Preheat an air fryer to 390 F (199 C). Place the egg rolls in the bowl, make sure they do not touch; if possible, cook them in batches. Fry for eight minutes; flip and cook until the skins are crispy, around four more minutes.

NUTRITIONAL   INFORMATION

Per Serving: 216 calories; 7.7 g fat; 27 g carbohydrates; 10.6 g protein; 25 mg cholesterol; 628 mg sodium.

27. ROASTED RAINBOW VEGETABLES

INGREDIENTS

- 1 red bell pepper, seeded and cut into 1-inch pieces
- 1 yellow summer squash, cut into 1-inch pieces
- 1 zucchini, cut into 1-inch pieces
- 4 ounces fresh mushrooms, cleaned and halved
- 1/2 sweet onion, cut into 1-inch wedges
- 1 tablespoon extra-virgin olive oilsalt and pepper to taste

INSTRUCTIONS

Preheat an air fryer, as suggested by the manufacturer.

In a broad bow put red bell pepper, summer squash, courgettes, mushrooms, and onion. Add olive oil, salt and black pepper and mix to shake.

Place the vegetables in the air fryer basket on a even plate. Air-fry vegetables until fried, stirring halfway through cooking time, about 20 minutes.

NUTRITIONAL INFORMATION

Per Serving: 69 calories; 3.8 g fat; 7.7 g carbohydrates; 2.6 g protein; 0 mg cholesterol; 48 mg sodium.

28. PURPLE YAM FRIES WITH SOUR CREAM SRIRACHA SAUCE

INGREDIENTS

- 1 1/3 pounds ube (purple yam), peeled and cut into 1/4-inch-thick fries
- 2 teaspoons olive oil
- 1 teaspoon sriracha-flavored salt
- 1/3 cup sour cream
- 2 teaspoons sriracha sauce, or more to taste

INSTRUCTIONS

Preheat an air fryer to 320 F (160 C).

Put the fried yams in a pot. Add olive oil and salt seasoned with sriracha; mix evenly to coat. Pour into the bucket of the air-fryer.

Cook 16 minutes in the preheated air fryer. Raising temperatures to 400 degrees F (200 degrees C). Shake pot, and cook for another 5 minutes.

Blend together the sour cream and sriracha sauce in a dish. Serve with fries of yam.

Note:

You can cut yams with a French fry cutter instead of a knife if preferred.

NUTRITIONAL INFORMATION

Per Serving: 242 calories; 6.7 g fat; 43.3 g carbohydrates; 2.9 g protein; 8 mg cholesterol; 719 mg sodium.

29.   APPLE PIES

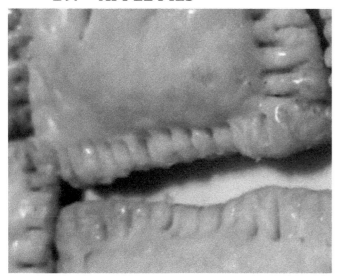

INGREDIENTS

- 4 tablespoons butter
- 6 tablespoons brown sugar
- 1 teaspoon ground cinnamon
- 2 medium Granny Smith apples, diced
- 1 teaspoon cornstarch2 teaspoons cold water
- 1/2 (14 ounce) package pastry for a 9-inch double crust piecooking spray
- 1/2 tablespoon grapeseed oil
- 1/4 cup powdered sugar
- 1 teaspoon milk, or more as needed

INSTRUCTIONS

In a non-stick pan, add the apples, butter, brown sugar and cinnamon. Cook over medium heat for about 5 minutes, until apples have softened.

Maize starch dissolves in cold water. Stir in apple mixture and cook for about 1 minute, until sauce thickens. Remove from heat the apple pie filling and set aside to cool while the crust is being prepared.

Unroll the pie crust on a lightly floured surface and gently roll out to smooth the dough surface. Cut the dough into small enough rectangles to allow 2 to fit at once in your air fryer.

Repeat with the remainder of the crust until you have 8 equal rectangles, re-rolling some of the dough scraps if necessary.

Wet the outer edges of 4 rectangles with water, and place some apple filling in the center about a half-inch from the edges. Roll the remaining 4 rectangles out so they're slightly larger than the ones packed.

Place those rectangles on top of the fill; crimp the edges with a sealing fork. Cut 4 tiny slits into the tops of the pies.

Oil an air fryer basket with cooking spray. Brush the 2-pie tops with grape seed oil and pass pastries using a spatula to the air fryer tray.

Attach a basket and set the temperature to 385 ° F (195 ° C). Bake for about 8 minutes, until golden brown. Remove the pies from the bowl and repeat with the 2 pies leftover.

NUTRITIONAL INFORMATION

Per Serving: 498 calories; 28.6 g fat; 59.8 g carbohydrates; 3.3 g protein; 31 mg cholesterol; 328 mg sodium.

30. POPCORN CHICKEN

INGREDIENTS

- 1 pound boneless, skinless chicken breast halves, cut into 1-inch pieces
- ¾ teaspoon salt
- ½ teaspoon paprika
- ¼ teaspoon black pepper
- ¼ teaspoon ground mustard
- ¼ teaspoon garlic powder
- ¼ teaspoon onion powder
- teaspoon ground thyme
- teaspoon dried basil
- teaspoon dried oregano
- teaspoon dried sage
- 3 tablespoons cornstarch

INSTRUCTIONS

Put pieces of chicken inside a medium bowl.

In a small bowl, mix cinnamon, paprika, black pepper, mustard, powdered garlic, onion powder, thyme, basil, oregano, and sage. Reserve 1 teaspoon of the seasoning mixture, and sprinkle on chicken the remaining seasoning. Equally, flip to cover.

In a resealable plastic bag, mix cornstarch and reserved 1 teaspoon seasoning; shake to blend. Place the pieces of chicken in the bag, seal the bag and shake for even coat. Pass chicken and shake to a fine mesh strainer to remove excess cornstarch. Let the corn starch rest for 5 to 10 minutes until it starts to dissolve into the chicken.

Preheat air fryer to 390 ° F (200 ° C).

Spray air fryer basket with oil and put pieces of chicken inside, making sure pieces don't overlap. Depending on the size of your air fryer you may have to do two batches. Mist chicken with spray to cook.

Cook for four minutes. Shake the air fryer basket and spray the chicken with oil again, so that dry or powdery areas are not present. Cook for about 4 to 5 more minutes until chicken is no longer pink on the inside. Serve straight away.

NUTRITIONAL INFORMATION

Per Serving:

152 calories; 2.9 g total fat; 65 mg cholesterol; 493 mg sodium. 6.1 g carbohydrates; 23.8 g protein

31.   TOSTONES

INGREDIENTS

- 2 green (unripe) plantains
- olive oil cooking spray

- 3 cups water, or as neededsalt to taste

INSTRUCTIONS

Preheat an air fryer to 400 F (200 C).

Slice the plantain's tips off. Create a vertical cut in the skin from end to end, making sure to cut into the flesh of the plantain only through the thick skin and not in it. Cut the plantain into 1-inch pieces, still with the peel. Peel off every chunk of skin starting from the slit you've created.

Place the chunks of plantain in your basket of air fryer and spray them with a spray of olive oil. Fry air for 5 minutes. In the meantime prepare a salted bowl of water.

Extract the bits of the plantain with tongs from the air fryer. Use a tostonera (plant smasher) to break to about 1/2 inch thickness. Soak the broken tostones in the salted water bowl while crushing the remainder.

Extract the bits of the plantain with tongs from the air fryer. Use a tostanera (plant smasher) to break to about 1/2 "thickness. Soak the broken tostones in the salted water bowl while crushing the remainder.

Take off the salted water tostones and pat dry with a paper towel.

Return tostones in batches to the air fryer, filling the basket each time with a single layer. Sprinkle the tops with a spray of olive oil and season with salt; air fry for 5 minutes. Flip with tongs, and spray olive oil spray on the other side. Season to salt. Fry the air for 4 to 5 minutes, until golden brown and crisp.

Notes: If your plantains are especially hard to cut, you can use a case knife to help remove the skin, or start peeling them while under warm water, which can help.

If you don't have a plantain smasher, then the base of a mason jar or big mug will also fit.

NUTRITIONAL INFORMATION

Per Serving: 110 calories; 0.4 g fat; 28.5 g carbohydrates; 1.2 g protein; 0 mg cholesterol; 48 mg sodium.

32.   ROASTED BANANAS

INGREDIENTS

- 1 banana, sliced into 1/8-inch thick diagonals
- avocado oil cooking spray

INSTRUCTIONS

Line parchment paper bowl with an air fryer.

Preheat an air fryer to 375 F (190 C).

Place banana slices inside the bowl, making sure they don't touch; if possible, cook in batches. Slices of misty banana with avocado oil.

Cook for 5 minutes in an air fryer. Carefully cut baskets and flip slices of bananas (they'll be soft). Cook for an additional 2 to 3 minutes until the banana slices are browning and caramelizing. Remove completely from the tub.

NUTRITIONAL INFORMATION

Per Serving: 107 calories; 0.7 g fat; 27 g carbohydrates; 1.3 g protein; 0 mg cholesterol; 1 mg sodium.

33. STEAK TIPS AND PORTOBELLO MUSHROOMS

INGREDIENTS

- 1/4 cup olive oil1 tablespoon coconut aminos (soy-free seasoning sauce)
- 2 teaspoons Montreal steak seasoning
- 1/2 teaspoon garlic powder
- 2 strip steaks, cut into 3/4-inch pieces

- 4 ounces portobello mushrooms, quartered

INSTRUCTIONS

In a small bowl, add the olive oil, coconut amino, steak seasoning, and garlic powder. Mix well, stir in steaks and marinate for 15 minutes.

Preheat an air fryer to 390 ° F (200 ° C). Line the bottom of the basket with perforated parchment paper for the air fryer.

Drain marinade Steak bits. Air fryer tray of steak and quartered portobello mushrooms.

Cook for 5 minutes in preheated air fryer. Remove the pot, toss the steak and the mushrooms and continue to cook for another 4 minutes.

NUTRITIONAL INFORMATION

Per Serving: 548 calories; 40.1 g fat; 4.9 g carbohydrates; 41 g protein; 98 mg cholesterol; 731 mg sodium.

34. HONEY-CAJUN CHICKEN THIGHS

INGREDIENTS

- ½ cup buttermilk
- 1 teaspoon hot sauce
- 1?½ pounds skinless, boneless chicken thighs
- ¼ cup all-purpose flour
- cup tapioca flour

- 2½ teaspoons Cajun seasoning
- ½ teaspoon garlic salt
- ½ teaspoon honey powder
- ¼ teaspoon ground paprika
- teaspoon cayenne pepper
- 4 teaspoons honey

INSTRUCTIONS

mix buttermilk and hot sauce into a plastic resealable bag. Add chicken thighs and marinate in a small bowl for 30 minutes. Mix rice, tapioca, cajun seasoning, garlic salt, honey powder, paprika, and cayenne pepper. Remove thighs from buttermilk mixture and dredge by mixing with flour. Shake excess flour off.

Preheat an air fryer to 360 F (175 C).

Place the thighs of chicken in the basket of air fryer, and cook for about 15 minutes. Flip the thighs over and cook until the chicken thighs in the middle are no longer pink and the juices run clear, about 10 minutes longer. A center-inserted instant-read thermometer will read at least 165 degrees F (74 degrees C).

Remove the chicken thighs from the air fryer and drizzle with 1 teaspoon honey on each leg.

NUTRITIONAL   INFORMATION

Per Serving:

248 calories; 11.5 g total fat; 65 mg cholesterol; 430 mg sodium. 16.4 g carbohydrates; 19.1 g protein

35. BLACKENED CHICKEN BREAST

INGREDIENTS

- 2 teaspoons paprika
- 1 teaspoon ground thyme
- 1 teaspoon cumin
- ½ teaspoon cayenne pepper
- ½ teaspoon onion powder
- ½ teaspoon black pepper
- ¼ teaspoon salt
- 2 teaspoons vegetable oil
- 2 (12 ounce) skinless, boneless chicken breast halves

INSTRUCTIONS

In a cup, add the paprika, thyme, cumin, cayenne pepper, onion powder, black pepper, and salt. Move the spice mix to a flat plate.

Rub oil over each breast until completely covered. Roll each piece of chicken in blackening spice mixture, making sure that the spice sticks are pressed down on all sides. Let them sit for 5 minutes while the air fryer is preheated.

Preheat an air fryer for 5 minutes, at 360 degrees F (175 degrees C).

Put the chicken in the air fryer basket and cook for about ten minutes. Flip over and cook for 10 minutes. Move the chicken to a plate and allow 5 minutes to rest before serving.

NUTRITIONAL INFORMATION

Per Serving:

432 calories; 9.5 g total fat; 198 mg cholesterol; 516 mg sodium. 3.2 g carbohydrates; 79.4 g protein

36.   CRISPY RANCH AIR FRYER NUGGETS

INGREDIENTS

- 1 pound chicken tenders, cut into 1.5 to 2-inch pieces
- 1 (1 ounce) package dry ranch salad dressing mix
- 2 tablespoons flour
- 1 egg, lightly beaten
- 1 cup panko bread crumbs
- 1 serving olive oil cooking spray

INSTRUCTIONS

Put the chicken in a pot, sprinkle with the seasoning of the ranch and shake to mix. Let them sit for about 5-10 minutes.

Place the flour into a resealable bag. Layer the egg and panko bread crumbs in a small bowl on a platter. Preheat air fryer to 390 ° F (200 ° C).

Place the chicken in the bag, then toss it to cover. Dip the chicken gently into a mixture of the eggs, letting the excess drip away. Roll up pieces of chicken in panko, rubbing crumbs into the meat.

Spray the air fryer basket with oil and put pieces of chicken inside, making sure that they do not overlap. Depending on the size of your air fryer you may have to do two batches. Lightly mist the chicken with spray for cooking.

Cook for four minutes. Turn pieces of chicken and cook until the chicken is no longer pink on the inside, about 4 minutes more. Serve straight away.

NUTRITIONAL   INFORMATION

Per Serving: 244 calories; 3.6 g total fat; 112 mg cholesterol; 713 mg sodium. 25.3 g carbohydrates; 31 g protein

37. TARTAR SAUCE-BATTERED FISH STICKS

INGREDIENTS

- 3/4 cup mayonnaise
- 2 tablespoons dill pickle relish
- 1 teaspoon seafood seasoning
- 1 pound cod fillets, cut into 1x3-inch sticks
- 1 1/2 cups panko bread crumbs

INSTRUCTIONS

In a large bowl, mix mayonnaise, savor, and seafood seasoning. combine fish, then mix gently to brush.

Preheat an air fryer to 400 F (200 C).

Put the crumbs of bread over a tray. Coat each fish stick 1 at a time in bread crumbs.

Place fish sticks in a single layer in the air fryer basket to make sure that none of them strike. Cook for a further 12 minutes. Remove the basket and let rest for 1 minute before the fish sticks are moved to a towel-lined sheet of paper. Repeat with leftover fish sticks.

NUTRITIONAL INFORMATION

Per Serving: 401 calories; 34.1 g fat; 29.8 g carbohydrates; 4.7 g protein; 16 mg cholesterol; 634 mg sodium.

38. HONEY-SRIRACHA AIR FRYER WINGS

INGREDIENTS

- 12 fresh chicken wing drumettes
- ½ teaspoon salt
- ½ teaspoon garlic powder
- 1 tablespoon butter
- ¼ cup honey
- 2 teaspoons rice vinegar
- 1 tablespoon sriracha sauce

INSTRUCTIONS

Preheat an air fryer to 360 F (182 C).

In a cup, put the chicken wings and sprinkle with salt and garlic powder, tossing to cover.

Place wings in the basket of an air fryer. Set a 25-minute timer and cook the wings, shaking the basket every 7 to 8 minutes. Switch off the air fryer when the timer stops, and let wings stay in the basket for another 5 minutes.

Alternatively, melt the butter over medium heat in a small saucepan. Whisk the butter with the sugar, rice vinegar, and sriracha sauce and bring it to a boil. Reduce heat and simmer the sauce for 8 to 10 minutes over medium-low heat, whisking periodically. Turn heat off and set aside; sauce thickens as it cools.

Toss the fried wings together and sauce in a dish. Add extra sauce to serve next to wings.

NUTRITIONAL INFORMATION

Per Serving:

586 calories; 32.6 g total fat; 131 mg cholesterol; 1055 mg sodium. 36.2 g carbohydrates; 37.4 g protein

39. TEMPURA VEGGIES

INGREDIENTS

- 1/2 cup all-purpose flour
- 1/2 teaspoon salt, divided, or more to taste
- 1/2 teaspoon ground black pepper
- 2 eggs
- 2 tablespoons water
- 1 cup panko bread crumbs
- 2 teaspoons vegetable oil
- 1/2 cup whole green beans
- 1/2 cup whole asparagus spears
- 1/2 cup red onion rings
- 1/2 cup sweet pepper rings
- 1/2 cup avocado wedges
- 1/2 cup zucchini slices

INSTRUCTIONS

In a shallow dish, add the flour, 1/4 teaspoon salt, and pepper. Whisk the eggs and water together in another small platter. In a final, shallow dish, add panko and oil. Add either panko and/or flour mixture to the desired seasoning.

Sprinkle with remaining 1/4 teaspoon salt on the vegetables. Dip in mixture of rice, then in a mixture of eggs and eventually in a mixture of panko to paint.

Preheat the fryer to 400 degrees F (200 degrees C) and the oven to 95 degrees F.

In the air fryer basket, place half the vegetables in a single layer. Cook for about 10 minutes until golden brown. If needed, sprinkle with extra salt. Switch vegetables to the oven so that they keep warm. Repeat with other vegetables.

NOTES

Two seasoning ideas: Use 2 tablespoons of sesame seed to panko mixture and 1 teaspoon of ground ginger to flour mixture.

Apply 2 spoonfuls of shredded coconut to panko mix.

NUTRITIONAL INFORMATION

Per Serving: 247 calories; 10.1 g fat; 37.7 g carbohydrates; 9.3 g protein; 93 mg cholesterol; 464 mg sodium.

40.   PULL-APART PEPPERONI-CHEESE BREAD

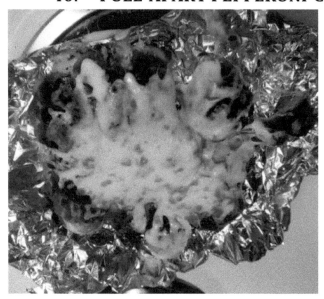

INGREDIENTS

- cooking spray
- 1 1/2 pounds fresh pizza dough
- 1 ounce sliced turkey pepperoni dried oregano to tasteground red pepper to tastegarlic salt to taste
- 1 teaspoon melted butter
- 1 teaspoon grated Parmesan cheese
- 1/2 cup shredded mozzarella cheese

INSTRUCTIONS

To suit the bottom of your air fryer, form a large sheet of aluminum foil into a pan with2-inch high sides. Spray cooking spray with nonstick.

Preheat air fryer for 15 minutes, to 390 degrees F (200 degrees C).

Roll the pizza dough into1-inch balls, and put in the aluminum foil pan in a single layer. Sprinkle with salt and pepperoni, oregano, red pepper and garlic. Melt butter in a bowl and sprinkle with Parmesan cheese.

Place the pan in the air fryer's bottom and cook for 15 minutes. Sprinkle bread with mozzarella cheese and cook for about 2 minutes, until cheese is melted and bubbled. Use tongs, detach from the air fryer to bring the pan sides up and out of the oven.

NUTRITIONAL INFORMATION

Per Serving: 478 calories; 8 g fat; 81.1 g carbohydrates; 17.4 g protein; 12 mg cholesterol; 1363 mg sodium.

41. PUMPKIN SEEDS

INGREDIENTS

- 1 3/4 cups pumpkin seeds
- 2 teaspoons avocado oil
- 1 teaspoon smoked paprika
- 1 teaspoon salt

INSTRUCTIONS

In a small colander put the pumpkin seeds, and rinse well.

Place onto a tray 2 sheets of paper towels. Place pumpkin seeds on towels and attach 2 more paper towels to cover. Press down to get most of the water drained. Let dry for at least 15 minutes.

Preheat the air fryer to 350 F (180 C).

Move seeds into a medium sized pot. Add the oil, paprika, and salt to the avocado. Use a small mixing spoon. Place the seeds in the basket with the air fryer and cook for 35 minutes, shaking the basket regularly.

Watch carefully over the last 5 minutes; the pumpkin seeds can go very easily from perfectly cooked to burnt.

Note: Olive oil may be substituted for avocado oil.

NUTRITIONAL INFORMATION

Per Serving: 233 calories; 20.2 g fat; 7.4 g carbohydrates; 9.9 g protein; 0 mg cholesterol; 395 mg sodium.

42. OLIVE-BRINED TURKEY BREAST

INGREDIENTS

- 3/4 cup brine from a can of olives
- 1/2 cup buttermilk
- 3 1/2 pounds boneless, skinless turkey breast
- 1 sprig fresh rosemary
- 2 sprigs fresh thyme

INSTRUCTIONS

Whisk the olive brine and the buttermilk together. Place the turkey breast into a plastic resealable bag and add the brine-buttermilk mix into the bag. Add sprigs of rosemary and thyme. Seal bottle, and cool for 8 hours.

Take the bag out of the refrigerator and allow the breast to rest until it reaches room temperature.

Preheat an air fryer to 350 F (175 C).

Cook the breast for 15 minutes at air fryer. Flip over the breast and cook for 5 minutes until the turkey breast in the center is no longer pink, and the juice runs clear. A center-inserted instant-read thermometer will read at least 165 degrees F (74 degrees C). If the internal temperature is lower, keep cooking at intervals of 5 minutes until the correct temperature is reached.

NUTRITIONAL   INFORMATION

Per Serving: 141 calories; 0.9 g fat; 1.4 g carbohydrates; 30.2 g protein; 82 mg cholesterol; 62 mg sodium.

43.   CHINESE FIVE-SPICE AIR FRYER BUTTERNUT SQUASH FRIES

INGREDIENTS

- 1 large butternut squash, peeled and cut into fries
- 2 tablespoons olive oil
- 1 tablespoon Chinese five-spice powder
- 1 tablespoon minced garlic
- 2 teaspoons sea salt
- 2 teaspoons black pepper

INSTRUCTIONS

The air fryer is preheated to 400 degrees F (200 degrees C).

Place squash cut into a large bowl. Add oil,5-spice powder, garlic, salt and black pepper to cover and shake.

In the preheated air fryer, cook butternut squash fries, shaking every 5 minutes, until crisp, taking 15 to 20 minutes. Cut the fries, and add extra sea salt to the season.

NUTRITIONAL INFORMATION

Per Serving: 150 calories; 4.9 g fat; 28.5 g carbohydrates; 2.5 g protein; 0 mg cholesterol; 596 mg sodium.

44.   PAKORAS

INGREDIENTS

- 2 cups chopped cauliflower
- 1 cup diced yellow potatoes
- 1 1/4 cups chickpea flour (besan)
- 3/4 cup water
- 1/2 red onion, chopped
- 1 tablespoon salt
- 1 clove garlic, minced
- 1 teaspoon curry powder
- 1 teaspoon coriander
- 1/2 teaspoon ground cayenne pepper, or more to taste
- 1/2 teaspoon cumin
- 1 serving cooking spray

INSTRUCTIONS

In a large bowl, mix cauliflower, carrots, chickpea flour, water, red onion, salt, garlic, curry powder, cayenne, coriander, and cumin. Set aside and let it rest for abouty 10-minutes.

Preheat air fryer to 350 ° F (175 ° C).

Oil air fryer basket with cooking spray. Spoon 2 cauliflower mixture tablespoon into a basket and flatten.

Do this as many times as your basket room permits without reaching the pakoras. Mist with non-stick spray to the top of each pakora.

Cook on for eight minutes. Flip over and cook for another 8 minutes. Move to a towel-lined sheet of paper. Repeat with batter other.

NUTRITIONAL INFORMATION

Per Serving: 81 calories; 1.2 g fat; 14.3 g carbohydrates; 4.3 g protein; 0 mg cholesterol; 891 mg sodium.

45. BANG-BANG CHICKEN

INGREDIENTS

- 1 cup mayonnaise
- ½ cup sweet chili sauce
- 2 tablespoons Sriracha sauce
- cup flour
- 1 pound chicken breast tenderloins, cut into bite-size pieces
- 1½ cups panko bread crumbs
- 2 green onions, chopped

INSTRUCTIONS

In a large bowl, mix mayonnaise, sweet chili sauce, and Sriracha. Spoon the mixture out 3/4 cup and set aside.

Drop the flour into a large plastic resealable bag. Add the chicken, close the jar, and cover with the shake. Move coated pieces of chicken with the mayonnaise mixture to the large bowl, and stir to combine.

Drop the crumbs of panko bread into another big resealable plastic bag. Working in hundreds, dropping pieces of chicken onto crumbs of bread, closing and shaking to cover.

Preheat an air fryer to 400 F (200 C).

Put as many pieces of chicken as you can in the air fryer bowl, without overcrowding. Cook for 10 minutes in a hot air fryer. Flip over and cook for another 5 minutes. Repeat with chicken leftover.

Move the fried chicken to a large bowl, and pour over the top reserved sauce. Sprinkle with the green onions and cover with a toss. Serve straight away.

NUTRITIONAL INFORMATION

Per Serving:

489 calories; 32.6 g total fat; 60 mg cholesterol; 818 mg sodium. 34.9 g carbohydrates; 20.9 g protein

46. KOREAN CHICKEN WINGS

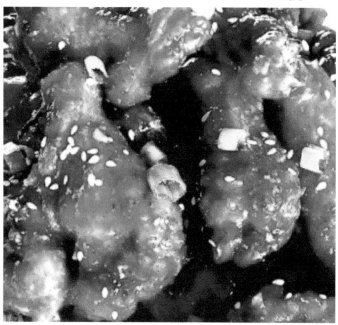

INGREDIENTS

- Sauce:
- 1/4 cup hot honey
- 3 tablespoons gochujang (Korean hot pepper paste)
- 1 tablespoon brown sugar
- 1 tablespoon soy sauce
- 1 teaspoon lemon juice
- 2 teaspoons minced garlic
- 1 teaspoon minced fresh ginger root
- 1/2 teaspoon salt
- 1/4 teaspoon black pepper
- 1/4 cup finely chopped green onions (green part only)
- Wings:
- 2 pounds chicken wings

- 1 teaspoon salt
- 1 teaspoon garlic powder
- 1 teaspoon onion powder
- 1/2 teaspoon black pepper
- 1/2 cup cornstarch
- Garnish:
- 2 tablespoons chopped green onions
- 1 teaspoon sesame seeds

INSTRUCTIONS

In a saucepan, add hot honey, gochujang, brown sugar, soya sauce, lemon juice, garlic, ginger, salt, and black pepper. At medium heat, bring the sauce to a boil, reduce heat and simmer for 5 minutes. Stir and incorporate green onions.

Air fryer preheats to 400 degrees F (200 degrees C).

In a large bowl, put the wings and mix with salt, garlic powder, onion powder, and black pepper. Apply the cornstarch, and throw the wings until completely covered. Shake will wing and put in the basket of the air fryer, making sure it doesn't touch; if possible, cook in batches.

Fry for 10 minutes in the preheated air fryer, shake the basket and fry for another 10 minutes. Flip the wings and fry until the chicken is cooked and the juice runs clear, 7 to 8 minutes longer.

Garnish with chopped green onions and sesame seeds with each wing in the sauce. Serve on the side with the rest of the sauce.

NUTRITIONAL   INFORMATION

Per Serving: 346 calories; 11.5 g fat; 44.8 g carbohydrates; 16.2 g protein; 48 mg cholesterol; 1247 mg sodium.

47.   CRISPY KETO FRIED CHICKEN

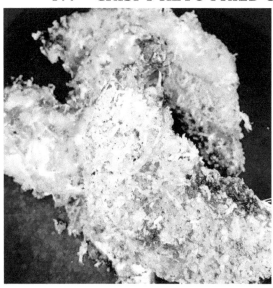

INGREDIENTS

- ½ cup whole-milk plain kefir
- 1 tablespoon hot sauce
- 1½ pounds chicken tenders
- 2 (3.25 ounce) packages pork rinds, crushed
- 3 ounces finely grated Parmesan cheese
- 1½ teaspoons garlic powder
- ¾ teaspoon cantanzaro herbs or Italian seasoning
- ½ teaspoon sweet smoked paprika

INSTRUCTIONS

In a shallow bowl, mix kefir and a hot sauce. Add the chicken tenders and marinate to 1 hour for 30 minutes, or longer if desired.

Pour the crushed pork rinds into a shallow resealable container. Mix in Parmesan cheese, garlic powder, herbs with cantanzaro, and paprika.

Preheat the air fryer, about 3 minutes, to 390 degrees F (200 degrees C).

Drain and dredge chicken from the kefir mixture through the mixture of pork rind.

Air fry for a minimum of 17 minutes in the preheated fryer, bringing chicken to halfway point.

NUTRITIONAL INFORMATION

Per Serving: 378 calories; 20.7 g total fat; 121 mg cholesterol; 563 mg sodium. 2.3 g carbohydrates; 47.4 g protein

48.   STUFFED MUSHROOMS WITH SOUR CREAM

INGREDIENTS

- 24 mushrooms, caps and stems diced
- 1/2 orange bell pepper, diced
- 1/2 onion, diced
- 1 small carrot, diced
- 2 slices bacon, diced
- 1 cup shredded Cheddar cheese
- 1/2 cup sour cream
- 1 1/2 tablespoons shredded Cheddar cheese, or to taste

INSTRUCTIONS

Place the stems of the mushroom, orange pepper bell, onion, carrot, and bacon in a medium-heat skillet. Cook and boil for about 5 minutes, until softened.

Stir in 1 cup Cheddar cheese and sour cream; cook for about 2 minutes until the stuffing is well mixed and cheese has melted.

Preheat air fryer to 350 ° F (175 ° C).

Use the baking tray to arrange mushroom caps. To each mushroom cap apply stuffing in a heaped pattern. Sprinkle over 1 1/2 spoonful of Cheddar cheese.

Drop the mushroom tray into the air-fryer tub. Cook, for about 8 minutes, until the cheese melts.

Notes:

You can use whatever cheese that you want.

You can also do this under the broiler: Bake for about 10 minutes until the cheese is in perfectly browned.

To bake: Bake at 325 degrees F (165 degrees C) until the cheese is melted, about 15 minutes.

NUTRITIONAL INFORMATION

Per Serving: 43 calories; 3.1 g fat; 1.7 g carbohydrates; 2.4 g protein; 8 mg cholesterol; 55 mg sodium.

49.   EASY SPRING ROLLS

INGREDIENTS

- 2 ounces dried rice noodles
- 1 tablespoon sesame oil
- 7 ounces ground beef
- 1 cup frozen mixed vegetables
- 1 small onion, diced
- 3 cloves garlic, crushed
- 1 teaspoon soy sauce
- 1 (16 ounce) package egg roll wrappers
- 1 tablespoon vegetable oil, or to taste

INSTRUCTIONS

Soak noodles in a bowl of hot water for about 5 minutes, until tender. Split in shorter lengths of noodles.

In a wok, heat the sesame oil over medium to high heat. Attach the ground beef, mixed vegetables, garlic, and onion. Cook for about 6 minutes, until the beef, is almost browned. Take off fire. Drop-in noodles; let stand until juices are absorbed. To the filling add soy sauce.

Preheat air fryer to 350 ° F (175 ° C).

Place 1 egg roll wrapper onto a flat work surface; put a filling strip diagonally across the wrapper. Fold over the filling at the top corner; fold in both side corners; brush center with cold water and roll spring roll over to cover. Continue and complete with remaining wrappers.

Apply vegetable oil to the tops of the spring rolls. Arrange a batch of spring rolls into the air fryer basket; cook for about 8 minutes until crisped and lightly browned. Repeat until it all cooks.

NUTRITIONAL   INFORMATION

Per Serving: 112 calories; 3.2 g fat; 16.4 g carbohydrates; 4.1 g protein; 8 mg cholesterol; 155 mg sodium.

50.   STUFFED AIR FRYER POTATOES

INGREDIENTS

- 4 baking potatoes, peeled and halved
- 3 teaspoons olive oil, divided
- 1/2 cup Cheddar cheese, divided
- 1/2 yellow onion, diced fine
- 2 slices bacon

INSTRUCTIONS

Preheat air fryer to 350 ° F (175 ° C).

Gently brown the potatoes with 1 teaspoon oil; place them in the air fryer basket and cook for 10 minutes.

Brush the potatoes with 1 extra teaspoon oil; continue cooking for 10 minutes in the air fryer. Coat with remaining oil and cook for about 10 minutes, until tender.

Halve the cooked potatoes. In a bowl, spoon the insides; add 1/4 cup Cheddar cheese and stir well.

Place the onion and bacon in a skillet and cook over medium-high heat, turning occasionally, around 10 minutes, until the bacon is evenly brown.

Fill the skins with a combination of potato-Cheddar cheese, onion, and bacon. Sprinkle over leftover milk. Return the stuffed potatoes to the air fryer; cook for about 6 minutes, until cheese is melted.

NUTRITIONAL INFORMATION

Per Serving: 288 calories; 10.3 g fat; 40.1 g carbohydrates; 9.8 g protein; 20 mg cholesterol; 206 mg sodium.

51. CELERY ROOT FRIES

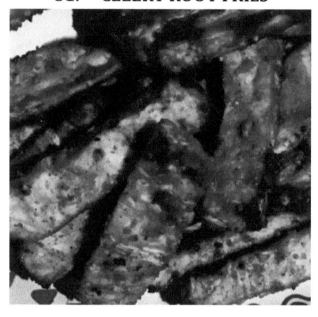

INGREDIENTS

- 1/2 celeriac (celery root), peeled and cut into 1/2-inch sticks
- 3 cups water
- 1 tablespoon lime juice
- Mayo Sauce:
- 1/3 cup vegan mayonnaise
- 1 tablespoon brown mustard
- 1 teaspoon powdered horseradish
- 1 tablespoon olive oil
- 1 pinch salt and ground black pepper to taste

INSTRUCTIONS

Place the root of celery into a dish. Garnish with water and lime juice. Mix for 20 minutes, and let it sit.

The air fryer is preheated to 400 degrees F (200 degrees C).

Make the sauce Mayo. Blend vegan mayonnaise, butter, and ground horseradish. Hold covered in the fridge until necessary.

Drain the sticks of the celery root, rinse, and place them back in a pot. Drizzle oil and season with salt and pepper over the fries. Equally toss to cover.

Remove celery root to basket of air fryer. Cook about 10 minutes, testing for doneness halfway through. Shake the basket and continue cooking, about 8 minutes longer, until the fries are crisp and browned.

Serve fries with vegan mayo on the side straight away.

NUTRITIONAL   INFORMATION

Per Serving: 168 calories; 12.9 g fat; 13 g carbohydrates; 1.8 g protein; 0 mg cholesterol; 259 mg sodium.

52.   TEX MEX HASH BROWNS

INGREDIENTS

- 1 1/2 pounds potatoes, peeled and cut into 1-inch cubes
- 1 tablespoon olive oil
- 1 red bell pepper, seeded and cut into 1-inch pieces
- 1 small onion, cut into 1-inch pieces
- 1 jalapeno, seeded and cut into 1-inch rings
- 1/2 teaspoon olive oil
- 1/2 teaspoon taco seasoning mix
- 1/2 teaspoon ground cumin
- 1 pinch salt and ground black pepper to taste

INSTRUCTIONS

20 Minutes to soak potatoes in cool water.

Preheat the air fryer to 320 ° F (160 ° C). Drain the potatoes, with a clean towel, dry them and move them to a large bowl. Drizzle over the potatoes 1 tablespoon of olive oil, and toss to coat. Remove them to the air fryer basket which is preheated. Set the timepiece for 18 minutes.

In the bowl used previously for the potatoes, put bell pepper, onion, and jalapeno. Sprinkle the olive oil, taco seasoning, ground cumin, salt, and pepper in 1/2 tablespoon. Toss to shirk.

Move potatoes with the vegetable mixture from the air fryer into the dish. Give the empty basket back to the air fryer and lift it to 356 degrees F (180 degrees C). Rapidly toss the bowl contents to uniformly blend the potatoes with the vegetables and season. Mixture moved into the tub. Cook for 6 minutes, shake the basket and cook till the potatoes are browned and crispy, about 5 more minutes. Serve straight away.

NUTRITIONAL INFORMATION

Per Serving: 186 calories; 4.3 g fat; 33.7 g carbohydrates; 4 g protein; 0 mg cholesterol; 79 mg sodium.

53. RATATOUILLE, ITALIAN-STYLE

INGREDIENTS

- 1/2 small eggplant, cut into cubes
- 1 zucchini, cut into cubes
- 1 medium tomato, cut into cubes
- 1/2 large yellow bell pepper, cut into cubes
- 1/2 large red bell pepper, cut into cubes
- 1/2 onion, cut into cubes
- 1 fresh cayenne pepper, diced
- 5 sprigs fresh basil, stemmed and chopped
- 2 sprigs fresh oregano, stemmed and chopped
- 1 clove garlic, crushedsalt and ground black pepper to taste
- 1 tablespoon olive oil
- 1 tablespoon white wine
- 1 teaspoon vinegar

INSTRUCTIONS

Preheat an air fryer to 400 F (200 C).

In a bowl, place the eggplant, zucchini, tomatoes, bell peppers, and onion. Attach the tomato, basil, oregano, garlic, salt, and pepper to taste. Mix well to get it evenly distributed. Drizzle in oil, wine, and vinegar, combining all vegetables to coat.

Pour the vegetable mixture into a baking platter and put into the air fryer bowl. Cook on for eight minutes. Stir; cook for an additional 8 minutes and continue to cook until tender, stirring 10 to 15 minutes more every 5 minutes. Switch off the air fryer, and put inside the pot. Leave to rest for five minutes before serving.

NUTRITIONAL INFORMATION

Per Serving: 79 calories; 3.8 g fat; 10.2 g carbohydrates; 2.1 g protein; 0 mg cholesterol; 48 mg sodium

54. STUFFING-FILLED PUMPKIN

INGREDIENTS

- 1/2 small pumpkinparsnip, diced
- 1 sweet potato, diced
- 1 onion, diced
- 1/2 cup peas
- 1 carrot, diced
- 1 egg
- 2 cloves garlic, minced
- 2 teaspoons dried mixed herbs

INSTRUCTIONS

Scrape the seeds halfway out of the pumpkin.

In a cup, add parsnip, sweet potato, onion, peas, carrot, egg, garlic, and blended herbs. Fill the pumpkin with a combination of vegetables.

Preheat an air fryer to 350 F (175 C). Put stuffed pumpkin in the pot, and cook for about 30 minutes until tender.

NUTRITIONAL INFORMATION

Per Serving: 247 calories; 3.3 g fat; 48.6 g carbohydrates; 9.3 g protein; 93 mg cholesterol; 210 mg sodium.

55. GUILT-FREE RANCH ZUCCHINI CHIPS

INGREDIENTS

- 2 zucchini, thinly sliced
- 1/4 cup all-purpose flour
- 1/8 teaspoon salt
- 1 pinch ground black pepper
- 1/2 cup ranch dressing
- 1/2 cup whole wheat bread crumbs
- 1/4 cup grated Parmesan cheese
- 1/4 teaspoon garlic powdercooking spray

INSTRUCTIONS

you will preheat an air fryer to 400degree F (200 C).

In a cup, add salt, rice, and pepper.

Pour dressing ranch into a tub.

In a third dish, add the crumbs of bread, Parmesan cheese, and garlic powder.

Dredge each piece of zucchini in a flour mixture and dip into a ranch dressing, cover the two sides and shake off excess dressing. Next, dip into the mixture of bread crumbs and press the breading gently onto each chip of zucchini.

Spray cooking spray on the air fryer bowl, then put breaded zucchini chips in a single layer in the container. Cook for 5 to 6 minutes, until browned. Repeat with the remaining chips of the courgette.

NUTRITIONAL INFORMATION

Per Serving: 243 calories; 17.8 g fat; 16.5 g carbohydrates; 5.3 g protein; 13 mg cholesterol; 522 mg sodium.

56. VEGETARIAN CHICKEN TENDERS

INGREDIENTS

- 1 cup all-purpose flour
- 3 eggs, beaten
- 2 cups panko bread crumbs
- 1 teaspoon garlic powder
- 3/4 teaspoon paprika
- 1/2 teaspoon cayenne pepper
- 1/2 teaspoon ground black pepper
- 1/2 teaspoon chili powder
- 1/4 teaspoon salt
- 2 (16 ounce) packages imitation chicken breast halves (seitan), cut into 1-inch wide strips
- cooking spray

INSTRUCTIONS

Pour flour over a large bowl. Put the eggs into a shallow bowl. In another shallow bowl, add the bread crumbs, garlic powder, paprika, cayenne pepper, black pepper, chili powder and salt.

Coat imitation strips of chicken in flour, dip in eggs, then dredge in a mixture of bread crumbs and put them on a tray.

Heat an air fryer up to 500 F (260 C).

Place a row of coated stripes in the basket of the air fryer. Spray with a light coat of spray to cook.

Cook strips for 6 minutes in the air-fryer. Open fryer with tongs to turn the pieces. Continue cooking until golden brown, for another 4 to 6 minutes.

NUTRITIONAL INFORMATION

Per Serving: 510 calories; 3.8 g fat; 49 g carbohydrates; 70.9 g protein; 123 mg cholesterol; 908 mg sodium

57. CHINESE PINEAPPLE PORK

INGREDIENTS

- 450 g pork loin, cut into cubes
- 1/2 teaspoon salt
- 1/2 teaspoon pepper
- 1/2 pineapple, cut into cubes
- 1 green pepper, cut into cubes
- 1 clove garlic, minced
- 1 teaspoon fresh ginger, minced
- 2 tablespoons soy sauce
- 1 tablespoon brown sugar
- 1 ActiFry spoon vegetable oil
- 1 small bunch fresh coriander leaves, chopped
- Toasted sesame seeds

INSTRUCTIONS

Season with salt and pepper over pork.

To the AirFry pan, add the seasoned pork, pineapple, green pepper, garlic, and ginger.

In a cup, add soy sauce and brown sugar. Pour in the ingredients above. Drizzle ingredients over vegetable oil.

Switch on your ActiFry and set the 17-minute cooking timer. Once you have completed the cooking process, test to ensure that all ingredients are cooked to your specifications.

Garnish with cilantro and sesame seeds. Serve with rice white, and enjoy!

NUTRITIONAL INFORMATION

Per Serving: 372 calories; 18.3 g fat; 28.6 g carbohydrates; 24.4 g protein; 71 mg cholesterol; 806 mg sodium.

58. POTATO-SKIN WEDGES

INGREDIENTS

- 4 medium russet potatoes
- 1 cup water
- 3 tablespoons canola oil
- 1 teaspoon paprika
- 1/4 teaspoon ground black pepper
- 1/4 teaspoon salt

INSTRUCTIONS

In a large pot put the potatoes and cover with salted water; bring to a boil. Reduce heat to medium-low, and simmer for about 20 minutes until fork-tender. Drain and drain. Place in a bowl and refrigerate for about 30 minutes, until completely cool.

In a mixing bowl, add butter, paprika, black pepper, and salt. Cut the cooled potatoes into quarters and stir in the mix.

you need to preheat the air fryer to 400degree F (200 C).

Attach 1/2 of the potato wedges to the basket of the air fryer, put them skin side down and be careful not to overcrowd.

Cook, for 13 to 15 minutes, until golden brown. Repeat with wedges leftover.

NUTRITIONAL INFORMATION

Per Serving: 259 calories; 10.8 g fat; 37.6 g carbohydrates; 4.4 g protein; 0 mg cholesterol; 160 mg sodium.

59. FALAFEL

INGREDIENTS

- 1 cup dry garbanzo beans
- 1 1/2 cups fresh cilantro, stems removed
- 3/4 cup fresh flat-leafed parsley, stems removed
- 1 small red onion, quartered
- 1 clove garlic
- 2 tablespoons chickpea flour
- 1 tablespoon ground coriander
- 1 tablespoon ground cumin
- 1 tablespoon sriracha saucesalt and ground black pepper to taste
- 1/2 teaspoon baking powder
- 1/4 teaspoon baking sodacooking spray

INSTRUCTIONS

Soak chickpeas for 24 hours in a large amount of cool water. Rub your fingers on soaked chickpeas to help loosen and remove skins. Rinse well, then clean. Spread chickpeas to dry onto a big, clean dish towel.

In a food processor, blend the chickpeas, cilantro, parsley, onion, and garlic until a rough paste develops. The mixture is moved to a large bowl. Add the flour, coriander, cumin, sriracha, salt, and pepper to chickpea and mix well. Cover the bowl and allow it to rest for 1 hour.

Preheat an air fryer to 375 F (190 C).

Add baking powder to the chickpea mixture, and baking soda. Use your hands to blend until you have already mixed. Shape 15 balls of equal size, and gently push to shape patties. Sprinkle falafel patties with spray for cooking.

In the preheated air fryer, place 7 falafel patties and cook for 10 minutes. Move cooked falafel to a plate and repeat for 10 to 12 minutes with the remaining 8 falafel.

Note:

you can also try harissa sauce in place of the sriracha.

NUTRITIONAL INFORMATION

Per Serving: 60 calories; 1.1 g fat; 9.9 g carbohydrates; 3.1 g protein; 0 mg cholesterol; 98 mg sodium.

60. SEXY MEATLOAF

INGREDIENTS

- 1/2 pound ground pork
- 1/2 pound ground veal
- 1 large egg
- 1/4 cup chopped fresh cilantro
- 1/4 cup gluten-free bread crumbs
- 2 medium spring onions, diced
- 1/2 teaspoon ground black pepper
- 1/2 teaspoon sriracha salt
- 1/2 cup ketchup
- 2 teaspoons gluten-free chipotle chili sauce
- 1 teaspoon olive oil
- 1 teaspoon blackstrap molasses

INSTRUCTIONS

The air fryer is preheated to 400 degrees F (200 degrees C).

Combine pork and veal in a non-stick baking dish that fits inside the basket of the air fryer. Put the potato, cilantro, bread crumbs, spring onions, black pepper, and 1/2 teaspoon of Sriracha salt into a well. Use your hands and blend well. Inside the baking dish shape a loaf.

In a small bowl, mix the ketchup, chipotle chili sauce, olive oil, and molasses and whisk well. Set aside but don't cool it down.

Cook meatloaf for 25 minutes in the air fryer, without opening the bowl. Cut meatloaf and top with ketchup mixture, completely covering the rim. Return the meatloaf to the fryer and bake until the heat reaches 160 degrees F (71 degrees C), Around 7 minutes. Turn off air fryer and let 5 minutes of meatloaf rest inside. Take the meatloaf out and let it rest for another 5 minutes before slicing and serving.

NUTRITIONAL INFORMATION

Per Serving: 272 calories; 14.4 g fat; 13.3 g carbohydrates; 22.1 g protein; 123 mg cholesterol; 536 mg sodium.

61.   TRIPLE-CHOCOLATE OATMEAL COOKIES

INGREDIENTS

- 3 cups quick-cooking oatmeal
- 1 1/2 cups all-purpose flour
- 1/4 cup cocoa powder
- 1 (3.4 ounce) package instant chocolate pudding mix
- 1 teaspoon baking soda1 teaspoon salt
- 1 cup butter, softened
- 3/4 cup brown sugar
- 3/4 cup white sugar
- 2 eggs
- 1 teaspoon vanilla extract
- 2 cups chocolate chips
- 1 cup chopped walnuts (optional)
- nonstick cooking spray

INSTRUCTIONS

Preheat an air fryer to 350 degrees F (175 degrees C), as directed by the manufacturer. Spray nonstick cooking spray to the air fryer pot.

In a cup, mix the oatmeal, flour, cocoa powder, pudding mixture, baking soda, and salt until well mixed. Deposit back.

Using an electric mixer, cream butter, brown sugar, and white sugar fall together in another cup. Remove vanilla extract and eggs. Attach the mixture of oatmeal and blend well. Stir in walnuts and chocolate chips.

Use a large cookie scoop to drop dough into the air fryer; flatten it out and leave about 1 inch between each cookie.

Cook for 6 to 10 minutes, until light brown. Before serving, cool onto a wire rack.

NUTRITIONAL INFORMATION

Per Serving: 199 calories; 10.9 g fat; 24.7 g carbohydrates; 2.9 g protein; 24 mg cholesterol; 180 mg sodium.

62. SHRIMP

INGREDIENTS

- 1 tablespoon butter, melted
- 1 teaspoon lemon juice
- 1/2 teaspoon garlic granules
- 1/8 teaspoon salt
- 1 pound large shrimp - peeled, deveined, and tails removed
- perforated parchment paper
- 1/8 cup freshly grated Parmesan cheese

INSTRUCTIONS

Put the butter in a medium container and allow it to melt. Blend together with the lemon juice, garlic granules, and salt. Add shrimp and cover with the toss.

Line air fryer basket with paper perforated to the parchment. Place shrimp in the basket of the air-fryer and sprinkle with Parmesan cheese.

Cook the shrimp at 400 degrees F (200 degrees C) in the air fryer until the shrimp is bright pink on the outside and the meat is opaque around 8 minutes.

NUTRITIONAL INFORMATION

Per Serving: 125 calories; 4.6 g fat; 0.5 g carbohydrates; 19.6 g protein; 182 mg cholesterol; 330 mg sodium.

63. PEANUT BUTTER & JELLY S'MORES

INGREDIENTS

- 1 chocolate-covered peanut butter cup
- 2 chocolate graham cracker squares, divided
- 1 teaspoon seedless raspberry jam
- 1 large marshmallow

INSTRUCTIONS

The air fryer is preheated to 400 degrees F (200 degrees C).

Put a cup of peanut butter on 1 square of graham cracker. Fill with Marshmallow and Jelly. Carefully place them in the basket of an air fryer.

Cook in a preheated air fryer, about 1 minute, until marshmallow is browned and softened. Remaining graham cracker square instantly tops up.

NUTRITIONAL INFORMATION

Per Serving: 249 calories; 8.2 g fat; 41.8 g carbohydrates; 3.9 g protein; 1 mg cholesterol; 281 mg sodium.

64.   JERK PORK SKEWERS WITH BLACK BEAN AND MANGO SALSA

INGREDIENTS

- Jamaican Jerk Seasoning:
- 2 tablespoons white sugar
- 4 1/2 teaspoons onion powder
- 4 1/2 teaspoons dried thyme, crushed
- 1 tablespoon ground allspice
- 1 tablespoon ground black pepper
- 1 1/2 teaspoons cayenne pepper, or to taste
- 1 1/2 teaspoons salt
- 3/4 teaspoon ground nutmeg
- 1/4 teaspoon ground cloves
- 1/4 cup shredded coconut
- 1 (1 pound) pork tenderloin, cut into 1 1/2-inch cubes
- 4 bamboo skewers, soaked in water for 30 minutes, drained
- 1 tablespoon vegetable oil1 mango - peeled, seeded, and chopped
- 1/2 (15 ounce) can black beans, rinsed and drained
- 1/4 cup finely chopped red onion
- 2 tablespoons fresh lime juice
- 1 tablespoon honey
- 1 tablespoon chopped fresh cilantro
- 1/4 teaspoon salt
- 1/8 teaspoon ground black pepper

INSTRUCTIONS

In a small bowl, blend together the sugar, onion powder, thyme, allspice, black pepper, cayenne pepper, salt, nutmeg and cloves for seasoning. Move rub to a small airtight container, reserving 1 spoonful of pork in a cup. Add the remaining 1 tablespoon of coconut to season; stir to combine.

Preheat the air fryer to 350 F (175 C).

Thread chunks of pork onto the skewers. Brush the pork with butter, sprinkle with seasoning mixture on all sides and put in the basket of the air fryer.

Cook in the preheated air fryer until 5 to 7 minutes for an instant-read thermometer inserted into the thickest part of the meat reads 145 degrees F (63 degrees C). In a medium bowl, mash 1/3 of the mango in the meantime. Add remaining mango, black beans, red onion, cilantro, lime juice, salt, and pepper. Serve the salsa alongside skewers of pork.

NUTRITIONAL INFORMATION

Per Serving: 313 calories; 10.8 g fat; 34.6 g carbohydrates; 22.3 g protein; 49 mg cholesterol; 1268 mg sodium.

65.   LOBSTER TAILS WITH LEMON-GARLIC BUTTER

INGREDIENTS

- 2 (4 ounce) lobster tails
- 4 tablespoons butter
- 1 teaspoon lemon zest
- 1 clove garlic, gratedsalt and ground black pepper to taste
- 1 teaspoon chopped fresh parsley
- 2 wedges lemon

INSTRUCTIONS

Butterfly lobster tails with kitchen shears cut lengthwise through the centers of the hard top shells and meat. Cut the bottoms of the shells, but not through. Split away from the tailpieces. Place the tails with lobster meat facing up into the air fryer basket.

allow the butter to melt at medium heat, in a small saucepan. Add lemon zest and garlic; heat for about 30 seconds, until the garlic is tender. Move 2 tablespoons of butter mixture to a small bowl and brush onto lobster tails; discard any remaining brushed butter to avoid uncooked lobster contamination. Season with salt and pepper.

Cook at 380 degrees F (195 degrees C) in an air fryer until the lobster meat is opaque, for 5 to 7 minutes. Spoon reserved butter over lobster meat from saucepan. Finish with parsley, and serve with wedges of lemon.

NUTRITIONAL INFORMATION

Per Serving: 313 calories; 25.8 g fat; 3.3 g carbohydrates; 18.1 g protein; 129 mg cholesterol; 590 mg sodium.

66. MEDITERRANEAN VEGETABLE MEDLEY

INGREDIENTS

- 1 small zucchini, cut into 1/4-inch slices
- 1 small summer squash, cut into 1/4-inch slices
- 1 cup shiitake mushrooms, stemmed and sliced
- 1 cup grape tomatoes2 tablespoons olive oil
- 2 cloves garlic, minced
- 1/2 teaspoon dried oregano
- 1/2 teaspoon kosher salt
- 1 teaspoon lemon zest

INSTRUCTIONS

Oven preheat to 200 degrees F (95 degrees C).

Cut slices of the eggplant into wedges and place them in a large bowl. Toss to blend with zucchini, summer squash, garlic, mushrooms, olive oil, oregano, and salt; Place vegetables in the air fryer basket in a single layer, and operate in small lots if necessary.

Cook the vegetables in the air fryer for 5 minutes at 360 degrees F (182 degrees C). Stir, and cook until tender and edges turn golden brown, about 5 more minutes. Move the vegetables to a baking pan and put the remaining vegetables in the preheated oven to keep them warm while cooking.

Upon serving sprinkle with lemon zest on vegetables.

Per Serving: 105 calories; 7.1 g fat; 8.9 g carbohydrates; 2.4 g protein; 0 mg cholesterol; 256 mg sodium.

67.   CAULIFLOWER WITH ALMONDS AND PARMESAN

INGREDIENTS

- 3 cups cauliflower florets
- 3 teaspoons vegetable oil, divided
- 1 clove garlic, minced
- 1/3 cup finely shredded Parmesan cheese
- 1/4 cup chopped almonds
- 1/4 cup panko bread crumbs
- 1/2 teaspoon dried thyme, crushed

INSTRUCTIONS

In a medium bowl, put cauliflower florets, 2 teaspoons of oil, and garlic; toss to coat. In an air-fryer tub, put in a single layer.

Cook in the air fryer for 10 minutes at 360 degrees F (180 degrees C), shaking the basket half way through.

Return the cauliflower to the bowl and toss with 1 tablespoon oil left over. Stir in Parmesan cheese, almonds, crumbs of bread and thyme; toss to coat. Return the cauliflower mixture to the air fryer basket and cook for about 5 minutes more until the mixture is crisp and browned.

NUTRITIONAL   INFORMATION

Per Serving: 148 calories; 10.1 g fat; 11 g carbohydrates; 6.7 g protein; 6 mg cholesterol; 158 mg sodium.

68.   CHOCOLATE CHIP COOKIE BITES

INGREDIENTS

- 1/2 cup butter, softened
- 1/2 cup packed brown sugar
- 1/4 cup white sugar
- 1/2 teaspoon baking soda
- 1/2 teaspoon salt1 egg
- 1 1/2 teaspoons vanilla extract
- 1 1/3 cups all-purpose flour
- 1 cup miniature semisweet chocolate chips
- 1/3 cup finely chopped pecans, toasted

INSTRUCTIONS

Cut a piece of parchment paper to fit into the tray of an air fryer.

Beat the butter for 30 seconds in a large bowl with a medium to a high-speed electric mixer. Add brown sugar, white sugar, baking soda, and salt; beat for 2 minutes at medium speed, sometimes scraping cup. Beat in the extract from the egg and vanilla until combined. Add flour, pound in as much as possible. Incorporate any leftover rice, chocolate chips, and pecan.

Drop dough onto the parchment paper 1 inch apart by teaspoonfuls. Carry the parchment paper carefully into the air fryer tub.

Turn the air fryer to 300 degrees F (150 degrees C) and cook for about 8 minutes, until golden brown and set. Remove parchment paper to cool onto a wire rack. Repeat with extra cookie dough.

NUTRITIONAL INFORMATION

Per Serving: 188 calories; 10.4 g fat; 23.6 g carbohydrates; 2 g protein; 24 mg cholesterol; 151 mg sodium.

69.   CRISPY FISH PO' BOYS WITH CHIPOTLE SLAW

INGREDIENTS

- cooking sprayCrispy Fish:
- 4 (4 ounce) fillets white fish, about 1/2- to 1-inch thick
- 1/4 cup all-purpose flour
- 1/2 teaspoon ground black pepper
- 1/4 teaspoon salt
- 1/4 teaspoon garlic powder
- 1 egg
- 1 tablespoon water
- 1/2 cup panko bread crumbs
- 1/4 cup cornmeal
- Chipotle Slaw:
- 1/3 cup sour cream
- 1/4 cup mayonnaise
- 1 tablespoon fresh lime juice
- 1/4 teaspoon salt
- 1/4 teaspoon ground dried chipotle pepper
- 3 cups shredded cabbage with carrot (coleslaw mix)
- 1/4 cup chopped fresh cilantro
- Sandwiches:
- 4 hoagie rolls, split lengthwise and toasted
- 2 tablespoons crumbled queso fresco
- 4 lime wedges

INSTRUCTIONS

Coat with cooking spray from an air fryer tub. Rinse fish fillets with paper towels, and pat dry.

In a shallow dish, add flour, black pepper, salt, and garlic powder. In a second, shallow dish, whisk egg and water together. In a final, shallow dish, mix bread crumbs and cornmeal.

Dip each fish fillet in the flour mixture, then in the mixture of the eggs and finally in the mixture of the bread crumbs. Sprinkle the fillets with a cooking spray and put them in a single layer in the prepared air fryer tray, cooking in lots if necessary.

Cook at 400 degrees F (200 degrees C) in the air fryer until the breaded coating is browned and the fish flakes are easily checked with a fork, 6 to 10 min. Alternatively, in a medium bowl, mix sour cream, mayonnaise, lime juice, salt, and dry chipotle pepper. Attach a mixture of coleslaw and cilantro; toss to cover.

Eat the fish fillets in rolls of hoagies. Top with fresh chipotle slaw and cheese, and eat with lime wedges.

NUTRITIONAL INFORMATION

Per Serving: 899 calories; 34 g fat; 106.1 g carbohydrates; 45.3 g protein; 145 mg cholesterol; 1312 mg sodium.

70. DONUT STICKS

INGREDIENTS

- 1 (8 ounce) package refrigerated crescent roll dough
- 1/4 cup butter, melted
- 1/2 cup white sugar
- 2 teaspoons ground cinnamon
- 1/2 cup any flavor fruit jam

INSTRUCTIONS

Unroll the dough sheet in a crescent roll and pat it to a rectangle of 8x12 inches. Cut the dough with a pizza cutter in half lengthwise and cut each piece cross-sectionally into 1/2-inch wide "sticks." Dip the doughnut sticks in melted butter and place in the air fryer basket one afterwards.

Cook 380 degrees F (195 degrees C) in the air fryer until well browned, for 4 to 5 minutes.

In a pie plate, or small cup, add sugar and cinnamon. Remove the doughnut sticks from the air fryer and roll into a mixture of cinnamon and sugar. Repeat with extra flour.

Serve with jam on doughnut sticks.

NUTRITIONAL INFORMATION

Per Serving: 266 calories; 11.8 g fat; 37.6 g carbohydrates; 2.2 g protein; 15 mg cholesterol; 267 mg sodium.

71.   DOUBLE CHERRY MINI EGG ROLLS

INGREDIENTS

- 1/2 (8 ounce) package cream cheese, softened
- 1/3 cup cherry jam
- 1/4 cup dried tart red cherries, chopped
- 16 (3.5 inch square) wonton wrapperswater, as needednonstick cooking spray
- 3 tablespoons white sugar
- 1/2 teaspoon ground cinnamon

INSTRUCTIONS

Preheat an air fryer to 400 F (200 C).

In a small bowl, whisk the cream cheese and jam together; stir in dried cherries.

Place a wonton wrapper on a surface of work with an angle pointing toward you. Moisten with water to the edges. Spoon a rounded cherry mixture teaspoon just below the wrapper center.

Fold the bottom corner over filling, tucking the other side under. Fold side corners over filling; roll the egg away to the remaining corner from you. Continue and fill with remaining wrappers.

Coat the egg rolls with cooking spray on both sides. Arrange the egg rolls in a single layer in the air fryer basket, in batches if necessary. Cook in a preheated air fryer for 4 to 5 minutes until well browned.

Meanwhile, blend sugar and cinnamon together in a shallow bowl.

Remove the egg rolls from the air fryer and roll into cinnamon sugar immediately, using two forks. Cool off for 5 to 10 minutes on a wire rack. Serving warm.

NUTRITIONAL INFORMATION

Per Serving: 83 calories; 2.6 g fat; 13.4 g carbohydrates; 1.5 g protein; 8 mg cholesterol; 69 mg sodium.

72. SESAME-CRUSTED COD WITH SNAP PEAS

INGREDIENTS

- 4 (5 ounce) cod filletssalt and ground black pepper to taste
- 3 tablespoons butter, melted
- 2 tablespoons sesame seedsvegetable oil
- 2 (6 ounce) packages sugar snap peas
- 3 cloves garlic, thinly sliced
- 1 medium orange, cut into wedges

INSTRUCTIONS

Brush the basket with vegetable oil to the air fryer and preheat to 400 degrees F (200 degrees C).

If frozen, thaw fish; wash with paper towels, and sprinkle lightly with salt and pepper.

In a small bowl, whisk butter and sesame seeds together. Set aside 2 butter mixture tablespoons for the fish. Place the peas and garlic in the air fryer basket with the remaining butter mixture.

Cook the peas in the preheated air fryer in lots, if necessary, tossing once, about 10 minutes, until just tender. Remove and keep the fish warm as they cook.

Brush the fish with 1/2 of the butter mixture leftover. Put fillets in the basket with the air fryer. Cook for 4 minutes; turn the fish over. Brush the remaining mixture with butter. Cook for another 5 to 6 minutes or until fish starts to flake when checked with a fork. Serve with orange wedges and snap peas.

NUTRITIONAL INFORMATION

Per Serving: 364 calories; 15.2 g fat; 22.9 g carbohydrates; 31.4 g protein; 75 mg cholesterol; 202 mg sodium.

73. SHORTBREAD COOKIE FRIES

INGREDIENTS

- 1 1/4 cups all-purpose flour
- 3 tablespoons white sugar
- 1/2 cup butter
- 1/3 cup strawberry jam
- 1/8 teaspoon ground dried chipotle pepper (optional)
- 1/3 cup lemon curd

INSTRUCTIONS

In a medium sized dish, mix flour and sugar. Use a pastry blender to cut butter until the mixture resembles fine crumbs and starts to adhere. Forme the mixture into a ball and knead to a smooth spot.

Preheat an air fryer to 350 F (190 C).

Roll the dough on a lightly floured surface to 1/4-inch thick. Cut into "fries," about 3-to4-inch long, 1/2-inch high. Sprinkle with added sugar.

Arrange fries in the air-fryer basket in a single layer. Cook for 3 to 4 minutes, until lightly brown. Let cool down in the basket before strong enough to cool completely to move to a wire rack. Repeat with leftover dough. To give strawberry "ketchup," use the back of a spoon to push jam through a fine-mesh sieve. Stir the chipotle into the table. Whip the lemon curd to make it a dippable consistency for the "mustard." Serve the strawberry ketchup and lemon curd mustard with the sugar cookie fries.

NUTRITIONAL INFORMATION

Per Serving: 75 calories; 3.9 g fat; 9.6 g carbohydrates; 0.7 g protein; 10 mg cholesterol; 27 mg sodium

74. TATER TOTS WITH GOCHUJANG CHEESE SAUCE

INGREDIENTS

- 1 (16 ounce) package frozen bite-size potato nuggets
- 1 (8 ounce) package shredded cheddar cheese
- 1/2 cup heavy whipping cream
- 1 tablespoon gochujang (korean hot pepper paste), or more to taste
- 1/4 teaspoon salt

INSTRUCTIONS

Preheat an air fryer to 370 ° F (188 ° C).

In the preheated air fryer, cook the potato nuggets until crispy and cooked through, about 15 minutes, shaking the air fryer basket halfway through cooking time.

In the meantime heat a casserole over medium-high heat. Add cheddar cheese and cream; whisk for about 5 minutes, until cheese is melted. Add salt and gochujang, and mix until mixed. Drizzle the potato nuggets over the sauce.

NUTRITIONAL INFORMATION

Per Serving: 265 calories; 20.1 g fat; 15.8 g carbohydrates; 8.6 g protein; 50 mg cholesterol; 495 mg sodium.

75.   EASY BAKED POTATOES

INGREDIENTS

- 4 large baking potatoes, scrubbed
- 2 tablespoons olive oil
- coarse kosher salt
- ground black pepper
- garlic powder
- dried parsley
- 4 tablespoons butter

INSTRUCTIONS

Preheat an air fryer to 400 F (200 C).

Brush the potatoes with the olive oil and season with salt, pepper, garlic powder, and parsley. Place potatoes in the basket of the air-fryer.

Cook in a preheated air fryer, depending on the size of the potato, until the potatoes are tender, 40 to 50 minutes.

Slice the potatoes longitudinally. Use your hands to pinch both sides of each potato and force the potatoes to open until the fluffy inside comes up. Put 1 spoonful of butter into each potato.

NUTRITIONAL INFORMATION

Per Serving: 448 calories; 18.6 g fat; 64.9 g carbohydrates; 7.7 g protein; 31 mg cholesterol; 205 mg sodium.

76. TURKEY BREAST

INGREDIENTS

- Herb Butter:
- 1 tablespoon finely chopped fresh rosemary
- 1 teaspoon finely chopped fresh chives
- 1 teaspoon finely minced fresh garlic
- 1/2 teaspoon salt, or to taste
- 1/4 teaspoon ground black pepper, or to taste
- 2 tablespoons cold unsalted butter
- 2 3/4 pounds skin-on, bone-in split turkey breast

INSTRUCTIONS

Preheat air fryer to 350 ° F (175 ° C).

In a cutting board put the rosemary, chives, garlic, salt and pepper. Cut butter on top of herbs and seasonings into thin slices, and mash until well blended.

Pat turkey breast dry, and rub on both sides and under the skin with herbal oil.

Put the turkey in the air fryer tub, skin side down, and fry for about 20 minutes.

Switch turkey carefully to the skin-side and continue to fry until an instant-read thermometer inserted near the bone reads 165 degrees F (74 degrees C), about 18 more minutes. Switch to an aluminum foil platter and tent; allow for 10 minutes to rest. Slice soft, and drink.

NUTRITIONAL INFORMATION

Per Serving: 263 calories; 10.1 g fat; 0.3 g carbohydrates; 40.2 g protein; 86 mg cholesterol; 913 mg sodium.

77. COCONUT CHICKEN

INGREDIENTS

- ½ cup canned coconut milk
- ½ cup pineapple juice
- 2 tablespoons brown sugar
- 1 tablespoon soy sauce
- 2 teaspoons Sriracha sauce
- 1 teaspoon ground ginger
- 1 pound boneless skinless chicken breasts, cut into strips
- 2 eggs
- 1 cup sweetened shredded coconut
- 1 cup panko bread crumbs
- 1?½ teaspoons salt
- ½ teaspoon ground black pepper
- nonstick cooking spray

INSTRUCTIONS

In a medium-sized bowl, put coconut milk, pineapple juice, brown sugar, soy sauce, Sriracha sauce, and ginger and whisk to mix. Attach strips of chicken, and toss to coat. Cover with plastic wrap, and cool 2 hours or overnight.

Preheat an air fryer to 375 F (190 C).

Whisk the eggs in a bowl. In a separate bowl, mix shredded coconut, panko, salt, and pepper.

Remove strips of chicken from the marinade, and shake off excess. Discard the marinade leftover. Dip strips of chicken in beaten egg, then in a mixture of coconut-panko, then again in a mixture of eggs and again in a mixture of coconut-panko, double-dipping and double coating per strip.

Sprinkle with a cooking spray on the air fryer pot. Sprinkle with a cooking spray on the air fryer basket.

Place breaded strips of chicken in the air fryer basket, making sure they don't touch; work in batches if necessary.

Cook for 6 minutes, flip strips and continue cooking until lightly browned and toasted, another 4 to 6 minutes.

NUTRITIONAL   INFORMATION

Per Serving:

418 calories; 17.4 g total fat; 158 mg cholesterol; 1493 mg sodium. 41.1 g carbohydrates; 31.1 g protein

78.   OLD BAY CHICKEN WINGS

INGREDIENTS

- 2 pounds chicken wings
- 2 tablespoons seafood seasoning
- 1/4 teaspoon freshly cracked black pepper
- 1/2 cup cornstarch
- Sauce:
- 4 tablespoons butter
- 1 teaspoon seafood seasoning

INSTRUCTIONS

The air fryer is preheated to 400 degrees F (200 degrees C).

In a large bowl, put the chicken wings and toss with 2 tablespoons of Old Bay(R) seasoning and black pepper. Remove the cornstarch, and throw the wings until completely covered. Shake each wing and put in the basket of the air fryer, making sure it doesn't touch; if possible, cook in batches.

Fry 10 minutes in the preheated air fryer, shake the basket and fry for another 8 minutes. Flip the wings over and fry until chicken is cooked and the juices run clear, 5 to 6 minutes longer.

Meanwhile, in a small saucepan, add butter and 1 teaspoon Old Bay(R) seasoning for a sauce. Over medium heat bring to a boil, stirring constantly.

Dip the sauce into each leg. Serve with extra sauce on the other side.

NUTRITIONAL   INFORMATION

Per Serving: 335 calories; 22.8 g fat; 15.8 g carbohydrates; 15.7 g protein; 78 mg cholesterol; 1083 mg sodium.

79.   BRATWURST BITES WITH SPICY BEER MUSTARD

INGREDIENTS

- 1/2 cup dark beer
- 3 tablespoons honey
- 1/2 teaspoon ground turmeric
- 1/8 teaspoon ground allspice
- 1/2 cup stone-ground spicy mustard
- 6 miniature multi-colored sweet peppers, halved lengthwise, seeds removed
- 5 links bratwurst, cut into 1-inch chunks

INSTRUCTIONS

In a small saucepan, add the malt, honey, turmeric, and allspice; bring to a boil. Reduce heat to medium, and simmer uncovered for about 8 minutes, until the volume has decreased by half. Rub in the mustard and allow to stand until ready to serve.

Place the sweet peppers and chunks of bratwurst in the air fryer basket in a single layer.

Cook 400 degrees F (200 degrees C) in the air fryer, flipping once halfway through the cooking until the peppers are tender and the edges of bratwurst are golden brown and crisp around 10 minutes. A thermometer instant-read inserted in the center of the brats would read 165 degrees F (75 degrees C). If need be, work in groups.

Serve warm with a sauce made with mustard.

NUTRITIONAL INFORMATION

Per Serving: 112 calories; 3.3 g fat; 15.2 g carbohydrates; 3.6 g protein; 16 mg cholesterol; 324 mg sodium

80.   ZUCCHINI CURLY FRIES

INGREDIENTS

- 1 zucchini1 egg, beaten
- 1 cup panko bread crumbs
- 1/2 cup grated Parmesan cheese
- 1 teaspoon Italian seasoning
- nonstick cooking spray

INSTRUCTIONS

Preheat an air fryer to 400 F (200 C).

Cut the zucchini into spirals by means of a modified shredding blade with a large blade

Drop the egg into a shallow platter. In a big resealable plastic bag, add the bread crumbs, Parmesan cheese, and Italian seasoning. In the beaten egg, dip 1/2 of the specialized zucchini and then put in the bag to cover with a mixture of bread crumbs.

Oil air fryer basket with cooking spray. Arrange breaded zucchini fries in the prepared basket, ensuring that they are not overcrowded. Oil cooking oil to the tips.

Cook for about 10 minutes, flipping halfway through cooking time, until crispy. Pass the fries to a plate lined with paper towels. Repeat process of breading and cooking with remaining spirals of the zucchini.

NUTRITIONAL INFORMATION

Per Serving: 136 calories; 5.1 g fat; 20.5 g carbohydrates; 8.6 g protein; 55 mg cholesterol; 305 mg sodium.

81. PORK MEATBALLS

INGREDIENTS

- 12 ounces ground pork8 ounces ground Italian sausage (mild or hot)
- 1/2 cup panko bread crumbs
- 1 egg
- 1 teaspoon salt
- 1 teaspoon dried parsley
- 1/2 teaspoon paprika

INSTRUCTIONS

Preheat the air fryer to 350 F (175 C).

In a large bowl, combine the pork, bacon, bread crumbs, egg, salt, parsley, and paprika and blend until evenly mixed. Use an ice cream scoop to form into 12 equally sized meatballs. Place the meatballs on a tray to bake.

Place 1/2 of the meatballs in the air fryer basket and cook for eight minutes. Shake the pot, and cook for another 2 minutes. Transfer to a serving plate, and allow 5 minutes to rest. Repeat with meatballs leftover.

NUTRITIONAL INFORMATION

Per Serving: 120 calories; 8.1 g fat; 3.8 g carbohydrates; 8.5 g protein; 41 mg cholesterol; 391 mg sodium.

82.   FRIED GREEN TOMATOES IN THE AIR FRYER

INGREDIENTS

- cooking spray
- 1 egg, beaten
- 1/2 cup cornmeal
- 1/3 cup self-rising flour
- 1/3 cup panko bread crumbs
- 1 teaspoon salt
- 1/2 teaspoon ground black pepper
- 2 green tomatoes, sliced

INSTRUCTIONS

You will Preheat the air fryer to 400 F (200 C). Oil air fryer basket with cooking spray.

Pour the egg onto a shallow platter. In a second, shallow dish, blend the cornmeal, rice, panko, salt, and pepper. Dip each tomato slice into an egg, then coat both sides in a mixture of cornmeal.

In the prepared tub, put tomato slices in a single layer and gently mist the tops with a cooking spray.

Cook for 8 minutes in a preheated air fryer. Flip the tomatoes and spray with a cooking spray on any dry spots. Cook 4 more minutes, and switch to a towel-lined sheet of paper. Repeat with slices of tomatoes leftover.

NUTRITIONAL   INFORMATION

Per Serving: 144 calories; 2.2 g fat; 28.7 g carbohydrates; 5.5 g protein; 46 mg cholesterol; 777 mg sodium.

83. MUSHROOMS

INGREDIENTS

- 8 ounces cremini mushrooms, halved or quartered
- 2 tablespoons avocado oil
- 1 teaspoon low-sodium soy sauce (such as Bragg)
- 1/2 teaspoon garlic granules
- salt and ground black pepper to taste

INSTRUCTIONS

You will Preheat the air fryer to 200 F (90 C).

In a cup, mix mushrooms, avocado oil, soy sauce, garlic granulates, salt, and pepper; shake to cover. Switch to bowl with the air fryer.

Fry the mushrooms in the air fryer, rotating periodically for 10 minutes.

NUTRITIONAL INFORMATION

Per Serving: 152 calories; 14.4 g fat; 4.5 g carbohydrates; 3.7 g protein; 0 mg cholesterol; 172 mg sodium.

84. VEGETARIAN CAULIFLOWER AND CHICKPEA TACOS

INGREDIENTS

- 1 tablespoon olive oil
- 1 tablespoon lime juice
- 1 teaspoon chili powder
- 1 teaspoon ground cumin
- 1 teaspoon sea salt
- 1/4 teaspoon garlic powder
- 1 (15 ounce) can chickpeas, drained
- 1 small head cauliflower, cut into bite-sized pieces
- Sauce:
- 1 cup sour cream
- 1/4 cup chopped fresh cilantro
- 1/8 cup lime juice
- 1 tablespoon Sriracha
- salt to taste
- 6 (6 inch) corn tortillas

INSTRUCTIONS

Preheat an air fryer to 370 ° F (190 ° C).

In a large bowl, whisk together olive oil, lime juice, chili powder, cumin, salt, and garlic powder. Remove chickpeas and cauliflower and mix until coated evenly.

In a cup, mix sour cream, cilantro, lime juice, and Sriracha. Season with to taste salt.

Place cauliflower mixture in the air fryer basket. Cook and mix for 10 minutes, then cook for another 10 minutes. stir it again and cook for about 5 minutes, until desired crispness.

Cauliflower spoon mixture into corn tortillas and sauce tip.

NUTRITIONAL INFORMATION

Per Serving: 232 calories; 11.8 g fat; 27.6 g carbohydrates; 6.1 g protein; 17 mg cholesterol; 616 mg sodium.

85.   FINGERLING POTATOES WITH DIP

INGREDIENTS

- 12 ounces fingerling potatoes, halved lengthwise
- 1 tablespoon olive oil
- 1 teaspoon garlic powder
- 1/4 teaspoon paprikasalt and ground black pepper to taste
- Dipping Sauce:
- 1/3 cup reduced-fat sour cream
- 2 tablespoons mayonnaise
- 2 tablespoons finely grated Parmesan cheese
- 1 1/2 tablespoons ranch dressing mix
- 1 tablespoon white vinegar
- 1 tablespoon chopped fresh parsley

INSTRUCTIONS

Preheat an air fryer for 5 minutes, at 390 degrees F (200 degrees C).

In a bowl, place potatoes and add olive oil, garlic powder, paprika, salt, and pepper. Toss until the potatoes are coated, and move to the basket of the air fryer.

Cook in the preheated air fryer until the potatoes are cooked through and crispy, 15 to 17 minutes, shaking the basket half way through.

When cooking the potatoes, blend in a small bowl sour cream, mayonnaise, Parmesan cheese, ranch dressing mix and vinegar.

Add to a plate the cooked potatoes, and garnish with the parsley. Serve with dipping sauce straight away.

NUTRITIONAL INFORMATION

Per Serving: 385 calories; 24.2 g fat; 36 g carbohydrates; 7 g protein; 25 mg cholesterol; 628 mg sodium.

86. FINGERLING POTATOES

INGREDIENTS

- 1 pound fingerling potatoes, halved lengthwise
- 1 tablespoon olive oil
- 1/2 teaspoon ground paprika
- 1/2 teaspoon parsley flakes
- 1/2 teaspoon garlic powder
- salt and ground black pepper to taste

INSTRUCTIONS

you will preheat the air fryer to 400 F (200 C).

Place halves of the potato in a large bowl. Add olive oil, paprika, parsley, garlic powder, salt, and pepper, then stir until coated evenly.

Place the potatoes in the preheated air fryer basket and cook for 10 minutes. Stir and cook for about 5 minutes, until target crispness is achieved.

NUTRITIONAL INFORMATION

Per Serving: 120 calories; 3.5 g fat; 20.3 g carbohydrates; 2.4 g protein; 0 mg cholesterol; 46 mg sodium.

87.   BLACKENED FISH TACOS

INGREDIENTS

- 1 (15 ounce) can seasoned black beans, rinsed and drained
- 2 ears corn, kernels cut from the cob
- 1 tablespoon olive oil1 tablespoon lime juice
- 1/2 teaspoon salt
- 1 pound tilapia filletscooking spray
- 1/4 cup blackened seasoning
- 4 (6 inch) corn tortillas
- 1 lime, cut into wedges
- 1 teaspoon Louisiana-style hot sauce (optional)

INSTRUCTIONS

Oven preheat to 400 degrees F (200 degrees C).

In a cup, mix black beans, corn, olive oil, lime juice and salt. Stir gently until the beans and the corn are coated evenly; set aside.

Place fish filets with paper towels on a clean work surface, and pat dry. Sprinkle each fillet lightly with a cooking spray and sprinkle 1/2 of the blackened seasoning over the rim. Flip the fillets over, spray and sprinkle with the remaining seasoning.

Place fish in the air fryer basket in a single layer and work in lots if needed. Cook for another 2 minutes. Flip the fish and cook for another 2 minutes; move to a platter.

Place the bean and maize mixture in the air fryer basket, and cook for 10 minutes, stirring halfway.

Layer the fish in tortillas of corn and cover with a mixture of beans and peas. Serve with hot sauce and the lime wedges.

Per Serving: 360 calories; 6.9 g fat; 43.3 g carbohydrates; 33.4 g protein; 42 mg cholesterol; 2210 mg sodium.

88. LATKES

INGREDIENTS

- 1 (16 ounce) package frozen shredded hash brown potatoes, thawed
- 1/2 cup shredded onion
- 1 eggkosher salt and ground black pepper to taste
- 2 tablespoons matzo mealavocado oil cooking spray

INSTRUCTIONS

you will Preheat an air fryer to 375 degrees F (190 degrees C), as directed by the manufacturer. Layout a parchment pad, or waxed paper.

Layer thawed potatoes on several layers of paper towels, and shredded onion. Fill with extra paper towels and press to squeeze most of the liquid out.

Whisk the egg, salt, and pepper together in a large bowl. In a pan, whisk in potatoes and onion. Sprinkle with the matzo meal on top and stir until the ingredients are distributed evenly.

Use your hands to shape a mixture into ten patties 3 to 4 inches wide. Place patties on a waxed paper or parchment.

Sprinkle with a cooking spray on the air fryer pot. Place half of the patties carefully in the basket and generously spray with a cooking spray.

Air-fry to the outside for 10 to 12 minutes, until crispy and dark golden brown. (If you want a softer latke, test for doneness at 8 minutes.) Remove latkes from the plate.

Repeat with remaining patties, before frying, spray them with a cooking spray.

NUTRITIONAL INFORMATION

Per Serving: 97 calories; 6.5 g fat; 18.6 g carbohydrates; 3.3 g protein; 33 mg cholesterol; 121 mg sodium.

89. SAUSAGE PATTIES

INGREDIENTS

- 1 (12 ounce) package sausage patties
- 1 serving nonstick cooking spray

INSTRUCTIONS

firstly you will need to heat the air fryer to 400 F (200 C).

Place sausage patties in 1 layer in the tub, and work in lots if necessary.

Cook for 5 minutes in a preheated air fryer. Take the basket out, turn the sausage over and cook until a thermometer inserted in the center of a patty reads about 3 minutes more than 160 degrees F (70 degrees C).

NUTRITIONAL INFORMATION

Per Serving: 145 calories; 9 g fat; 0.7 g carbohydrates; 14.1 g protein; 46 mg cholesterol; 393 mg sodium.

90.   CRISPY BREADED PORK CHOPS

INGREDIENTS

- olive oil spray
- 6 3/4-inch thick center cut boneless pork chops, fat trimmed (5 oz each)
- kosher salt
- 1 large egg, beaten
- 1/2 cup panko crumbs, check labels for GF
- 1/3 cup crushed cornflakes crumbs
- 2 tbsp grated parmesan cheese, omit for dairy free
- 1 1/4 tsp sweet paprika
- 1/2 tsp garlic powder
- 1/2 tsp onion powder
- 1/4 tsp chili powder
- 1/8 tsp black pepper

INSTRUCTIONS

Preheat the air fryer for 12 minutes to 400F, and spray the basket lightly with oil.

Coat the pork chops with 1/2 tsp kosher salt on both sides.

In a big shallow bowl, add the panko, cornflake crumbs, parmesan cheese, 3/4 tsp of kosher salt, paprika, garlic powder, onion powder, chili powder and black pepper.

Place the beaten egg in a different one. Dip the pork into the egg, then blend with the crumbs.

Once the air fryer is set, put 3 of the chops in the prepared basket and spritz with oil on top.

Cook 12 minutes halfway spinning, spritzing oil on both hands. Set aside, and with the rest repeat.

NUTRITIONAL INFORMATION

Serving: 1pork chop, Calories: 378kcal, Carbohydrates: 8g, Protein: 33g, Fat: 13g, Cholesterol: 121mg, Sodium: 373mg, Sugar: 1g

91.   BALSAMIC GLAZED CHICKEN WINGS

INGREDIENTS

- Coating:
- cooking spray
- 3 tablespoons baking powder
- 1 1/2 teaspoons salt
- 1 1/2 teaspoons freshly ground black pepper
- 1 teaspoon paprika
- 2 pounds chicken wings, split and tips discarded
- Glaze:
- 1/3 cup water
- 1/3 cup balsamic vinegar
- 2 tablespoons soy sauce
- 2 tablespoons honey
- 2 tablespoons chili sauce
- 2 cloves garlic, minced
- 1 teaspoon water
- 1/4 teaspoon cornstarch
- Garnish:
- 1 green onion, thinly sliced
- 1/4 teaspoon toasted sesame seeds

INSTRUCTIONS

Preheat an air fryer to 380 F (190 C). Coat the basket with cooking spray on the fryer.

In a small bowl, whisk together the baking powder, salt, pepper, and paprika. Put the mixture of baking powder in a container or bowl, add some of the chicken wings and shake the bag for the coat. Remove the wings from the bag, shake off excess powder and repeat until all wings are covered with a mixture of baking powder.

Spray the wings lightly with a cooking spray, put them in the prepared air fryer basket and cook for 20 minutes, shaking and flipping through the wings halfway.

Also, in a saucepan over medium heat, mix 1/3 cup water, balsamic vinegar, soy sauce, sugar, chili sauce, and garlic. Bring to a low boil and cook for about 15 minutes, until sauce is that. In a small bowl, whisk 1 teaspoon of water and cornstarch together and add into the sauce; stir until sauce thickens.

In a large bowl, put the crispy wings, drizzle with the sauce, and toss until well coated. Garnish and serve immediately with sliced green onion and sesame seeds.

NUTRITIONAL INFORMATION

Per Serving: 458 calories; 22.8 g fat; 32.8 g carbohydrates; 32.6 g protein; 95 mg cholesterol; 4269 mg sodium.

92. CHOCOLATE CAKE IN AN AIR FRYER

INGREDIENTS

- cooking spray
- 1/4 cup white sugar
- 3 1/2 tablespoons butter, softened1 egg
- 1 tablespoon apricot jam
- 6 tablespoons all-purpose flour
- 1 tablespoon unsweetened cocoa powder
- salt to taste

INSTRUCTIONS

firstly heat the air fryer to 320 F (160 C). Spray the cooking spray on a tiny fluted tube pan.

Use an electric mixer to pound sugar and butter together in a bowl until light and creamy; add the egg and jam; combine until mixed. Season with flour, cocoa powder, and salt; thoroughly mix. Pour batter into the ready-made tub. Level the batter's surface with a spoon in the back.

Place the pan in the basket for air fryer. Cook, about 15 minutes, until a toothpick inserted in the cake center, comes out cleanly.

NUTRITIONAL INFORMATION

'Per Serving: 214 calories; 11.7 g fat; 25.5 g carbohydrates; 3.2 g protein; 73 mg cholesterol; 130 mg sodium

93.   KOREAN FRIED CHICKEN WINGS

INGREDIENTS

- cup reduced-sodium soy sauce
- ¼ cup brown sugar
- 2 tablespoons gochujang (Korean hot pepper paste)
- 1 teaspoon sesame oil
- ½ teaspoon ginger paste
- ½ teaspoon garlic paste
- 2 green onions, chopped
- 1 pound chicken wings
- 1 teaspoon vegetable oil

INSTRUCTIONS

Preheat an air fryer to 400 F (200 C).

In a large casserole, add soya sauce, brown sugar, gochujang, sesame oil, ginger paste, garlic paste, and green onions and bring to a boil over medium-high heat. Reduce heat and simmer to about 4 minutes, until slightly thickened. Turn off heat, and set aside.

Put the chicken wings in a big bowl. Apply vegetable oil to the chicken, and rub until evenly coated. Place the wings in the air fryer pot, and cook for 10 minutes. Flip the wings, and cook for another 10 minutes.

Dip the wings into the mixture of the sauce, then whisk to paint. Return wings to the air fryer bowl, and cook for 2 minutes. Coat wings up again into the sauce. Return to the basket with the air fryer and cook for another 2 minutes. Serve straight away.

NUTRITIONAL INFORMATION

Per Serving: 356 calories; 14.3 g total fat; 40 mg cholesterol; 1638 mg sodium. 41.2 g carbohydrates; 15.5 g protein

94. SPICY ROASTED PEANUTS

INGREDIENTS

- 2 tablespoons olive oil
- 3 teaspoons seafood seasoning
- 1/2 teaspoon cayenne pepper
- 8 ounces raw Spanish peanuts
- salt to taste

INSTRUCTIONS

Preheat an air fryer to 320 F (160 C).

In a large bowl, mix olive oil, seafood seasoning, and cayenne pepper together. Remove the peanuts and stir until the peanuts are coated uniformly. Move the peanuts to the basket for air fryer.

Cook the peanuts for 10 minutes in air fryer. Place and cook for another 10 minutes.

Taking out the bowl to sample from the air fryer and salt peanuts. Toss the peanuts one last time and cook 5 minutes more. Move the peanuts to a lined sheet of paper towel and let it cool.

NUTRITIONAL INFORMATION

Per Serving: 193 calories; 17.4 g fat; 4.9 g carbohydrates; 7.4 g protein; 0 mg cholesterol; 229 mg sodium.

95. ONION BHAJI

INGREDIENTS

- 1 small red onion, thinly sliced
- 1 small yellow onion, thinly sliced
- 1 tablespoon salt
- 1 jalapeno pepper, seeded and minced
- 1 clove garlic, minced
- 1 teaspoon coriander
- 1 teaspoon chili powder
- 1 teaspoon ground turmeric
- 1/2 teaspoon cumin
- 2/3 cup chickpea flour (besan)
- 4 tablespoons water, or as needed
- cooking spray

INSTRUCTIONS

In a large bowl, combine red onion, yellow onion, salt, jalapeno, garlic, coriander, chili powder, turmeric, and cumin. Stir until the mixture is even. Add the flour and water to chickpea. Stir it into a thick batter to mix. Add more water if need be. Let the blend rest for 10 minutes.

Preheat air fryer to 350 ° F (175 ° C).

Spray nonstick cooking spray to the air fryer pot. Spoon 2 tablespoons of batter and flatten in the basket. Repeat as many times as your basket permits without touching the bhajis.

Cook for 6 minutes in a preheated air fryer. Mist every bhaji's tops with a cooking spray. Flip over and cook for another 6 minutes. Switch to a tray covered with paper towels. Repeat with the extra batter.

NUTRITIONAL INFORMATION

Per Serving: 40 calories; 0.7 g fat; 6.8 g carbohydrates; 2.1 g protein; 0 mg cholesterol; 882 mg sodium.

96. LUMPIA

INGREDIENTS

- 1 tablespoon sesame oil
- 1 pound ground pork
- 1/3 cup chopped water chestnuts
- 3 green onions, chopped
- 4 tablespoons reduced sodium soy sauce
- 2 tablespoons rice vinegar
- 3 cups shredded cabbage
- 2 large carrots, grated
- 18 lumpia wrappers
- olive oil cooking spray

INSTRUCTIONS

Heat the oil over medium to high heat in a large skillet. add the pork and cook for about 5 minutes, until browned, breaking it into small pieces. Add chestnuts, green onion, soy sauce, and vinegar; cook for 5 minutes.

Increase to high heat and add cabbage. Cook for about 2 minutes, until cabbage, is soft and liquid has evaporated. Turn off heat, then whisk in rubbed carrots. Let the blend cool for 3 minutes.

Air fryer preheats to 400 degrees F (200 degrees C).

In the meantime, put a diamond-shaped lumpia wrapper on a clean surface, with one corner at the bottom. Put 2 tablespoons in the wrapper for filling. Fold in half at the bottom and then fold tightly in hands. Both hands. Roll and seal softly with a few droplets of water. Repeat and fill with remaining wrappers.

Each roll is lightly misted with olive oil. Arrange as many lumpia as possible without hitting them in your air-fryer tub. Cook for 5 minutes in a preheated air fryer. Flip over and cook for another 3 minutes. Switch to a plate covered with paper towels. Repeat with remaining lumpia.

NUTRITIONAL INFORMATION

Per Serving: 92 calories; 4.5 g fat; 6.9 g carbohydrates; 5.7 g protein; 17 mg cholesterol; 185 mg sodium.

97. MINI SCOTCH EGGS

INGREDIENTS

- 1/2 cup Greek yogurt
- 1/4 cup stone-ground mustard
- 1/2 teaspoon garlic powder
- 1/4 teaspoon ground cayenne pepper
- 1/3 cup all-purpose flour
- 12 ounces spicy pork sausage
- 12 quail eggs, hard-boiled and peeled
- 1 egg, beaten
- 1 cup panko bread crumbs
- 1 serving cooking spray

INSTRUCTIONS

In a small bowl, mix yogurt, mustard, garlic powder and cayenne. Cover and refrigerate until ready to use a mustard dipping sauce.

now heat the air fryer to 400 F (200 C) and Set a meal on a flat plate. Divide the sausage into 12 balls which are equal. Use your hands to flatten each ball into a thin-paper patty. Coat all sides of each patty with flour; one side of the flour will help the sausage bind to the egg, and the other side of the flour will prevent the sausage from sticking to your hands. Shape each sausage patty around a hard-boiled quail egg making sure the inside of the egg is sealed completely. Dip each one of them into the beaten egg and coat in crumbs of bread.

Spray nonstick cooking spray to the air fryer pot. Place 6 eggs in the basket and mist cooking spray on tops. Cook on for eight minutes. Flip, then spray again. Cook for 6 minutes. Repeat with eggs left over.

Slice each egg in half to cook, then serve with mustard dipping sauce.

NUTRITIONAL INFORMATION

Per Serving: 143 calories; 8.9 g fat; 9.9 g carbohydrates; 7.6 g protein; 109 mg cholesterol; 382 mg sodium.

98. KETO THUMBPRINT COOKIES

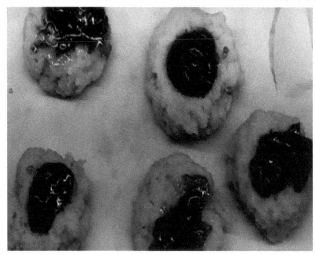

INGREDIENTS

- 1 cup almond flour
- 2 ounces cream cheese, softened
- 3 tablespoons low-calorie natural sweetener
- 1 egg
- 1 teaspoon baking powder
- 3 1/2 tablespoons reduced sugar raspberry preserves

INSTRUCTIONS

In a mixer, add the flour, cream cheese, sweetener, egg, and baking powder until wet dough forms.

Place the bowl in the freezer for about 20 minutes, until the dough is cool and you can shape it into balls.

Preheat an air fryer to 400 degrees F (200 degrees C), as directed by the manufacturer. Fill the Parchment Paper tub.

Roll dough into 10 balls and put in the basket. Create a thumbprint in each cookie halfway through. In each indention, place 1 teaspoon of preserves in.

Cook in a preheated air fryer for about 7 minutes, until the edges, are golden brown.

Cool cookies completely before you move out of the parchment paper, about 15 minutes or you'll have a crumbly mess.

NUTRITIONAL INFORMATION

Per Serving: 112 calories; 8.6 g fat; 9.1 g carbohydrates; 3.7 g protein; 25 mg cholesterol; 73 mg sodium.

99.   BUTTERNUT SQUASH HOME FRIES

INGREDIENTS

- 1 pound butternut squash, peeled and cut into 1/2-inch pieces
- 1 tablespoon extra-virgin olive oil
- 2 teaspoons bage
- l seasoning
- 1 teaspoon chopped fresh rosemary

INSTRUCTIONS

firstly you will Preheat an air fryer to 400 F (200 C).

with olive oil in a large bowl toss butternut squash. Attach bits of squash to the bowl of an air fryer. Cook until browned lightly, stirring every 3 to 4 minutes, taking about 22 minutes.

Transfer to a bowl or serving plate, and sprinkle evenly over the top seasoning blend. Finish with a fresh rosemary garnish.

NUTRITIONAL INFORMATION

Per Serving: 92 calories; 3.5 g fat; 13.3 g carbohydrates; 1.1 g protein; 0 mg cholesterol; 165 mg sodium.

100. VEGAN CHILI CHEESE FRIES

INGREDIENTS

- 25 ounces russet potatoes
- Vegan Chili:
- 1/4 cup texturized vegetable protein
- 1/2 cup hot vegetable broth2 tablespoons olive oil
- 1/4 cup diced onion
- 1/4 cup diced carrot
- 1/4 cup diced celery
- 1 clove garlic, minced
- 1 (10 ounce) can Mexican-style diced tomatoes with green chilescanned black beans, drained
- 1/3 cup canned kidney beans, drained
- 1/3 cup canned white beans, drained
- 1/3 cup canned pinto beans, drained
- 1/2 tablespoon blackstrap molasses
- 1 teaspoon New Mexico chili powder
- 1 teaspoon dried Mexican oregano
- 1/2 teaspoon ground cumin
- 1/2 teaspoon smoked paprika
- 1/2 teaspoon smoked salt
- 1/2 teaspoon ground black pepper
- 1 tablespoon olive oilsalt and ground black pepper to taste
- Cheese Sauce:
- 1/2 cup shredded vegan Cheddar flavored cheese
- 1/4 cup unsweetened soy milk, or more as needed1 teaspoon vegan butter
- Toppings:
- 1/4 cup minced red onion
- 1 jalapeno pepper, sliced into rings
- 3 tablespoons minced cilantro

INSTRUCTIONS

Wash the potatoes and remove any eyes or discoloration. Just peel. Slice thinly into fries in the shoestring instructionS, or use a fry cutter. Place the fries in a large bowl and rinse with cool water before clear water runs out. Fill with 1 inch of water over fries. Cover for 30 minutes, and let stand.

In a bowl location TVP. Cover with a hot frying pan.

Place over the medium place 2 tablespoons of olive oil in a bowl. Add onion, carrot, and celery; cook and mix, for 3 to 5 minutes, until fragrant. Add garlic. Remove the Broth and TVP. Add tomatoes, drained beans, molasses, powdered chili, oregano, cumin, paprika, smoked salt, and pepper. Simmer for about 15 minutes, until thickened.

Preheat an air fryer to 320 F (160 C). Drain the soaked potatoes with a clean towel and rinse. Place them back in the bowl, drizzle with 1 spoonful of olive oil and toss to coat.

Prep, untouched, in the air fryer for 18 minutes. Shake for 6 minutes and boil. Shake again and continue cooking for another 6 minutes. Mix with pepper and salt.

In a microwave safe bowl, combine vegan Cheddar, soy milk, and vegan butter. Microwave for 30 seconds, at 360W. Stir and check the level. Attach more microwave and soy milk for another 30 seconds, if necessary. Briskly stir to form a creamy sauce.

Put the fries on a large saucepan. Stack on chili.

NUTRITIONAL INFORMATION

Per Serving: 468 calories; 15.6 g fat; 66.4 g carbohydrates; 18.9 g protein; 0 mg cholesterol; 1245 mg sodium.

101. PAO DE QUEIJO

INGREDIENTS

- 3/4 cup sweet manioc starch (polvilho doce)
- 3/4 cup sour manioc starch (polvilho azedo)
- 1/4 cup whole milk
- 1/4 cup water

- 1/4 cup olive oil
- 1 teaspoon salt
- 2 eggs, lightly beaten
- 3/4 cup shredded Cheddar cheese
- 1/2 cup finely grated Parmigiano-Reggiano cheese

INSTRUCTIONS

You will warm the air fryer to 325 degrees F (165 C).

In a tub, add together the sweet manioc and sour manioc starches until thoroughly mixed.

In a saucepan, add the milk, water, olive oil, and salt and bring it to a boil. Reduce heat and stir in starch. Extract until the liquid is absorbed; the mixture gets very dry. Remove from heat and allow cooling of the mixture until safe to handle.

In a saucepan, add eggs to the starch mixture; mix until smooth and dough pull away from the sides. Remove Cheddar and Parmigiano-Reggiano cheese; blend well.

Pinch off a golfball-sized piece of dough, roll into a ball, and place it on a plate using gloved or lightly oiled hands. Repeat with extra dough.

NUTRITIONAL INFORMATION

Per Serving: 97 calories; 5.5 g fat; 9.2 g carbohydrates; 2.7 g protein; 24 mg cholesterol; 185 mg sod

102. OVEN PORK JERKY

INGREDIENTS

- 2 pounds ground pork
- 1 tablespoon sesame oil
- 1 tablespoon Sriracha1 tablespoon soy sauce
- 1 tablespoon rice vinegar
- 1/2 teaspoon salt
- 1/2 teaspoon black pepper
- 1/2 teaspoon onion powder
- 1/2 teaspoon pink curing salt

INSTRUCTIONS

In a large bowl, mix ground pork, sesame oil, Sriracha, soy sauce, rice vinegar, salt, black pepper, onion powder, and pink salt; mix until evenly combined. Refrigerate and cover for 8 hours.

Forme as many sticks as you can fit on all three air fryer oven racks using a jerky gun. Both will almost instantly shrink so you can put them together tightly and use the racks ' full length. The first time I could get 21 sticks I would go back.

Set the oven to 160 degrees Fahrenheit with the air fryer. Put all 3 racks in and cook 1 hour.

Clear racks from the oven, and use paper towels to scrub excess moisture. Flip each stick and continue cooking for 1 hour.

Repeat step 4 for a total of 3 hours of cooking time. Switch jerky sticks to a baking sheet covered with paper towels. Cover with another layer of paper towels and allow for the final drying to sit out 8 hours. Repeat with any jerky mix leftover.

Move jerky to an airtight container and put in a fridge for 30 days.

103. DRY RUB CHICKEN WINGS

INGREDIENTS

- 1 tablespoon dark brown sugar
- 1 tablespoon sweet paprika
- ½ tablespoon kosher salt
- 1 teaspoon garlic powder
- 1 teaspoon onion powder
- 1 teaspoon poultry seasoning
- ½ teaspoon mustard powder
- ½ teaspoon freshly ground black pepper
- 8 chicken wings, or more as needed
- Preheat the air fryer to 350 ° F (175 ° C).

INSTRUCTIONS

In a large bowl, whisk together brown sugar, paprika, cinnamon, garlic powder, onion powder, poultry seasoning, mustard powder, and pepper. Throw in the wings of the chicken and rub the seasonings with your hands until completely covered.

Arrange wings in the preheated air fryer's bowl, stand up at their ends and lean against each other and basket wall.

Cook for about 35 minutes, until the wings are tender inside and golden brown and crisp outside. Place the wings on a plate and serve hot.

NUTRITIONAL   INFORMATION

Per Serving:

318 calories; 18.7 g total fat; 77 mg cholesterol; 1520 mg sodium. 11.3 g carbohydrates; 25.9 g protein;

104. BBQ CHICKEN TENDERS

INGREDIENTS

- 3½ ounces barbecue-flavored pork rinds
- 1 cup all-purpose flour
- 1 tablespoon barbecue seasoning
- 1 egg, beaten
- 1½ pounds chicken breast tenderloins
- cooking spray

INSTRUCTIONS

Warm the air fryer to 370 ° F (190 ° C).

In a food processor, put pork rinds and pulse to the size of bread crumbs. Place yourself in a shallow bowl. In a shallow dish, season with the flour and barbecue. Beat the egg in a small, third dish.

Next coat each chicken tender in the flour mixture, then dip in beaten egg and finally coat in crumbs of pork rind.

Spray nonstick cooking spray to the air fryer pot. Arrange 1/2 of the chicken tenders in the basket of the air fryer, ensuring that none strike. Spray cooking spray to the top of each tender. Cook, about 15 minutes, until chicken is cooked through and no longer pink in the middle. Repeat for leftover tenders.

NUTRITIONAL INFORMATION

Per Serving:

327 calories; 11.8 g total fat; 124 mg cholesterol; 649 mg sodium. 16.9 g carbohydrates; 38.1 g protein

105. BUTTERMILK FRIED CHICKEN

INGREDIENTS

- 1½ pounds boneless, skinless chicken thighs
- 2 cups buttermilk
- 1 cup all-purpose flour
- 1 tablespoon seasoned salt
- ½ tablespoon ground black pepper
- 1 cup panko bread crumbs
- 1 serving cooking spray

INSTRUCTIONS

Put the thighs of the chicken in a shallow dish. Pour buttermilk over chicken, then cool for 4 hours, or overnight.

Preheat an air fryer to 380 F (190 C).

In a big gallon-sized resealable bag, add the flour, seasoned salt and pepper. Thighs of chicken dredged in seasoned flour. Sprinkle back into the buttermilk, then cover with crumbs of panko crust.

Spray nonstick cooking spray to the air fryer pot. Arrange 1/2 of the chicken thighs inside the basket to ensure that no one hits. Spray cooking spray to the top of each chicken thigh.

Cook for 15 minutes in the preheated air-fryer. Flip back. Sprinkle chicken tops, again.

NUTRITIONAL INFORMATION

Per Serving:

335 calories; 12.8 g total fat; 67 mg cholesterol; 687 mg sodium. 33.2 g carbohydrates; 24.5 g protein

106. GOLDEN FRIEDCHICKEN TENDERS

INGREDIENTS

- 1 egg
- ½ teaspoon salt
- teaspoon ground black pepper
- 2 cornbread muffins, crumbled
- ¼ cup panko bread crumbs
- 2 teaspoons honey powder
- 1 tablespoon tropical poultry rub
- 1 pound chicken tenders

INSTRUCTIONS

In a shallow bowl, whip egg, salt, and pepper, until well mixed. In a small, shallow bowl, bring together the cornbread crumbs, panko, honey powder and poultry polish.

Dip growing tender chicken into the mixture of eggs. Shake off excess and dredge in coating with the cornbread.

Preheat an air fryer to 380 F (190 C). Cook 6 minutes for chicken tender. Flip over and cook for 6 minutes.

NUTRITIONAL INFORMATION

Per Serving: 256 calories; 7.6 g total fat; 127 mg cholesterol; 579 mg sodium. 19.2 g carbohydrates; 29.8 g protein

107. MAPLE CHICKEN THIGHS

INGREDIENTS

- 1 cup buttermilk
- ½ cup maple syrup
- 1 egg
- 1 teaspoon granulated garlic
- 4 skin-on, bone-in chicken thighs
- Dry Mix:
- ½ cup all-purpose flour
- ¼ cup tapioca flour
- 1 tablespoon salt
- 1 teaspoon sweet paprika
- ½ teaspoon smoked paprika
- 1 teaspoon granulated onion
- ¼ teaspoon ground black pepper
- ¼ teaspoon cayenne pepper
- ½ teaspoon granulated garlic
- ½ teaspoon honey powder

INSTRUCTIONS

In a resealable bag, mix buttermilk, maple syrup, egg, and 1 teaspoon of granulated garlic. Add the chicken thighs and marinate in the refrigerator for at least 1 hour or until overnight.

In a shallow bowl, add flour, tapioca meal, salt, sweet paprika, smoked paprika, granulated onion, pepper, cayenne pepper, 1/2 teaspoon of granulated garlic, and honey powder.

Preheat an air fryer to 380 F (190 C).

Drain from the chicken thighs and discard marinade. Dredge chicken by mixing with the flour and shake off excess. Place skin-side-down chicken in the preheated air fryer and cook for 12 minutes. Switch thighs and fry for another 13 minutes.

NUTRITIONAL   INFORMATION

Per Serving:

415 calories; 13.4 g total fat; 113 mg cholesterol; 1885 mg sodium. 50.8 g carbohydrates; 23.3 g protein

108. CHICKEN THIGH SCHNITZEL

INGREDIENTS

- 1 pound skinless, boneless chicken thighs, trimmed of fat
- ½ cup seasoned bread crumbs
- 1 teaspoon salt
- ½ teaspoon ground black pepper
- ¼ cup flour
- 1 egg, beaten
- avocado oil cooking spray

INSTRUCTIONS

Place the thighs of the chicken, 1 at a time, between 2 sheets of parchment paper and flatten with a trim.

In a shallow bowl, mix brown crumbs, salt, and black pepper. In a different, shallow bowl, put the flour and beat the egg in a third, shallow bowl. Dip chicken thighs in flour first, then in beaten egg, and then coat with a mixture of bread crumbs.

Preheat an air fryer to 375 F (190 C).

Place breaded thighs in the basket of the air fryer, make sure they do not touch; operate in batches if necessary. Avocado oil spray, and cook for 6 minutes. Flip each leg, mist the oil and cook for another 3 to 4 minutes.

NUTRITIONAL INFORMATION

Per Serving:

293 calories; 14 g total fat; 117 mg cholesterol; 927 mg sodium. 16.5 g carbohydrates; 23.6 g protein

109. SESAME CHICKEN THIGHS

INGREDIENTS

- 2 tablespoons sesame oil
- 2 tablespoons soy sauce
- 1 tablespoon honey
- 1 tablespoon sriracha sauce
- 1 teaspoon rice vinegar
- 2 pounds chicken thighs
- 1 green onion, chopped
- 2 tablespoons toasted sesame seeds

INSTRUCTIONS

In a large bowl, mix sesame oil, soy sauce, butter, sriracha, and vinegar. Add the chicken, and mix to stir. Refrigerate and cover for at least 30 minutes.

Preheat the air fryer to 400 F (200 C). Drain the chicken marinade.

Put skin-side up chicken thighs in the air-fryer tub. Cook for five minutes. Flip and cook for another 10 minutes.

Place the chicken on a plate and let rest for 5 minutes before serving. Garnish with sesame seeds and green onion.

NUTRITIONAL   INFORMATION

Per Serving:

485 calories; 32.6 g total fat; 141 mg cholesterol; 739 mg sodium. 6.6 g carbohydrates; 39.5 g protein

110. BBQ CHEDDAR-STUFFED CHICKEN BREASTS

INGREDIENTS

- 3 strips bacon, divided
- 2 ounces Cheddar cheese, cubed, divided
- ¼ cup barbeque sauce, divided
- 2 (4 ounce) skinless, boneless chicken breasts
- salt and ground black pepper to taste

INSTRUCTIONS

Preheat the air fryer to 380 F (190 C). Cook 1 strips of bacon 2 minutes in the air fryer. Cut into small bits and remove them from the air fryer. Line the air fryer basket with parchment paper and raise the temperature to 400 F (200 C).

In a bowl, combine cooked bacon, Cheddar cheese and 1 tablespoon of barbeque sauce.

Use a long, sharp knife to make a1-inch horizontal cut at the top of each chicken breast, creating a small pocket within. Fill each breast with a bacon-cheese mixture in equal measure. Wrap remaining bacon strips around each breast. Coat the chicken breast with the remaining barbecue sauce and place it in the fryer basket prepared for air.

NUTRITIONAL INFORMATION

Per Serving:

379 calories; 18.9 g total fat; 114 mg cholesterol; 987 mg sodium. 12.3 g carbohydrates; 37.7 g protein

111. KOREAN FRIED CHICKEN

INGREDIENTS

- ½ cup tapioca starch
- ½ teaspoon garlic powder
- ¾ teaspoon salt
- ½ teaspoon black pepper
- 1 pound boneless, skinless chicken breasts, cut into 1-inch pieces
- cooking spray
- Sauce:
- 4 ounces tomato sauce
- 2 tablespoons gochujang (Korean hot pepper paste)
- 2 tablespoons honey
- 1 tablespoon soy sauce

INSTRUCTIONS

Air fryer preheats to 400 degrees F (200 degrees C).

In a shallow dish, mix the tapioca starch, garlic powder, salt, and pepper. Dredge bits of chicken over the mixture.

Line a baking sheet with a cooling rack, and position the chicken on the rack to allow the excess dredge to fall. Lightly grease chicken with spray for cooking and put it in the basket for the air fryer.

Cook for 10 minutes in the preheated air fryer, shaking the basket halfway through.

In a small bowl, mix tomato sauce, gochujang sauce, honey and soy sauce, and drizzle over pieces of chicken.

NUTRITIONAL   INFORMATION

Per Serving:

244 calories; 2.9 g total fat; 65 mg cholesterol; 931 mg sodium. 29.6 g carbohydrates; 24.4 g protein

112. HEALTHIER BANG BANG CHICKEN IN THE AIR FRYER

INGREDIENTS

- Egg wash:
- 1 egg
- ½ cup milk
- 1 tablespoon hot pepper sauce
- Dry Mix:
- ½ cup flour
- ½ cup tapioca starch
- 1½ teaspoons seasoned salt
- 1 teaspoon garlic granules
- ½ teaspoon cumin
- 1 pound boneless, skinless chicken breasts, cut into 1-inch pieces
- cooking spray
- Sauce:
- ¼ cup plain Greek yogurt
- 3 tablespoons sweet chili sauce
- 1 teaspoon hot sauce

INSTRUCTIONS

Heat the fryer to 380 ° F (190 ° C).

In a shallow bowl, whisk the potato, milk and hot sauce together. In a second bowl, add a meal, tapioca starch, salt, garlic, and cumin. Dip pieces of chicken in the egg mixture first, then dredge in the dry mix and shake off the waste. Place in the air fryer basket in batches, be careful not to overload and spray chicken lightly with oil.

Cook after 5 minutes, shaking bowl until chicken is no longer pink in the center and the juices run clear, around 10 minutes per pan.

In a small bowl, add the Greek yogurt, sweet chili sauce, and hot sauce. Serve with chicken sauce.

NUTRITIONAL   INFORMATION

Per Serving: 313 calories; 6.1 g total fat; 111 mg cholesterol; 665 mg sodium. 34.4 g carbohydrates; 28.7 g protein

113. CORNFLAKE CRUSTED CHICKEN TENDERS

INGREDIENTS

- Egg wash:
- 1 egg
- 1 tablespoon pesto
- 1 pinch salt
- Dry mix:
- 1 cup crushed cornflakes
- 1 ounce finely shredded Parmesan cheese
- ½ teaspoon cantanzaro herbs
- ½ teaspoon granulated garlic
- 1 pinch salt
- 1 pound chicken tenders

INSTRUCTIONS

The air fryer is preheated to 400 degrees F (200 degrees C).

In a shallow dish, add the potato, pesto, and salt together. Mix the cornflake crumbs, Parmesan cheese, Catanzaro herbs, garlic, and salt together in a separate bowl.

Dip each piece of the chicken piece into egg wash first, then dredge through the mixture of cornflakes, shaking off excess breading. Place pieces of chicken in the basket for the air fryer.

Fry air for 5 minutes, rearrange pieces of chicken and fry until the center is no longer pink and the juices run clear, about 5 minutes more.

NUTRITIONAL INFORMATION

Per Serving: 220 calories; 7.8 g total fat; 119 mg cholesterol; 340 mg sodium. 7.1 g carbohydrates; 29.1 g protein

114. POPCORN-CRUSTED POPCORN CHICKEN

INGREDIENTS

- ¼ cup cornstarch
- 1 teaspoon salt
- ¾ teaspoon paprika
- ½ teaspoon ground mustard
- ¼ teaspoon black pepper
- 1½ pounds boneless, skinless chicken breasts, cut in bite-sized pieces
- 6 cups popped popcorn
- 2 eggs, beaten
- Butter flavored cooking spray

INSTRUCTIONS

In a big resealable plastic bag, add the cornstarch, salt, paprika, ground mustard, and pepper. Drop half of the pieces of chicken into the bag, seal the container, shake and let sit for 5 minutes while preheating your air fryer.

Set the air fryer to 350 F (175 C) and preheat for 5 minutes.

In the meantime, put the popped popcorn in a food processor and pulse to a consistency similar to crumbs. Place the crumbs into a separate plastic resealable bag.

Dip seasoned pieces of chicken in beaten egg first, then drop them into the crumbs of popcorn. Shake to touch.

Place the chicken in the air fryer tub. Rub gently with a cooking spray flavored with butter. Cook for 8 minutes, in batches, if desired. Flip again, mist with spray and cook for another 6 minutes.

Switch chicken to a sheet of the paper towel-lined plate using tongs. Repeat with pieces of chicken leftover. Serve with the dipping sauce you like.

NUTRITIONAL INFORMATION

Per Serving:

219 calories; 5.7 g total fat; 131 mg cholesterol; 473 mg sodium. 11.9 g carbohydrates; 28.6 g protein

115. GLUTEN FREE FRESH CHERRY CRUMBLE

INGREDIENTS

- 1/3 cup butter
- 3 cups pitted cherries
- 10 tablespoons white sugar, divided
- 2 teaspoons lemon juice
- 1 cup gluten-free all purpose baking flour
- 1 teaspoon vanilla powder
- 1 teaspoon ground nutmeg
- 1 teaspoon ground cinnamon

INSTRUCTIONS

Cube butter and place in a freezer for about 15 minutes, until firm.

Preheat air fryer to 325 ° F (165 ° C).

In a cup, add pitted cherries, 2 tablespoons of sugar, and lemon juice; blend well. Pour the mixture of cherry into baking dish.

In a cup, add the flour and 6 tablespoons of sugar. Using fingers to cut in butter until the flakes are pea-sized. Distribute over the cherries, then gently press down.

Stir together in a bowl 2 tablespoons of sugar, vanilla powder, nutmeg, and cinnamon. Toping with dust sugar over the cherries and flour.

Bake in the air fryer which is preheated. Test at 25 minutes; if not browned, continue cooking and testing at intervals of 5 minutes until lightly browned. close the drawer and turn the air fryer off. For 10 minutes leave collapsing within. Remove and allow to cool slightly, 5 minutes or so.

NUTRITIONAL INFORMATION

Per Serving: 459 calories; 17.8 g fat; 76.4 g carbohydrates; 4.9 g protein; 41 mg cholesterol; 109 mg sodium

116. CRISPY NACHOS PRAWNS

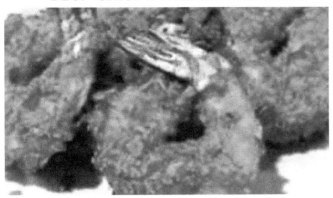

INGREDIENTS

- 1 egg18 large prawns, peeled and deveined, tails left on
- 1 (10 ounce) bag nacho-cheese flavored corn chips, finely crushed

INSTRUCTIONS

Rinse prawns, and dry pat.

Whisk the egg in a saucepan. Place the broken chips in a different tub.

In the whisked egg, dip a prawn and then in the crushed chips; put it on a plate; Repeat for prawns left over.

Preheat an air fryer to 350 F (180 C).

Place prawns in the air fryer and set the timer for eight minutes. Cook until the prawns have become opaque.

NUTRITIONAL   INFORMATION

Per Serving: 286 calories; 14.5 g fat; 28.9 g carbohydrates; 12.8 g protein; 95 mg cholesterol; 312 mg sodium.

117. CHEESY GARLIC BREAD

INGREDIENTS

- 2 dinner rolls
- 1/2 cup grated Parmesan cheese
- 2 tablespoons butter, melted
- 2 tablespoons garlic and herb seasoning, or more to taste

INSTRUCTIONS

Cut a crisscross into every roll nearly all the way down, leaving the crusts at the bottom intact. Fill with Parmesan cheese on all slits.

Paint the roll tops with melted butter; sprinkle with garlic seasoning in equal measure.

Preheat an air fryer to 350 F (180 C).

Put the rolls in the air fryer tub. Cook for about 5 minutes, until cheese, is melted.

NUTRITIONAL INFORMATION

Per Serving: 188 calories; 17.2 g fat; 0.8 g carbohydrates; 7.8 g protein; 48 mg cholesterol; 388 mg sodium.

118. VEGAN STUFFED BELL PEPPERS

INGREDIENTS

- 1 potato, diced
- 1/2 cup peas
- 1 small onion, diced
- 1 carrot, diced
- 1 vegan bread roll, diced
- 2 cloves garlic, minced
- 2 teaspoons dried mixed herbs
- 6 green bell peppers - tops, seeds, and membranes removed (tops reserved)
- 1/3 cup shredded vegan cheese

INSTRUCTIONS

In a cup, add the potatoes, peas, onion, carrot, egg, garlic and mixed herbs. Dice the pepper on the tops of the green bell and apply it to the dish. Mix together well.

Preheat the air fryer to 350 F (180 C).

Fill the filler fairly with peppers. Put stuffed peppers inside the basket of the air fryer.

Cook all through until tender and soft, about 20 minutes. Add shredded vegan cheese and cook for about 5 minutes, until melted.

NUTRITIONAL INFORMATION

Per Serving: 110 calories; 2.3 g fat; 19.3 g carbohydrates; 3.9 g protein; < 1 mg cholesterol; 170 mg sodium

119. APPLE DUMPLINGS

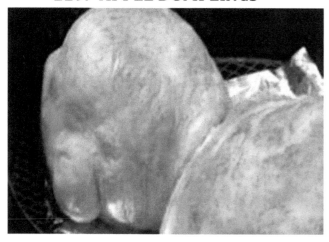

INGREDIENTS

- 2 tablespoons sultana raisins
- 1 tablespoon brown sugar
- 2 sheets puff pastry
- 2 small apples, peeled and cored
- 2 tablespoons butter, melted

INSTRUCTIONS

Preheat an air fryer to 320 F (180 C). Attach aluminum foil to the air fryer tub.

In a dish, add the sultanas and brown sugar.

Place a sheet of puff pastry on a clean work surface. Put an apple on the pastry and fill the heart with a mixture of sultanas.

Fold the pastry around the fruit, to cover it entirely. Repeat with leftover pastry, apple and fill.

Place the dumplings and brush with melted butter into the prepared bowl.

Set timer for 25 minutes; cook the dumplings until the apples are soft and golden brown.

NUTRITIONAL   INFORMATION

Per Serving: 384 calories; 25.9 g fat; 34.2 g carbohydrates; 4.5 g protein; 8 mg cholesterol; 172 mg sodium.

120. TACO DOGS

INGREDIENTS

- 2 jumbo hot dogs
- 1 teaspoon taco seasoning mix
- 2 hot dog buns
- 1/3 cup guacamole
- 4 tablespoons salsa
- 6 pickled jalapeno slices

INSTRUCTIONS

Preheat an air fryer to 390 ° F (200 ° C). Make sure the air fryer is at a minimum temperature of 4 minutes.

Cut every hot dog into 5 slits. Rub 1/2 teaspoon of taco seasoning evenly over each hot dog.

Cook the hot dogs for 5 minutes in the air-fryer tub. Put hot dogs in buns and get back to basketball. Cook for about 4 minutes, until buns are toasted and hot dogs are crisp.

Top hot dogs with equal amounts of guacamole, jalapenos and salsa.

NUTRITIONAL INFORMATION

Per Serving: 418 calories; 28 g fat; 28.7 g carbohydrates; 14 g protein; 44 mg cholesterol; 1261 mg sodium.

121. AIR FRYER PORK CHOPS (NO BREADING)

INGREDIENTS

- 2 tablespoons brown sugar
- 1 tablespoon Worcestershire sauce1 tablespoon reduced-sodium soy sauce
- 1 teaspoon lemon juice
- 1 clove minced garlic
- 1/4 teaspoon freshly ground black pepper
- 1 dash Sriracha sauce (optional)
- 4 (5 ounce) boneless, center-cut pork chops

INSTRUCTIONS

In a small bowl, add brown sugar, Worcestershire sauce, soya sauce, lemon juice, garlic, pepper and Sriracha sauce.

Preheat an air-fryer for 2 minutes to 400 degrees F (200 degrees C).

In a 6-inch silicone cake pan, put pork chops and pour 1/2 of the brown sugar-soy sauce on top. Move the silicone saucepan to the basket in air fryer.

Cook for 9 minutes in a preheated air fryer. Turn the pork chops and continue to cook for another 9 minutes. Pour the remaining sauce over the pork chops and serve straight away.

NUTRITIONAL INFORMATION

Per Serving: 192 calories; 9.2 g fat; 8.3 g carbohydrates; 18.2 g protein; 48 mg cholesterol; 225 mg sodium.

122. STUFFING BALLS

INGREDIENTS

- 1 tablespoon butter
- 1/4 cup finely chopped onion
- 1/2 cup finely chopped celery
- 5 cups stale bread, cut into cubes
- 1 teaspoon dried parsley
- 1/2 teaspoon poultry seasoning
- 1/2 teaspoon salt
- 1/4 teaspoon ground black pepper
- 1 egg, well beaten
- 1/4 cup no-salt-added chicken broth
- cooking spray

INSTRUCTIONS

Let the butter melt over medium heat, in a very small skillet. Add celery and onion, and cook for about 5 minutes, until softened.

In a bowl, add the flour, parsley, seasoning poultry, salt, and pepper. Add in cooked celery and onion. Slowly pour egg with one hand into the bowl when mixing with the other to ensure even coating of the mixture. Continue and blend everything together with the chicken broth until well mixed. Divide the mixture of the stuffing into 8 equal portions, roll into balls and put it on a plate. Chill for at least 15 minutes.

Preheat an air fryer to 350 F (180 C).

Remove the stuffing balls from the fridge and brush lightly with spray for cooking.

NUTRITIONAL INFORMATION

Per Serving: 167 calories; 5.6 g fat; 24 g carbohydrates; 5.2 g protein; 49 mg cholesterol; 645 mg sodium.

123. OKRA FRIES

INGREDIENTS

1 pound fresh okra, about 3-inches long

1 1/2 teaspoons extra-virgin olive oil

1/2 teaspoon seasoned salt, or to taste

INSTRUCTIONS

Warm the air fryer to 400 degrees F (200 C).

Wash and dry the okra, cut the stems and ends, and slice lengthwise in half. Put in a bowl and sprinkle with salt and olive oil.

Put the okra slices, cut-sides down, in the air fryer, in batches if necessary, and cook for 12 to 15 minutes until crispy.

NUTRITIONAL INFORMATION

Per Serving: 103 calories; 3.7 g fat; 16.2 g carbohydrates; 4.6 g protein; 0 mg cholesterol; 248 mg sodium

124. HASSELBACK POTATOES

INGREDIENTS

- 4 (6 ounce) russet potatoes, scrubbed and dried
- 2 chopsticks
- 4 tablespoons olive oil, or as needed
- salt and ground black pepper to taste
- 1/2 teaspoon chopped fresh chives (optional)

INSTRUCTIONS

Preheat the air fryer to 350 F (180 C).

From the flattest side of 1 potato cut a very thin slice lengthwise.

On a cutting board lie potato, cut-side down so it rests uniformly without rolling.

Place lengthwise chopsticks along the top and bottom edges of potatoes.

Slice thinly across the entire length of the potato to make 1/4-inch slices, making sure that each time the knife gets to rest on chopsticks, leaving the potato bottom intact. Repeat with potatoes leftover.

Brush with oil on the outsides and between the cuts. Sprinkle with pepper and salt.

Place the potatoes in the air fryer bowl and simmer for 15 minutes.

NUTRITIONAL INFORMATION

Per Serving: 250 calories; 13.7 g fat; 29.7 g carbohydrates; 3.4 g protein; 0 mg cholesterol; 49 mg sodium.

125. SALMON NUGGETS

INGREDIENTS

- 1/3 cup maple syrup
- 1/4 teaspoon ground dried chipotle pepper
- 1 pinch sea salt
- 1 1/2 cups butter- and garlic-flavored croutons
- 1 large egg
- 1 (1 pound) skinless, center-cut salmon fillet, cut into 1 1/2-inch chunks cooking spray

INSTRUCTIONS

In a saucepan, mix maple syrup, chipotle powder, and salt and bring to a simmer over medium heat. Reduce heat to low to preserve the warmth.

Place the croutons in a mini food processor's bowl; pulse until they crumble into fine crumbs. Switch to a shallow saucepan. Whisk the egg in a separate saucepan.

The air fryer is preheated to 390 degrees F (200 degrees C).

Lightly dust with sea salt. Dip salmon gently into a mixture of the sperm, making excess drip away. Coat salmon in breading crouton and extra shake off. Put gently on a plate and mist with cooking spray.

Oil Air Fryer basket with cooking spray. Put salmon nuggets inside, working in batches if necessary to avoid overcrowding.

Cook for 3 minutes in preheated air fryer. Turn the salmon pieces gently, spray lightly with oil and cook for 3 to 4 more minutes until salmon is cooked throughout. Put the warm chipotle-maple syrup on a serving platter and drizzle. Serve straightaway.

NUTRITIONAL INFORMATION

Per Serving: 364 calories; 16.4 g fat; 27.2 g carbohydrates; 25.8 g protein; 115 mg cholesterol; 353 mg sodium.

126. CRISPY COD

INGREDIENTS

- 1 pound cod, about 1-inch thick, cut into 4 pieces
- 1/4 cup polenta
- 1/4 cup all-purpose flour
- 1 1/2 teaspoons seafood seasoning
- 1 1/2 teaspoons garlic salt
- 1 teaspoon onion powder
- 1/2 teaspoon ground black pepper
- 1/2 teaspoon paprika
- olive oil cooking spray

INSTRUCTIONS

Preheat an air fryer to 380 F (195 C). Dry bits of pat cod with paper towels.

In a shallow dish, mix polenta, pasta, seasoning with kinds of seafood, garlic salt, onion powder, pepper, and paprika. Coat the breading mixture with each slice of cod, pressing the breading on each side of the fish until well coated.

Spray olive oil cooking sprays on the air fryer pot. Arrange cod in a basket, so that air can circulate, leaving space between each piece. Spray cooking spray to the top of each slice of cod.

Cook on for eight minutes. Turn each bit, spray with spray and cook for another 4 minutes.

NUTRITIONAL INFORMATION

Per Serving: 171 calories; 1.8 g fat; 14.8 g carbohydrates; 22.7 g protein; 42 mg cholesterol; 1057 mg sodium

127. CORN DOGS

INGREDIENTS

- 6 bamboo skewers, soaked in water 20 minutes parchment paper
- 1 (6.5 ounce) package corn bread mix
- 2/3 cup milk
- 1 egg
- 1 teaspoon white sugar
- 8 hot dogs, cut in half

INSTRUCTIONS

Split skewers of soaked bamboo into thirds. To suit the bottom of the air-fryer tub, cut a piece of parchment paper.

The air fryer is preheated to 400 degrees F (200 degrees C).

In a cup, whisk the cornbread, milk, egg, and sugar together until smooth; pour into a tall glass.

Put a skewer into any slice of the hot dog. Remove the air fryer basket, and put the cut parchment paper on the bowl bottom.

Dunk 4 hot dogs in the glass with the batter, and put the alternating INSTRUCTIONS of the stick end on top of the parchment paper.

Cook for 8 minutes in the preheated air fryer, or until brownness is desired. Move to a tray, and repeat with other hot dogs.

NUTRITIONAL INFORMATION

Per Serving: 259 calories; 16.6 g fat; 18.7 g carbohydrates; 8.4 g protein; 49 mg cholesterol; 901 mg sodium.

128. TORI'S PUMPKIN BAGELS

INGREDIENTS

- Cooking spray
- 1 cup all-purpose flour or more as needed
- 1 tablespoon brown sugar
- 2 teaspoons baking powder
- 1/2 teaspoon salt
- 1/2 cup pumpkin puree
- 1/2 cup fat-free Greek yogurt
- Topping:
- 1/4 cup quick oats
- 1 tablespoon quick oats
- 1 pinch ground cinnamon, or to taste
- 1 egg white
- 2 teaspoons honey
- 1 teaspoon water
- 1/4 cup mild shredded Cheddar cheese (optional)

INSTRUCTIONS

Preheat an air fryer to around 3 minutes, at 280 degrees F (140 degrees C) as instructed by the manufacturer. Fill the parchment paper basket for the air fryer and spray it with the cooking spray.

In a medium bowl, add the flour, brown sugar, baking powder, and salt. Remove yogurt and pumpkin puree. Stir to combine.

Place the dough on a floured surface; break into 4 balls. Roll each ball into ropes which are 8 inches long. Attach the ends and form bagels together.

In a small bowl, combine the oats and cinnamon together. In another small bowl, whisk egg white, honey, and water together until smooth. Brush the bagels with a mixture of eggs; brush both sides with oats and cinnamon.

Place the bagels in the basket ready and bake for 13 minutes. Sprinkle Cheddar cheese over bagels, and bake for another 2 minutes.

NUTRITIONAL INFORMATION

Per Serving: 222 calories; 3.2 g fat; 39.1 g carbohydrates; 9.6 g protein; 7 mg cholesterol; 679 mg sodium

129. STEAK AND CHEESE MELTS

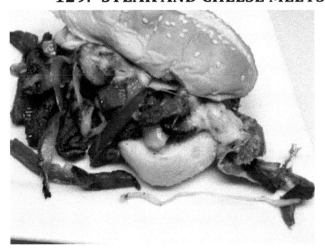

INGREDIENTS

- 1 pound beef rib-eye steak, thinly sliced
- 2 tablespoons Worcestershire sauce
- 1 tablespoon reduced-sodium soy sauce
- 1 medium onion, sliced into petals
- 4 ounces sliced baby portobello mushrooms
- 1/2 green bell pepper, thinly sliced
- 1 tablespoon olive oil
- 1/2 teaspoon salt
- 1/2 teaspoon ground mustard
- 1/4 teaspoon ground black pepper
- 4 hoagie rolls
- 4 slices Provolone cheese

INSTRUCTIONS

Place the steak in a bowl and add the Worcestershire sauce and soy. Cover and refrigerate to overnight for 4 hours. Remove from the refrigerator and allow about 30 minutes to arrive at room temperature.

Preheat the air fryer to 380 F (190 C).

In a large bowl, add the onion, mushrooms, and bell pepper. Add the olive oil, salt, mustard ground, and pepper; mix to coat.

Place the hoagie rolls in the air fryer basket and cook for about 2 minutes, until toasted. Rolls are moved to a tray.

Put stake in the air fryer pot, and cook for 3 minutes. Remove and simmer for another 1 minute. Move onto a platform.

Add vegetable mix to air fryer basket and cook for 5 minutes. Stir and cook for about 5 more minutes, until softened.

NUTRITIONAL INFORMATION

Per Serving: 679 calories; 26.4 g fat; 75.4 g carbohydrates; 33.4 g protein; 82 mg cholesterol; 1541 mg sodium.

130. STEAK FOR FAJITAS

INGREDIENTS

- 2 tablespoons olive oil
- 2 teaspoons salt
- 1/2 teaspoon garlic powder
- 1/2 teaspoon ground cumin
- 1/2 teaspoon jalapeno chili powder (optional)
- 1/4 teaspoon chili powder
- 1/4 teaspoon ground coriander
- 1 pound skirt steak, sliced into strips against the grain
- 1 onion, sliced into strips
- 1 bell pepper, seeded and sliced into strips

INSTRUCTIONS

In a resealable plastic bag, add olive oil, salt, garlic powder, cumin, jalapeno chili powder, chili powder, and coriander. Add steak, onion, and bell pepper, marinade cover, squeeze excess air and seal the container. Marinate for 8 hours to overnight in the refrigerator.

Line a basket of air fryers with a sheet of perforated parchment paper. Marinated onions, peppers, and steak are included.

Fry the air to 400 degrees F (200 degrees C) for 5 minutes. Take the basket from the air fryer and mix to ensure even cooking. Air fried, about 4 minutes longer, before the steak is cooked through.

NUTRITIONAL INFORMATION

Per Serving: 193 calories; 11.6 g fat; 7.4 g carbohydrates; 14.7 g protein; 25 mg cholesterol; 1198 mg sodium.

131. PORK RIBS WITH GINGER GLAZE

INGREDIENTS

- 2 pounds country-style pork ribs
- 2 tablespoons vegetable oil
- 1/4 teaspoon salt
- 1/4 teaspoon ground black pepper
- 2 teaspoons vegetable oil
- 1 shallot, finely chopped
- 1/3 cup chili sauce
- 1/3 cup apricot preserves
- 1 tablespoon reduced-sodium soy sauce
- 1 teaspoon grated fresh ginger
- 1/8 teaspoon ground chipotle pepper
- 2 tablespoons chopped fresh chives (optional)

INSTRUCTIONS

Preheat an air fryer to 350 F (175 C). Oven preheats to 200 degrees F (95 degrees C).

Brush 2 tablespoons of oil to the ribs and season with salt and pepper. In the air fryer bowl, place 1/2 of the ribs in a single layer.

Cook in the preheated air fryer for 15 to 20 minutes, until ribs are fork-tender and fully cooked. A center-inserted instant-read thermometer will read 145 degrees F (63 degrees C). Move ribs to a baking pan, and put them in the preheated oven to keep the remaining ribs warm while cooking.

In the mean time, heat 2 teaspoons of oil over medium heat in a small saucepan. Add shallot; stir and cook for about 3 minutes, until tender. Stir in chili sauce, apricot preserves, soy sauce, chipotle pepper and ginger. Heat and stir for 3 to 5 minutes, until bubbly.

Move ribs onto a serving dish. Greatly dust with glaze, and garnish with chives.

NUTRITIONAL   INFORMATION

Per Serving: 337 calories; 22.9 g fat; 17 g carbohydrates; 16.3 g protein; 61 mg cholesterol; 431 mg sodium

132. TAJIN SWEET POTATO FRIES

INGREDIENTS

- Cooking spray
- 2 medium sweet potatoes cut into 1/2-inch-thick fries
- 3 teaspoons avocado oil
- 1 1/2 teaspoons chili-lime seasoning
- Dipping Sauce:
- 1/4 cup mayonnaise
- 1 tablespoon fresh squeezed lime juice
- 1 teaspoon chili-lime seasoning
- 4 lime wedges

INSTRUCTIONS

Preheat the air fryer for 5 minutes, to 400 degrees F (200 degrees C). Sprinkle loosely with a cooking spray on the fryer bowl.

In a large bowl, put the sweet potato fries, drizzle with the avocado oil and mix. Sprinkle the chili-lime seasoning with 1 1/2 teaspoons and mix well. Switch to the air fryer container, where possible, operating in batches.

Cook the sweet potato friezes until brown and crispy, for 8 to 9 minutes, after 4 minutes, shaking and turning.

When cooking sweet potatoes, whisk mayonnaise, lime juice, and chili-lime seasoning together in a small bowl to dip in sauce. Serve sweet potato fries with lime wedges and dipping sauce.

NUTRITIONAL INFORMATION

Per Serving: 233 calories; 14.8 g fat; 24.1 g carbohydrates; 2 g protein; 5 mg cholesterol; 390 mg sodium.

133. INDIAN OKRA IN THE AIR FRYER (KURKURI BHINDI)

INGREDIENTS

- 2 cups frozen cut okra, thawed
- 2 tablespoons oil
- 2 tablespoons gram flour (besan)
- 1 teaspoon salt, or to taste1 teaspoon red chili powder
- 1 teaspoon ground coriander1 teaspoon chaat masala
- 1/2 teaspoon ground cumin
- 1/2 teaspoon amchoor (dried mango powder) (optional)

INSTRUCTIONS

Layer thawed okra in a saucepan. Preheat an air fryer for 5 minutes before 400 degrees F (200 degrees C).

In the meantime, heat oil over medium heat in a skillet. Stir in gram flour, cinnamon, chili powder, coriander, masala chaat, cumin, and amchoor. Mix to mix and start stirring for about 2 minutes, until fragrant. Remove and apply to the okra from the heat; blend to paint. Move okra to the basket of an air fryer.

Cook for 5 minutes in a preheated air fryer. Flip okra and air-fry, tossing at intervals of 5 minutes until fried, and crispy, 5 to 10 minutes.

NUTRITIONAL INFORMATION

Per Serving: 194 calories; 14.8 g fat; 12.9 g carbohydrates; 3.4 g protein; 0 mg cholesterol; 1334 mg sodium.

134. TURKEY BREAKFAST SAUSAGE LINKS

INGREDIENTS

1 (9.6 ounce) package turkey breakfast sausage links

INSTRUCTIONS

Preheat the air fryer to 350 F (175 C).

Put all 12 ties in one single layer in the air fryer tub.

Cook for a further 6 minutes.

NUTRITIONAL   INFORMATION

Per Serving: 74 calories; 4.5 g fat; 0 g carbohydrates; 8.4 g protein; 34 mg cholesterol; 375 mg sodium.

135. SALMON PATTIES

INGREDIENTS

- Aioli Dipping Sauce:
- 1/2 cup mayonnaise1 teaspoon finely minced garlic
- 1/2 teaspoon fresh lemon juice
- 2 pinches Cajun seasoning
- Patties:
- 12 ounces salmon, minced
- 1 tablespoon snipped fresh chives
- 1 teaspoon dried parsley
- 1 teaspoon finely minced garlic
- 1/2 teaspoon salt
- 1 tablespoon all-purpose flour, or more as needed
- 1 lemon
- cooking spray

INSTRUCTIONS

In a small bowl, mix mayonnaise, garlic, lemon juice, and cajun seasoning together and refrigerate until necessary.

In a medium bowl, place the salmon, chives, parsley, garlic, and salt and combine well. Stir in flour and stir well. Divide into four equal parts, and mold into patties.

Preheat air fryer to 350 ° F (175 ° C). Slice the lemon into four slices.

Place the lemon slices in the bottom of the air-fryer basket and top with the salmon patties. Sprinkle the patties gently with a cooking spray.

Place the basket in the preheated fryer and drop the temperature in the air fryer to 275 degrees F (135 degrees C) until a thermometer inserted in the center of a patty reads 145 degrees F (63 degrees C), 10 to 15 minutes. Serve with sauce.

NUTRITIONAL INFORMATION

Per Serving: 351 calories; 30.2 g fat; 6.1 g carbohydrates; 15.6 g protein; 52 mg cholesterol; 568 mg sodium.

136. COCONUT CHICKEN IN THE AIR FRYER

INGREDIENTS

- 2 pounds chicken tenderloins, tendons removed
- Dry Mix:
- 1/2 cup tapioca starch
- 1 1/2 teaspoons jerk seasoning
- 1/2 teaspoon granulated garlic
- Egg Wash:
- 1 egg
- 1 teaspoon hot sauce
- Crust:1 cup cornflakes, finely crushed
- 1/4 cup unsweetened coconut flakes

INSTRUCTIONS

Preheat the air fryer for 5 minutes, to 400 degrees F (200 degrees C).

Alternatively, in a shallow bowl, add tapioca starch, jerk seasoning and garlic for the dry mix. Beat egg and hot sauce together in a small, shallow bowl for washing the eggs. In a final, shallow bowl, mix corn flakes and coconut flakes for the crust.

Dip each tender chicken into the dry mixture and shake off excess spice. Dip into a wash of sperm, remove waste, and dredge through the mixture of crust. Repeat every tender move.

Put crushed chicken tenders in the basket of the air fryer and cook for 6 minutes on warm. Turn the tenders and cook for an additional 6 minutes until the chicken is cooked and the coating is crisp.

Per Serving: 201 calories; 6.1 g fat; 8.7 g carbohydrates; 26.5 g protein; 92 mg cholesterol; 156 mg sodium.

137. BURGERS

INGREDIENTS

- 1 (16 ounce) package ground beef
- 1/2 red onion, diced
- 1 teaspoon minced garlic
- 1 teaspoon salt
- 1 teaspoon ground black pepper
- 1 teaspoon Worcestershire sauce
- 1 teaspoon hot English mustard

INSTRUCTIONS

Preheat an air fryer to 350 F (175 C).

In a mixing bowl, bring together the beef, red onion, garlic, salt, pepper, Worcestershire and English mustard.

Form patties by putting your hand on a ball of ground beef and rounding the sides to the size you want.

Cook burgers in the preheated air fryer for about 10 minutes, until firm and no longer pink in the centers. A center-inserted instant-read thermometer will read at least 160 degrees F (70 degrees C).

NUTRITIONAL   INFORMATION

Per Serving: 215 calories; 13.8 g fat; 2.2 g carbohydrates; 19.4 g protein; 71 mg cholesterol; 678 mg sodium.

138. FRIED GREEN TOMATOES

INGREDIENTS

- 2 green tomatoes, cut into 1/4-inch slices
- salt and freshly ground black pepper to taste
- 1/3 cup all-purpose flour
- 1/2 cup buttermilk
- 2 eggs, lightly beaten
- 1 cup plain panko bread crumbs
- 1 cup yellow cornmeal
- 1 teaspoon garlic powder
- 1/2 teaspoon paprika
- 1 tablespoon olive oil, or as needed

INSTRUCTIONS

Tomato slices are flavored with salt and pepper.

Set up a breading station in 3 shallow dishes: pour the flour into the first dish; stir in the second dish buttermilk and eggs together; and mix in the third dish breadcrumbs, cornmeal, garlic powder and paprika.

Dredge slices of tomatoes in flour, shake the excess off. Dip the tomatoes into the mixture of the peas, then into the mixture of the bread crumb, making sure all sides are coated.

The air fryer is preheated to 400 degrees F (200 degrees C). Brush the basket with olive oil to the fryer. Place the breaded tomato slices in the fryer basket, make sure they do not touch each other; if possible, cook them in batches. Brush with olive oil over the tomato tops. Cook for 12 minutes, then turn over the tomatoes and brush with olive oil again. Cook, for 3 to 5 minutes, until crisp and golden brown. Transfer the tomatoes onto a towel-lined rack of paper to keep them crisp. Repeat with tomatoes left over.

NUTRITIONAL INFORMATION

Per Serving: 219 calories; 5.3 g fat; 39.6 g carbohydrates; 7.6 g protein; 63 mg cholesterol; 166 mg sodium

139. KETO CHICKEN WINGS

INGREDIENTS

- 3 pounds chicken wings
- 1 tablespoon taco seasoning mix
- 2 teaspoons olive oil

INSTRUCTIONS

In a resealable plastic bag, add the chicken wings, taco seasoning, and butter. Shake to touch.

Preheat the air fryer for 2 minutes, at 350 degrees F (175 degrees C).

Put the wings in the air fryer, cook for 12 minutes, turning 6 minutes later. Serve straightaway.

NUTRITIONAL INFORMATION

Per Serving: 220 calories; 15.1 g total fat; 57 mg cholesterol; 187 mg sodium. 1.2 g carbohydrates; 18.3 g protein

140. VEGAN BUFFALO TOFU BITES

INGREDIENTS

- 1 (8 ounce) container extra-firm tofu
- 4 tablespoons cornstarch
- 4 tablespoons unsweetened rice milk
- 3/4 cup panko bread crumbs
- 1/8 teaspoon garlic powder
- 1/8 teaspoon paprika
- 1/8 teaspoon onion powder
- 1/8 teaspoon freshly ground black pepper
- 2/3 cup vegan Buffalo wing sauce

INSTRUCTIONS

Cut block tofu from the packet and discard milk. Place tofu on a plate and cover with a heavy pot until the remaining liquid is squeezed out about 10 minutes. Cut the cheesecloth and cut it into 201-inch pieces of bite-sized tofu. Put in a container that is suitable for freezers and freeze, 8 hours to overnight.

Remove tofu and thaw on paper towels or a dry cheesecloth from the freezer. Dry Pat.

Place cornstarch in a resealable plastic bag while tofu is thawing. Pour in a small bowl, rice milk.

Preheat an air fryer to 375 F (190 C).

Place tofu with cornstarch in the bag, seal and shake to fully cover the tofu bits. Cut pieces of tofu and dredge each piece into rice milk.

Place the bread crumbs, garlic powder, paprika, onion powder, and pepper with the cornstarch residue in the resealable plastic bag; shake until well combined.

Place each piece of tofu, with the bread crumbs, one at a time, back into the bag. Shake the bag until the piece of tofu is completely covered, tap gently to shake off waste, and put tofu on a wire rack while repeating with remaining pieces of tofu.

Remove powdered tofu to the basket of the air fryer, and cook 10 minutes. Shake the basket to let the bits loose. Cook 3 more minutes, or until browned.

Put 1/3 cup buffalo sauce in a bowl, add bites of cooked tofu and swirl to cover. Drizzle the leftover buffalo sauce over tofu and toss to coat again. Serve straight away.

NUTRITIONAL INFORMATION

Per Serving: 35 calories; 1 g fat; 6.2 g carbohydrates; 1.6 g protein; 0 mg cholesterol; 243 mg sodium.

141. ZUCCHINI FRIES

INGREDIENTS

- 1 large zucchini, ends trimmed1 egg
- 1/4 cup melted butter
- 1/4 cup all-purpose flour
- 1 teaspoon dried oregano
- 1 teaspoon garlic powderfreshly ground black pepper to taste
- 1 cup panko bread crumbs
- 1/4 cup freshly grated Parmesan cheese

INSTRUCTIONS

Cut to two or three 3-inch pieces of zucchini, then spiralize each piece.

Whip the egg in a shallow bowl until it becomes foamy. Pour the melted butter carefully into the egg and whip until combined.

In a second, a shallow bowl, add flour, oregano, garlic powder, and pepper. In a third cup, mix panko bread crumbs and Parmesan cheese.

Spirals of dredge zucchini in seasoned meal mixture, shaking off excess flour. Dip the spirals in the wash of the whites, allowing the excess wash to run off, then dredge the spirals in the crumbs of Parmesan-bread. Place on a plate with a clean sheet.

Set the temperature of an air fryer to 400 degrees F (200 degrees C). Set 12 minutes with a timer. Move breaded zucchini fries in batches without crowding into the air fryer basket. Cook, for about 12 minutes, until crispy. Serve straight away.

NUTRITIONAL INFORMATION

Per Serving: 510 calories; 30.7 g fat; 57.3 g carbohydrates; 16.8 g protein; 163 mg cholesterol; 632 mg sodium.

142. MEATBALLS

INGREDIENTS

- 16 ounces lean ground beef
- 4 ounces ground pork
- 1 teaspoon Italian seasoning
- 1/2 teaspoon salt
- 2 cloves garlic, minced
- 1 egg
- 1/2 cup grated Parmesan cheese
- 1/3 cup Italian seasoned bread crumbs

INSTRUCTIONS

Preheat the air fryer to 350 F (175 C).

Combine beef, pork, Italian seasoning, in a large bowl, salt, garlic, egg, Parmesan cheese, and bread crumbs. Mix well, until mixed evenly. Use an ice cream scoop to shape 16 meatballs of equal size, and put them on a baking sheet.

Place 1/2 of the meatballs in the air fryer basket and cook for 8 minutes. Shake the pot, and cook for another 2 minutes. Switch to a serving plate, and allow 5 minutes to rest. Repeat with meatballs left over.

NUTRITIONAL INFORMATION

Per Serving: 96 calories; 6.1 g fat; 2 g carbohydrates; 7.9 g protein; 36 mg cholesterol; 170 mg sodium.

143. BACON-CHORIZO TATER TOT DRESSING

INGREDIENTS

- nonstick cooking spray
- 1/4 pound bacon, cut into 1-inch pieces
- 9 ounces ground chorizo
- 1/2 pound frozen bite-size potato nuggets
- 1 stalk celery, sliced
- 1/4 cup water
- 1 egg
- 1 teaspoon garlic base

INSTRUCTIONS

Oven preheats to 370 degrees F (190 degrees C). Allow 2 minutes to preheat. Spray the cooking spray into a 7-inch springform pan.

Put Tater Tots(R) in the basket of air fryer and bake for 15 minutes, shaking the basket halfway through.

Meanwhile, cook the pieces of bacon over medium-high heat in a small skillet until crisp, around 5 minutes. Attach slices of chorizo and celery to compare. Saute for 3 minutes, about. Drain extra grease.

Move the Tater Tots(R) to a bowl and pour a mixture of bacon-chorizo on top. Combine the base with water, egg, and garlic; stir to coat thoroughly. Full in prepared springform cup.

Reduce Air Fryer temperature to 320 degrees F (160 degrees C). Fill the air fryer with a springform pan and cook for 7 minutes until the dressing is cooked through. Cook an extra 3 minutes if dressing doesn't look right.

NUTRITIONAL INFORMATION

Per Serving: 459 calories; 35.3 g fat; 16.3 g carbohydrates; 21.1 g protein; 113 mg cholesterol; 1378 mg sodium.

144. CRISPY RANCH MAC AND CHEESE BALLS IN THE AIR FRYER

INGREDIENTS

- 1 (7.25 ounce) package macaroni and cheese dinner mix
- 3/4 cup milk, divided
- 1/4 cup margarine, cut into pieces
- 1/2 cup shredded sharp Cheddar cheese
- 2 cups cheese-flavored crackers
- 1 (1 ounce) envelope ranch dressing mix
- 2 eggs, beatennonstick cooking spray

INSTRUCTIONS

Switch to a plate covered with paper towels. Repeat with balls left over.. Cook the macaroni in boiling water, stirring occasionally for 7 to 8 minutes, until tender. Drain the macaroni and return to the bowl without rinsing. Packet 1/4 cup of milk, margarine, and cheese sauce; blend until well mixed.

Add the cheddar cheese and remaining 1/2 cup of milk to the mac and cheese and stir until melted. Put a lid into a bowl and refrigerate for 2 hours.

Line a parchment-papered baking sheet. Out of the cold mac and cheese, use an ice cream scoop to shape 1 1/2 inch balls. Place the balls on the baking sheet ready and freeze for 1 hour. Pulse cheese crackers in a food processor's bowl and become small crumbs until they become. Switch crumbs to a bowl and stir in a mixture of ranch dressing. Put the broken eggs in a bowl. you will heat air fryer to 360 degrees F (180 ° C). Oil air fryer basket with cooking spray.

Then dip the mac and cheese balls into the egg and then coat them in the cracker mixture. Place in the air fryer basket, attach as many balls as your basket allows to operate in batches, if appropriate, without touching. Spray cooking spray on tops of the shells.

Cook for 10 minutes in the preheated air-fryer. Sprinkle the tops of the ball with a cooking spray again and cook for 3 more minutes. Switch to a plate covered with paper towels. Repeat with extra balls.

NUTRITIONAL INFORMATION

Per Serving: 147 calories; 7.5 g fat; 14.7 g carbohydrates; 5.1 g protein; 31 mg cholesterol; 375 mg sodium.

145. KETO SALMON CAKES WITH SRIRACHA MAYO

INGREDIENTS

- Sriracha Mayo:
- 1/4 cup mayonnaise
- 1 tablespoon Sriracha
- Salmon Cakes:
- 1 pound skinless salmon fillets, cut into 1-inch pieces
- 1/3 cup almond flour
- 1 egg, lightly beaten
- 1 1/2 teaspoons seafood seasoning
- 1 green onion, coarsely choppedcooking spray
- 1 pinch seafood seasoning (optional)

INSTRUCTIONS

Put whisk mayonnaise and sriracha together in a small container or bowl. Put 1 Sriracha mayo tablespoon in a food processor's bowl and refrigerate the rest until ready for use.

Add to the Sriracha mayo salmon, almond flour, egg, 1 1/2 teaspoons of seafood seasoning, and green onion; pulse quickly for 4 to 5 seconds until the ingredients are just mixed, but there are still tiny chunks of salmon. (Do not over-process as the mixture is mushy.) Line the waxed paper tray, and spray the cooking spray hands. Shape the mixture of salmon into 8 small patties; move to a tray. Put in the refrigerator for about 15 minutes, until chilled and strong.

The air fryer is preheated to 390 degrees F (200 degrees C). Sprinkle with a cooking spray on the air fryer pot.

Remove salmon pastries from the fridge. Mist with cooking spray on both sides and put gently in the air fryer tub, operating in batches if necessary to avoid overcrowding.

Cook for 6 to 8 minutes in the preheated air-fryer. Place on a serving platter and serve with the remaining Sriracha mayo and a light sprinkling of Old Bay seasoning as necessary.

NUTRITIONAL INFORMATION

Per Serving: 340 calories; 24.7 g fat; 3.6 g carbohydrates; 25.5 g protein; 107 mg cholesterol; 513 mg sodium.

146. ROOT VEGETABLES WITH VEGAN AIOLI

INGREDIENTS

- Garlic Aioli:
- 1/2 cup vegan mayonnaise
- 1 clove garlic, minced
- 1/2 teaspoon fresh lemon juicesalt and ground black pepper to taste
- Root Vegetables:
- 4 tablespoons extra virgin olive oil
- 1 tablespoon minced fresh rosemary

- 3 cloves garlic, finely minced
- 1 teaspoon kosher salt, or to taste
- 1/2 teaspoon ground black pepper, or to taste
- 1 pound parsnips, peeled and cut vertically into uniform pieces
- 1 pound baby red potatoes, cut lengthwise into 4 or 6 pieces
- 1/2 pound baby carrots, split lengthwise
- 1/2 red onion, cut lengthwise into 1/2-inch slices
- 1/2 teaspoon grated lemon zest, or to taste (optional)

INSTRUCTIONS

For the garlic aioli, mix mayonnaise, garlic, lemon juice, salt and pepper in a small bowl; put in the refrigerator until ready to serve.

If your air-fryer manufacturer suggests preheating, preheat the air fryer to 400 degrees F (200 degrees C)

In a small bowl, combine olive oil, rosemary, garlic, salt, and pepper; set aside to allow the flavours to blend.

In a large bowl, add parsnips, onions, carrots, and onion. Attach a mixture of olive oil and rosemary and whisk until vegetables are uniformly coated. Place a portion of the vegetables in a single layer in the air fryer tub, then add a rack and a separate layer of vegetables.

Fry air for 15 minutes.

When the timer rings, you can plate the veggies and keep warm, or continue cooking in 5-minute intervals until the desired doneness and browning of the vegetable hits.

Place the remaining vegetables 15 minutes into the bottom of the air fryer basket and air fry, checking for doneness as required. Use the rack again, if a single layer includes more vegetables than the suit.

Serve with garlic aioli when all the vegetables have cooked, and garnish with lemon zest.

NUTRITIONAL INFORMATION

Per Serving: 228 calories; 13.8 g fat; 25.5 g carbohydrates; 2.2 g protein; 0 mg cholesterol; 98 mg sodium.

147. HUSH PUPPIES

INGREDIENTS

- nonfat cooking spray
- 1 cup yellow cornmeal
- 3/4 cup all-purpose flour
- 1 1/2 teaspoons baking powder
- 1/2 teaspoon salt
- 1/4 teaspoon cayenne pepper, or more to taste
- 1/4 teaspoon garlic powder
- 2 tablespoons minced onion
- 2 tablespoons minced green bell pepper
- 3/4 cup low-fat buttermilk
- 1 large egg

INSTRUCTIONS

Put whisk mayonnaise and sriracha together in a small container or bowl. Put 1 Sriracha mayo tablespoon in a food processor's bowl and refrigerate the rest until ready for use.

Add salmon, almond meal, egg, 1 1/2 teaspoons of seafood seasoning and green onion to the Sriracha mayo; pulse quickly for 4 to 5 seconds until the ingredients are easily mixed, but there are still tiny chunks of salmon. (Do not over-process as the mixture is mushy.) Line the waxed paper tray, and spray the cooking spray hands. Shape the mixture of salmon into 8 small patties; move to a tray. Put in the refrigerator for about 15 minutes, until chilled and strong.

The air fryer is preheated to 390 degrees F (200 degrees C). Sprinkle with a cooking spray on the air fryer pot.

Remove salmon pastries from the fridge. Mist with cooking spray on both sides and put gently in the air fryer tub, operating in batches if necessary to avoid overcrowding.

Cook for 6 to 8 minutes in the preheated air-fryer. Place on a serving platter and serve with the remaining Sriracha mayo and a light sprinkling of Old Bay seasoning as necessary.

NUTRITIONAL   INFORMATION

Per Serving: 85 calories; 0.9 g fat; 16.3 g carbohydrates; 2.8 g protein; 16 mg cholesterol; 181 mg sodium.

148.   CRUMBED CHICKEN TENDERLOINS (AIR FRIED)

INGREDIENTS

- 1 egg
- ½ cup dry bread crumbs
- 2 tablespoons vegetable oil
- 8 chicken tenderloins

INSTRUCTIONS

Preheat an air fryer to 350 F (175 C).

Whisk the egg in a medium bowl.

In a second bowl, blend together the bread crumbs and oil until the mixture is loose and crumbly.

Dip every tenderloin of chicken into the egg bowl; shake off any remaining egg. Dip the chicken into the crumb mixture, ensuring it is filled evenly and fully. Place the chicken tenderloins into the air fryer bowl. Cook, about 12 minutes, until the middle, is no longer pink. A center-inserted instant-read thermometer will read at least 165 degrees F (74 degrees C).

NUTRITIONAL   INFORMATION

Per Serving:

253 calories; 11.4 g total fat; 109 mg cholesterol; 171 mg sodium. 9.8 g carbohydrates; 26.2 g protein

149. OREOS

INGREDIENTS

- 1/2 cup complete pancake mix
- 1/3 cup watercooking spray
- 9 chocolate sandwich cookies
- 1 tablespoon confectioners' sugar, or to taste

INSTRUCTIONS

Blend the pancake mixture with the water until well mixed.

Fill a parchment paper basket with the air fryer. Spray nonstick cooking spray on parchment paper. Dip each cookie into the mixture of the pancake, and put it in the bowl. Make sure they do not touch; if possible cook in batches.

The air fryer is preheated to 400 degrees F (200 degrees C). Remove the basket and cook for 4 to 5 minutes; flip until golden brown, 2 to 3 more minutes. Sprinkle with sugar from candy-makers.

NUTRITIONAL INFORMATION

Per Serving: 77 calories; 2.1 g fat; 13.7 g carbohydrates; 1.2 g protein; 0 mg cholesterol; 156 mg sodium.

150. CRUMBED FISH

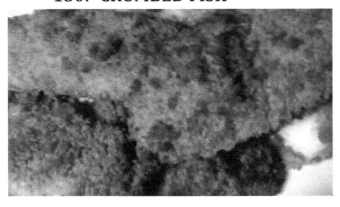

INGREDIENTS

- 1 cup dry bread crumbs
- 1/4 cup vegetable oil
- 4 flounder fillets
- 1 egg, beaten1 lemon, sliced

INSTRUCTIONS

Preheat an air fryer to 350 F (180 C).

In a cup, add the bread crumbs and the oil. Stir until the mixture is crumbly and loose.

Dip in the egg fish fillets; shake off any excesses. Dip the fillets into a mixture of bread crumbs; cover evenly and fully.

Gently lay coated fillets in the preheated air fryer. Cook, about 12 minutes, with a fork, until fish flakes easily. Garnish with sliced lemon.

NUTRITIONAL INFORMATION

Per Serving: 354 calories; 17.7 g fat; 22.5 g carbohydrates; 26.9 g protein; 107 mg cholesterol; 309 mg sodium.

151. BREAKFAST FRITTATA

INGREDIENTS

- 1/4 pound breakfast sausage, fully cooked and crumbled
- 4 eggs, lightly beaten
- 1/2 cup shredded Cheddar-Monterey Jack cheese blend
- 2 tablespoons red bell pepper, diced
- 1 green onion, chopped
- 1 pinch cayenne pepper (optional)cooking spray

INSTRUCTIONS

Combine the sausage, eggs, cheese from Cheddar-Monterey Jack, pepper. Ointment, and cayenne in a container, and blend.

Preheat the air fryer to 360 ° F (180 ° C). Sprinkle a 6x2-inch non-stick cake pan with a cooking spray.

Bring the mixture of the eggs in the prepared cake pan.

Cook in the air fryer for 18 to 20 minutes until the frittata is set.

NUTRITIONAL INFORMATION

Per Serving: 380 calories; 27.4 g fat; 2.9 g carbohydrates; 31.2 g protein; 443 mg cholesterol; 694 mg sodium.

152. LEMON PEPPER SHRIMP

INGREDIENTS

- 1 tablespoon olive oil
- 1 lemon, juiced
- 1 teaspoon lemon pepper
- 1/4 teaspoon paprika
- 1/4 teaspoon garlic powder

- 12 ounces uncooked medium shrimp, peeled and deveined
- 1 lemon, sliced

INSTRUCTIONS

Preheat an air fryer to 400 F (200 C).

In a small bowl, mix olive oil with lemon juice, lemon pepper, paprika, and garlic powder. Add the shrimp and then toss until coated.

Put the shrimp in the air fryer and cook for 6 to 8 minutes, until pink and strong. Serve with sliced lemon.

NUTRITIONAL INFORMATION

Per Serving: 215 calories; 8.6 g fat; 12.6 g carbohydrates; 28.9 g protein; 255 mg cholesterol; 528 mg sodium.

153. CORN ON THE COB

INGREDIENTS

- 1/4 cup mayonnaise
- 2 teaspoons crumbled cotija cheese
- 1 teaspoon lime juice
- 1/4 teaspoon chili powder

- 2 ears corn, shucked and halved
- 4 sprigs fresh cilantro, or to taste (optional)

INSTRUCTIONS

Preheat an air fryer to 400 F (200 C).

In a shallow dish, mix mayonnaise, cotija cheese, lime juice and chilli powder.

Roll each piece of corn in a mixture of mayonnaise before covering all sides.

Place all 4 pieces of corn in air fryer basket and cook for eight minutes. Top with cilantro.

NUTRITIONAL INFORMATION

Per Serving: 144 calories; 11.9 g fat; 9.3 g carbohydrates; 1.9 g protein; 7 mg cholesterol; 103 mg sodium.

154. FRENCH TOAST STICKS

INGREDIENTS

- 2 large eggs
- 1/3 cup milk
- 1 tablespoon butter, melted
- 1 teaspoon vanilla extract
- 1 teaspoon ground cinnamon
- 4 slices day-old bread, cut into thirds
- 1 teaspoon confectioners' sugar, or to taste

INSTRUCTIONS

In a cup, bring together the eggs, milk, butter, vanilla extract, and cinnamon.

Fill a parchment paper basket with the air fryer. Dip each piece of bread into a mixture of milk and place it in the basket. Make sure they do not touch; if possible cook in batches.

Preheat the air fryer to 370 ° F (188 ° C). Remove the basket and cook bread for 6 minutes; turn over and cook for another 3 minutes. Sprinkle with sugar from the confectioners on each piece.

NUTRITIONAL INFORMATION

Per Serving: 48 calories; 2.2 g fat; 5 g carbohydrates; 1.9 g protein; 34 mg cholesterol; 78 mg sodium.

155. KETO GARLIC CHEESE BREAD

INGREDIENTS

- 1 cup shredded mozzarella cheese
- 1/4 cup grated Parmesan cheese
- 1 large egg
- 1/2 teaspoon garlic powder

INSTRUCTIONS

Fill the basket with a piece of parchment paper to the air fryer.

In a bowl, add mozzarella cheese, Parmesan cheese, egg, and garlic powder; mix well until mixed. Press the air-fryer basket into a round circle on the parchment.

The air fryer is heated to 350 degrees F (175 degrees C). 10 Minutes to cook the bread. Take leave. Serve warm, but not dry, bread with garlic cheese.

NUTRITIONAL INFORMATION

Per Serving: 225 calories; 14.3 g fat; 2.7 g carbohydrates; 20.8 g protein; 138 mg cholesterol; 538 mg sodium.

156. SWEET POTATO HASH

INGREDIENTS

- 2 large sweet potato, cut into small cubes
- 2 slices bacon, cut into small pieces
- 2 tablespoons olive oil
- 1 tablespoon smoked paprika
- 1 teaspoon sea salt
- 1 teaspoon ground black pepper
- 1 teaspoon dried dill weed

INSTRUCTIONS

Preheat an air fryer to 400 F (200 C).

In a large bowl, toss the sweet potato, bacon, olive oil, paprika, salt, pepper, and dill. Place the mixture in the air fryer with preheating. Cook for about 12 -16 minutes. After 10 minutes test and stir, and then every 3 minutes until crispy and brown.

NUTRITIONAL   INFORMATION

Per Serving: 191 calories; 6 g fat; 31.4 g carbohydrates; 3.7 g protein; 3 mg cholesterol; 447 mg sodium.

157. CINNAMON AND SUGAR DOUGHNUTS

INGREDIENTS

- 1/2 cup white sugar
- 2 1/2 tablespoons butter, at room temperature
- 2 large egg yolks
- 2 1/4 cups all-purpose flour
- 1 1/2 teaspoons baking powder
- 1 teaspoon salt
- 1/2 cup sour cream
- 1/3 cup white sugar
- 1 teaspoon cinnamon
- 2 tablespoons butter, melted, or as needed

INSTRUCTIONS

In a mug, mix 1/2 cup of white sugar and butter together until crumbly. Add the yolks of the eggs and mix well until mixed.

Sew the flour into a separate bowl, baking powder, and salt. Put 1/3 of the flour mixture in the sugar-egg mixture, and 1/2 of the sour cream; stir until mixed. Add in the remainder of the flour and the sour cream. Cool the dough to ready for use.

In a mug, add 1/3 cup sugar and cinnamon.

Roll the dough out to 1/2-inch thick onto a gently floured work surface. In the dough, cut 9 large circles; cut out a small circle from the middle of each large circle to make doughnut shapes. Preheat an air fryer to 350 F (175 C).

Brush 1/2 over both sides of the doughnuts with the melted butter.

Place 1/2 doughnuts in air fryer basket; cook for eight minutes. With the remaining butter melted, paint fried donuts and immerse immediately in the cinnamon-sugar mixture. Repeat with doughnuts left over.

NUTRITIONAL INFORMATION

Per Serving: 276 calories; 9.7 g fat; 43.5 g carbohydrates; 4.3 g protein; 66 mg cholesterol; 390 mg sodium.

158. BREAKFAST TOAD-IN-THE-HOLE TARTS

INGREDIENTS

- 1 sheet frozen puff pastry, thawed
- 4 tablespoons shredded Cheddar cheese
- 4 tablespoons diced cooked ham
- 4 eggschopped fresh chives (optional)

INSTRUCTIONS

The air fryer is preheated to 400 degrees F (200 degrees C).

Unfold the sheet of pastry on a flat surface and cut it into 4 sq.

Place 2 squares of pastry in the basket of air fryer, and cook 6 to 8 minutes.

Disable Air Fryer pot. Use a tablespoon of metal to gently force every square to create an indentation. Place 1 spoonful of Cheddar cheese and 1 spoonful of ham in each hole and pour 1 egg over each.

Return to the air-fryer basket. Cook about 6 minutes more to optimal doneness. Remove tarts from basketball, and let them cool for 5 minutes. Repeat with squares of bread, cheese, bacon, and eggs left over.

NUTRITIONAL   INFORMATION

Per Serving: 446 calories; 31 g fat; 27.9 g carbohydrates; 14.2 g protein; 199 mg cholesterol; 377 mg sodium.

159. CHURROS

INGREDIENTS

- 1/4 cup butter
- 1/2 cup milk
- 1 pinch salt
- 1/2 cup all-purpose flour
- 2 eggs
- 1/4 cup white sugar
- 1/2 teaspoon ground cinnamon

INSTRUCTIONS

Melt the butter over medium to high heat in a saucepan. Pour the milk over and add salt. Lower to medium heat, and bring to a boil, stirring continuously with a wooden spoon. Quickly add all the flour in one go. Keep stirring until the dough joins in.

Remove from heat and allow it to cool for five to seven minutes. Mix the wooden spoon in the eggs until the choux pastry joins in. Spoon dough fitted with a large star tip into a pastry bag. Pip dough straight into the air-fryer basket into pieces.

Air fried churros for 5 minutes, at 340 degrees F (175 degrees C).

Meanwhile, in a small bowl, mix sugar and cinnamon and pour onto a shallow plate.

Remove the fried churros from the air fryer and roll in the mixture of cinnamon and sugar.

NUTRITIONAL INFORMATION

Per Serving: 172 calories; 9.8 g fat; 17.5 g carbohydrates; 3.9 g protein; 84 mg cholesterol; 112 mg sodium.

160. ONION RINGS

INGREDIENTS

- 1/2 cup all-purpose flour
- 1 tsp paprika
- 1 tsp salt, divided
- 1/2 cup buttermilk, see tips above for making your own
- 1 egg
- 1 cup panko breadcrumbs
- 2 Tbsp olive oil
- 1 large yellow sweet onion, sliced 1/2-inch thick and separated into rings
- Oil Spray, optional

INSTRUCTIONS

You'll need 3 shallow bowls or deep plates. Combine rice, paprika, and 1/2 tsp of salt in the first. Combine buttermilk (or milk and vinegar/lemon juice) and egg in the second, then add 1/4 cup of flour from the first bowl. Combine 1/2 tsp salt and olive oil with a fork in the third panko breadcrumbs, until the oil is evenly distributed.

In the flour mixture, dredge the onion rings, drop them in the buttermilk mixture, then dredge them in the panko mixture.

Place the onion rings into the Air Fryer basket in a single layer. If required, you can put smaller rings inside larger rings, just make sure that there's space between them.

Cook for about 12-15 minutes, at 400 ° F until golden brown and crispy. After about 6 minutes spray with some cooking spray.

161. ROASTED ASIAN BROCCOLI

INGREDIENTS

- 1 Lb Broccoli, Cut into florets
- 1 1/2 Tbsp Peanut oil
- 1 Tbsp Garlic, minced
- Salt
- 2 Tbsp Reduced sodium soy sauce
- 2 tsp Honey (or agave)
- 2 tsp Sriracha
- 1 tsp Rice vinegar
- 1/3 Cup Roasted salted peanuts
- Fresh lime juice (optional)

INSTRUCTIONS

Toss the broccoli, peanut oil, garlic and sea salt season together in a large bowl. Make sure all the broccoli florets are coated with oil. I like using my hands to wipe each one off quickly.

Spread the broccoli as much as possible into your air fryer's wire bowl, trying to leave a little gap between each floret as possible.

Cook until golden brown and crispy at 400 degrees, about 15-20 minutes, stirring halfway.

Mix the honey, soy sauce, sriracha, and rice vinegar in a hot, microwave-safe bowl while the broccoli and peanuts cook.

When combined, microwave the mixture for 10-15 seconds until the honey is cooled, and blended evenly. Move the cooked broccoli to a bowl, and add the mixture of soy sauce. Toss to coat and, if necessary, season to taste more salt with a pinch. Attach the peanuts and squeeze lime over the top (if desired).

162. PARMESAN POTATOES RECIPE

INGREDIENTS

- 1 Lb Baby Potatoes (the smaller the better)
- 1 Tablespoon Olive Oil
- 1 teaspoon Dried Italian Seasoning
- Pinch Salt
- 1/2 Cup Shredded Parmesan Cheese

INSTRUCTIONS

Spray nonstick air fryer dish, and preheat for 5 minutes at 370oF.

Toss potatoes, butter, salt, and parmesan in Italian season.

Move potatoes and cheese to the basket for an air fryer.

Air fry 15-18 minutes at 370oF (depending on the size of the potatoes)-toss every 5 minutes.

NUTRITIONAL INFORMATION:

Yield: 4 Serving Size: 1 Amount Per Serving: Calories: 178 Total Fat: 6g Saturated Fat: 2g Trans Fat: 0g Unsaturated Fat: 4g Cholesterol: 7mg Sodium: 214mg Carbohydrates: 24g Fiber: 3g Sugar: 1g Protein: 7g

163. PALEO FISH STICKS

INGREDIENTS

- 1-1/2 pound cod (or other white fish)
- 1/2 cup tapioca starch
- 2 eggs
- 1 cup almond flour
- 1-1/2 teaspoon dried dill
- 1-1/2 teaspoon onion powder
- 1 teaspoon fine sea salt
- 1 teaspoon ground black pepper
- 1/2 teaspoon mustard powder
- 2 tablespoons avocado oil
- avocado oil spray
- For Tartar Sauce
- 1/3 cup avocado oil mayo
- 1 tablespoon dill relish
- 1 tablespoon chopped fresh or dried herbs (dill, parsley, scallions are great here)
- 2 teaspoons lemon juice
- 1/4 teaspoon salt

INSTRUCTIONS

heat the air fryer to 390 degrees F.

Spray fish with a paper towel dry and pinch salt and pepper to season.

Cut into small fish sticks, roughly 1/2"x 1/2"x 2 "(see note) In a medium bowl position tapioca starch. In a second medium bowl whisk eggs. Whisk almond flour, dill, onion powder, salt, chili pepper and mustard powder in a large bowl. Dip the sliced fish into the tapioca, shake off any excess, then into the egg and then dredge in a mixture of flour. Add the avocado oil to the basket and sprinkle generously with avocado spray on the air fryer basket and put as many fish sticks in the basket that suit with plenty of space in between. Oil the fish sticks to brush gently with additional avocado oil.

Fry for 11 minutes, tossing at 5 minutes once with delicacy.

Alternatively, mix all the ingredients into a medium bowl to make tartar sauce. Deposit back.

Repeat with remaining fish until all are cooked to reach an inner temperature of 145oF. Be careful not to overcook, or the fish will disintegrate.

Serve immediately or cool completely with tartar sauce until freezing.

NUTRITIONAL INFORMATION

Serving Size 2 Amount Per Serving, Calories 598Calories from fat 198% Daily Value Total Fat 22.5g35% Saturated Fat 3.3g 17% Cholesterol 285mg 95% Sodium 1600mg   67% Carbohydrate 35.2g 12% Dietary Fiber 2.9g 12% Sugars 1.1g Protein 61.7g

164. THAI SALMON PATTIES

INGREDIENTS

- 14 oz/ 400 g canned salmon drained and bones removed (if desired)
- 1/2 cup Panko breadcrumbs
- 1/4 teaspoon salt
- 1 1/2 tablespoon Thai red curry paste
- 1 1/2 tablespoons brown sugar
- zest from 1 lime
- 2 eggs
- spray oil

INSTRUCTIONS

Mix all ingredients together until the red curry paste is evenly distributed via the mixture of fish.

Shape into 1/4 cup patties, 1 inch thick and 2-3 inches thick across.

Heat air fryer up to 360 ° F/ 180 ° C.

Spray oil patties; turn on and spray on the other side.

Place patties gently inside the basket; you can only cook 3 at a time). Cook 4 minutes, turn over, and cook 4 minutes more.

Move to a clean plate and repeat until all are finished, with remaining patties.

Serving: 1salmon pattie, Calories: 108kcal, Carbohydrates: 6g, Protein: 12g, Fat: 6g, Saturated Fat: 1g, Cholesterol: 71mg, Sodium: 323mg, Sugar: 3g

165. TANDOORI PANEER NAAN PIZZA

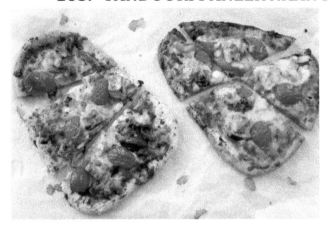

INGREDIENTS

- 2 Garlic Naan
- 1/4 cup Pizza sauce or Marinara sauce
- 1/4 cup Grape Tomatoes cut into halves
- 1/4 cup Red Onions sliced
- 1/4 cup Bell pepper sliced
- 3/4 cup Mozzarella grated
- 2 tbsp Feta (optional)
- 2 tbsp Cilantro chopped
- For Tandoori Paneer
- 1/2 cup Paneer small cubes
- 1 tbsp Yogurt thick
- 1/2 tsp Garam Masala
- 1/2 tsp Garlic powder
- 1/4 tsp Ground Turmeric (Haldi powder)
- 1/2 tsp Kashmiri Red Chili powder or mild paprika, adjust to taste
- 1/4 tsp Salt adjust to taste

INSTRUCTIONS

Mix all of the listed ingredients into a bowl for Tandoori Paneer.

Fill a parchment-papered baking tray. Place naans on the baking tray and add sauce and spread evenly on each. Layer the two naans with a little mozzarella.

Place the cubes of the paneer on the two naans (mixed with yogurt and spices) The red onions, bell peppers and grape tomatoes are spread next.

Next, a further layer of mozzarella spreads over the vegetables. Sprinkle some feta cheese on top, as an alternative. Finally, add some cilantro chopped.

Air Fryer: Cook 8-10 minutes on a 350F. After 7 minutes, start the test and crisp it to your choice.

Temperature: Preheat to 400F temperature. Bake ten-15 minutes or until the cheese has melted. If you like, you can broil to a crisper cheese finish for 2-3 minutes. You 're ready to pull out and enjoy when the cheese's melted!

Chili flakes top and enjoy!

NUTRITIONAL INFORMATION

Calories: 738kcal, Carbohydrates: 67g, Protein: 30g, Fat: 37g, Saturated Fat: 18g, Cholesterol: 96mg, Sodium: 1783mg, Potassium: 216mg, Fiber: 3g, Sugar: 8g, Vitamin A: 1455IU, Vitamin C: 28.5mg, Calcium: 657mg, Iron: 0.8mg

166. CAULIFLOWER CHICKPEA TACOS (VEGAN)

INGREDIENTS

- 4 cups cauliflower florets cut into bite-sized pieces
- 19 oz can of chickpeas drained and rinsed
- 2 tablespoons olive oil
- 2 tablespoons taco seasoning
- To serve
- 8 small tortillas
- 2 avocados sliced
- 4 cups cabbage shredded
- coconut yogurt to drizzle

INSTRUCTIONS

Air fryer pre-heat to 390 ° F/200 ° C.

Toss the chickpeas and the cauliflower with the olive oil and taco seasoning in a large bowl.

Dump it all into your air-fryer tub.

Cook in the air fryer, sometimes shaking the pot, for 20 minutes or until it is cooked through. Cauliflower is going to be golden but not charred.

Serve in slices of avocado, cod and coconut yogurt (or standard yogurt) in tacos.

167. PERFECT SALMON

INGREDIENTS

2 wild caught salmon fillets with comparable thickness, mine were 1-1/12-inches thick

2 tsps teaspoons avocado oil or olive oil

2 tsps paprika

generously seasoned with salt and coarse black pepper

lemon wedges

INSTRUCTIONS

If possible, remove any bones from your salmon, and allow the fish to sit on the counter for an hour. Spice each filet with olive oil and paprika, salt, and pepper.

Place filets in air fryer basket. Set air fryer for 1-1/2-inch filets at 390 degrees for 7 minutes.

When the timer stops, open the basket and test the filets with a fork to ensure that they are finished to your desired doneness.

NUTRITIONAL INFORMATION

Perfect Air Fryer Salmon Amount Per Serving (1 fillet) Calories 288Calories from Fat 170% Daily Value Fat 18.9g29% Saturated Fat 2.6g16% Polyunsaturated Fat 0.8g Monounsaturated Fat 10.3g Cholesterol 78mg26% Sodium 80.6mg4% Potassium 52.5mg2% Carbohydrates 1.4g0% Fiber 0.8g3% Sugar 0.3g0% Protein 28.3g57% Vitamin A 1135IU23% Vitamin C 2.5mg3% Calcium 25mg3% Iron 1.4mg8%

168. VEGAN BUFFALO CAULIFLOWER

INGREDIENTS

- 1 large head cauliflower
- 1 cup unbleached all-purpose flour
- 1 teaspoon vegan chicken bouillon granules
- 1/4 teaspoon cayenne pepper
- 1/4 teaspoon chili powder
- 1/4 teaspoon paprika
- 1/4 teaspoon dried chipotle chile flakes
- 1 cup soy milk
- canola oil spray
- 2 tablespoons nondairy butter
- 1/2 cup Frank's RedHot Original Cayenne Pepper Sauce or your favorite
- 2 cloves garlic, minced

INSTRUCTIONS

Cut the bite-sized cauliflower into bits. Rinse and rinse the parts of the cauliflower.

Combine the flakes in a large bowl with the rice, bouillon granules, cayenne, chili powder, paprika and chipotle. Slowly whisk in the milk until they form a thick batter.

Spray canola oil on the air fryer basket and preheat the air fryer to 390 ° F for 10 minutes.

Toss the cauliflower in the batter whilst the air fryer is preheating. Move the battered cauliflower to the basket for an air fryer. Cook them at 390 ° F for 20 minutes. Turn the cauliflower pieces at 10 minutes using tongs (do not be alarmed if they hang). Steam the butter, hot sauce and garlic in a small saucepan over medium-high steam after turning the cauliflower. Take the mixture to a boil, reduce heat to cool, and spray.

When cooked, move the cauliflower to a large bowl. Pour the cauliflower over the sauce and play gently with tongs. Serve straight away.

169. STEAK AND ASPARAGUS BUNDLES

INGREDIENTS

- 2 - 2 1/2 pounds Flank steak - cut into 6 pieces
- kosher salt/black pepper
- 1/2 cup Tamari sauce
- 2 cloves garlic - crushed
- 1 pound asparagus - trimmed
- 3 bell peppers - seeded and sliced thinly
- 1/4 cup balsamic vinegar
- 1/3 cup beef broth
- 2 tablespoons unsalted butter
- Olive oil spray

INSTRUCTIONS

Season the steaks with pepper and salt.

Place steaks in a large bag with a zip-top. Add Sauce with tamari, and garlic. Seal container.

Massage the steaks so they're fully covered. Switch to the refrigerator and allow up to overnight marinating for at least 1 hour.

Remove steaks from marinade when ready to clean, and put them on a cutting board or tray. Reject marinade.

Split asparagus and bell peppers evenly, then put them in the center of each piece of steak.

Roll the steak around the vegetables and take the tooth firmly.

Preheat the fryer to warm.

Depending on the size of your air fryer operating in batches, put bundles in the air fryer bag.

Mist vegetables with a mist of olive oil.

Cook for 5 minutes, at 400 degrees.

Remove bundles of steak and let stand for 5 minutes before serving/slicing.

WHILE steak rests in medium-sized saucepan heat: medium-heat balsamic vinegar, broth, and butter. Whisk to combine.

Continue to cook until sauce has thickened and halved. Season with salt and pepper.

Pour sauce over bundles of steaks before eating.

170. LOW CARB TANDOORI CHICKEN

INGREDIENTS

- 5 Chicken Drumsticks de-skinned (about 1.6 lbs)
- 1 tbsp Oil
- 2 tbsp Cilantro leaves to garnish
- 4 Lemon wedges
- For Marinade
- 1/4 cup Yogurt thick
- 1 tbsp Garlic paste
- 1 tbsp Ginger paste
- 1 tsp Cayenne or Red Chili powder Kashmiri chili powder preferred
- 1/2 tsp Ground Turmeric (Haldi powder)
- 1/2 tsp Garam Masala

- 1 tsp Ground Cumin (Jeera powder)
- 1 tbsp Dried Fenugreek leaves (Kasoori Methi) (optional)
- 1 tsp Salt adjust to taste
- 1 tbsp Lime juice

INSTRUCTIONS

Allow three or four slots on each drumstick.

Blend all the ingredients together for the marinade.

Apply evenly to the chicken drumsticks and allow them to marinate in the refrigerator for 1 hour (you can keep it cooled for up to 10 hours).

When ready to cook remove marinated chicken from the fridge. Arrange the air fryer pan or basket into a single layer. Baste with a bit of cooking oil.

Cook for 10 minutes in the air fryer, at 360 ° F. Flip the chicken over, then baste with butter. Then, another 5 minutes of cooking.

Use a serving plate to cover. Garnish with the coriander. Serve with wedges of lemon and sliced onion.

NUTRITIONAL INFORMATION

Calories: 231kcal, Carbohydrates: 4.3g, Protein: 22.6g, Fat: 12.7g, Saturated Fat: 3.2g, Cholesterol: 113mg, Sodium: 957mg, Potassium: 101mg, Fiber: 0.5g, Sugar: 1.4g, Calcium: 30mg, Iron: 1.6mg

171. SWEET POTATO TOTS

INGREDIENTS

- 2 small (14 oz. total) sweet potatoes, peeled
- 1 tablespoon potato starch
- 1/8 teaspoon garlic powder
- 1 1/4 teaspoons kosher salt, divided
- 3/4 cup no-salt-added ketchup Cooking spray

INSTRUCTIONS

Put a medium pot of water up over high heat to a boil. Remove potatoes, and cook for about 15 minutes until just fork tender. Move potatoes to a cool plate, about 15 minutes.

Using the large holes of a box grater, grate potatoes over a medium bowl. Throw away gently with potato starch, garlic powder, and 1 teaspoon salt. Form the mixture into approximately 24(1-inch) cylinders of tot.

Coat the air fryer basket lightly with spray for cooking. Place 1/2 of the tots (about 12) into the basket in a single layer, and spray with the spray. Cook until lightly browned at 400 ° F, 12 to 14 minutes, turning tots halfway through cooking time. Lift from the fry basket and add 1/8 teaspoon salt to sprinkle.

NUTRITIONAL INFORMATION

Calories 78 Fat 0g Satfat 0g Unsatfat 0g Protein 1g Carbohydrate 19g Fiber 2g Sugars 8g Added sugars 0g Sodium 335mg Calcium 1% DV Potassium 9% DV

172. BANANA BREAD

INGREDIENTS

- 3/4 cup (3 oz.) white-whole wheat flour
- 1 teaspoon cinnamon
- 1/2 teaspoon Kosher salt
- 1/4 teaspoon Baking soda
- 2 medium (12 oz. total) ripe bananas, mashed (about 3/4 cup)
- 2 large eggs, lightly beaten
- 1/2 cup granulated sugar
- 1/3 cup plain nonfat yogurt
- 2 tablespoons vegetable oil
- 1 teaspoon Vanilla extract
- 2 tablespoons (3/4 oz.) toasted walnuts, roughly chopped Cooking spray

INSTRUCTIONS

Line the bottom of a6-inch round cake pan with parchment paper; brush the pan lightly with spray for cooking. In a medium bowl, whisk together the flour, cinnamon, salt and baking soda; set aside.

Mashed bananas, bacon, sugar, milk, oil and vanilla are whisked together in a separate medium bowl. Stir wet ingredients gently into a mixture of flour until well mixed. Sprinkle with walnuts and pour the batter into the prepared pan.

Heat up a 5.3-qt air fryer to 310 ° F and then put pan in air fryer and cook until browned and a wooden pick inserted in the center comes out clean, 30 to 35 minutes, turning pan halfway through cooking time.

NUTRITIONAL Information

Calories 180 Fat 6g Satfat 1g Unsatfat 5g Protein 4g Carbohydrate 29g Fiber 2g Sugars 17g Added sugars 13g Sodium 184mg Calcium 3% DV Potassium 4% D

173. AVOCADO FRIES

INGREDIENTS

- 1/2 cup (about 2 1/8 oz.) all-purpose flour
- 1 1/2 teaspoons black pepper
- 2 large eggs
- 1 tablespoon water
- 1/2 cup panko (Japanese-style breadcrumbs)
- 2 avocados, cut into 8 wedges each Cooking spray
- 1/4 teaspoon kosher salt
- 1/4 cup no-salt-added ketchup
- 2 tablespoons canola mayonnaise
- 1 tablespoon apple cider vinegar
- 1 tablespoon Sriracha chili sauce

INSTRUCTIONS

In a shallow dish, mix the flour and pepper together. In a second shallow dish, gently beat eggs and water. Place the panko in a shallow third platter. Dredge wedges of avocado in flour and shake off the waste. Dip the mixture of the eggs, allowing any excess to drop off. Dredge in panko and click to stick. Avocado coat wedges well with spray cooking.

Place avocado wedges in air fryer basket and cook for 7 to 8 minutes at 400 ° F until golden, turning the avocado wedges over halfway through cooking. Remove from the frying pan; sprinkle with salt.

As avocado wedges cook, ketchup, mayonnaise, vinegar, and Sriracha are whisked together in a small bowl. To serve, put 4 avocado fries with 2 spoonfuls of sauce on each plate.

NUTRITIONAL INFORMATION

Calories 262 Fat 18g Satfat 3g Unsatfat 14g Protein 5g Carbohydrate 23g Fiber 7g Sugars 5g Added sugars 1g Sodium 306mg Calcium 2% DV Potassium 14% DV

174. SOUTHERN STYLE CATFISH WITH GREEN BEANS

INGREDIENTS

- 12 ounces fresh green beans, trimmed Cooking spray
- 1 teaspoon light brown sugar
- 1/2 teaspoon crushed red pepper (optional)
- 3/8 teaspoon kosher salt, divided
- 2 Unit (6-oz.) catfish fillets
- 1/4 cup all-purpose flour
- 1 large egg, lightly beaten
- 1/3 cup panko (Japanese-style breadcrumbs)
- 1/4 teaspoon black pepper
- 2 tablespoons mayonnaise
- 1 1/2 teaspoons finely chopped fresh dill
- 3/4 teaspoon dill pickle relish
- 1/2 teaspoon apple cider vinegar
- 1/8 teaspoon granulated sugar Lemon wedges

INSTRUCTIONS

In a medium bowl, put green beans and spray with cooking spray. Sprinkle with brown sugar, crushed red pepper (if used), and salt for 1/8 teaspoon. Put in air fryer bowl, and cook for about 12 minutes at 400oF until well browned and tender. Switch to a bowl; cover it with foil to keep it warm.

Elsewhere, throw catfish to cover in flour, shaking off excess fish. Dip bits, 1 at a time, in an egg to cover, then brush with panko, pressing on all sides to coat evenly. Place the fish in the basket for air fryer; spray with spray for frying. Cook at 400oF until browned, about 8 minutes, then cook through. Sprinkle the pepper and the remaining 1/4 teaspoon salt evenly on top. When frying fish, in a small bowl, whisk together mayonnaise, dill, relish, vinegar, and sugar. Serve the lemon wedges with the cod and green beans and the tartar sauce.

NUTRITIONAL INFORMATION

Calories 416 Fat 18g Satfat 3.5g Unsatfat 12g Protein 33g Carbohydrate 31g Fiber 7g Sugars 8g Added sugars 8g Sodium 677mg Calcium 10% DV Potassium 26% DV

175. MAKES DELICIOUS ROASTED BROCCOLI WITH CHEESE SAUCE

INGREDIENTS

- 6 cups broccoli florets (about 12 oz.)
- Cooking spray
- 10 tablespoons low-fat evaporated milk
- 1 1/2 ounces queso fresco (fresh Mexican cheese), crumbled (about 5 Tbsp.)
- 4 teaspoons aj amarillo paste
- 6 lower-sodium saltine crackers

INSTRUCTIONS

Coat broccoli with a cooking spray flourishes well. Place half of the broccoli in the air fryer basket and cook at 375 ° F for 6 to 8 minutes, until tender-crisp. Repeat with Broccoli remaining.

In the meantime, put evaporated milk, fresh cheese, ají Amarillo paste and saltines in a blender; process for about 45 seconds until smooth. Pour sauce into a bowl that is microwaveable. Microwave up on HIGH, about 30 seconds until wet. Serve with broccoli cheese sauce.

NUTRITIONAL INFORMATION

Calories 108 Fat 2g Satfat 1g Unsatfat 1g Protein 8g Carbohydrate 15g Fiber 4g Sugars 6g Added sugars 0g Sodium 159mg Calcium 20% DV Potassium 13% DV

176. STRAWBERRY POP TARTS

INGREDIENTS

- 8 ounces quartered strawberries (about 1 3/4 cups)
- 1/4 cup granulated sugar
- 1/2 (14.1-oz.) pkg. refrigerated piecrusts Cooking spray
- 1/2 cup (about 2 oz.) powdered sugar
- 1 1/2 teaspoons fresh lemon juice (from 1 lemon)
- 1/2 ounce rainbow candy sprinkles (about 1 Tbsp.)

INSTRUCTIONS

In a small microwavable bowl, add strawberries and granulated sugar. Let stand for 15 minutes, often stirring. On HIGH microwave until bright and reduced, about 10 minutes, stirring halfway through cooking. Completely Fantastic, about 30 minutes.

Roll pie crust over a lightly floured surface into a 12-inch shell. Cut dough into rectangles of 12 (21/2-x3-inch), reroll scraps, if necessary. Spoon about 2 teaspoons strawberry mixture into the middle of 6 rectangles of the dough, leaving a border of 1/2 inches. Brushes the edges of rectangles of filled dough with water; top with rectangles of the remaining dough, pressing the edges with a sealing fork. Coat tart well with spray to cook. Put 3 single-layer tarts in the air fryer basket and cook for about 10 minutes at 350 ° F until golden brown. Save the rest of the tarts. Place completely, about 30 minutes, on a wire rack.

Whisk powdered sugar and lemon juice together, until smooth in a small bowl. Glaze spoon over cooled tarts, and sprinkle uniformly with sprinkles of sugar.

NUTRITIONAL INFORMATION

Calories 229 Fat 9g Satfat 4g Unsatfat 3g Protein 2g Carbohydrate 39g Fiber 1g Sugars 22g Added sugars 20g Sodium 174mg Calcium 1% DV Potassium 1% DV

177. LIGHTEN UP EMPANADAS

INGREDIENTS

- 1 tablespoon olive oil 3 ounces (85/15) lean ground beef
- 1/4 cup finely chopped white onion
- 3 ounces finely chopped cremini mushrooms
- 2 teaspoons finely chopped garlic
- 6 pitted green olives, chopped
- 1/4 teaspoon paprika
- 1/4 teaspoon ground cumin
- 1/8 teaspoon ground cinnamon
- 1/2 cup chopped tomatoes
- 8 square gyoza wrappers
- 1 large egg, lightly beaten

INSTRUCTIONS

team oil over medium-high in medium-sized skillet. Attach the beef and onion; cook for 3 minutes, stirring to crumble, until brown. Add mushrooms; cook for 6 minutes, stirring occasionally, until mushrooms start to brown. Add garlic, olives, paprika, cumin, and cinnamon; cook for 3 minutes until the mushrooms are very tender and released most of their liquid. Add tomatoes, then cook for 1 minute, stirring occasionally. Move to fill into a bowl and allow it to cool for 5 minutes.

Arrange on the surface of work 4 gyoza wrappers. In the center of each wrapper, put around 1 1/2 tablespoons filling. Brush edges with egg; fold wrappers over, pinch edges to seal.Repeat with extra empanadas.

NUTRITIONAL INFORMATION

Calories 343 Fat 19g Satfat 5g Unsatfat 12g Protein 17g Carbohydrate 25g Fiber 2g Sugars 3g Added sugars 0g Sodium 605mg Calcium 6% DV Potassium 12% DV

178. PEACH HAND PIES

INGREDIENTS

- 2 (5-oz.) fresh peaches, peeled and chopped
- 1 tablespoon fresh lemon juice (from 1 lemon)
- 3 tablespoons granulated sugar
- 1 teaspoon vanilla extract
- 1/4 teaspoon table salt
- 1 teaspoon cornstarch
- 1 (14.1-oz.) pkg.
- refrigerated piecrusts
- Cooking spray

INSTRUCTIONS

A medium bowl, mix peaches, lemon juice, sugar, vanilla and salt. Let stand for 15 minutes, and stir occasionally. Drain peaches, with 1 tablespoon liquid reserved. Whisk cornstarch into reserved liquid; whisk in peaches that have drained.

Cut piecrusts into circles of 8 (4). Place approximately 1 tablespoon fill in the center of each circle. Brush dough edges with water; fold dough over fill to form half-moons. Crimp edges with a sealing fork; cut 3 tiny slits on top of the pies. Coat the pies well with spray for cooking.

In air fryer tray, put 3 pies in a single layer, and cook at 350 ° F until golden brown, 12 to 14 minutes. Repeat with pies left over.

NUTRITIONAL INFORMATION

Calories 314 Fat 16g Satfat 7g Unsatfat 7g Protein 3g Carbohydrate 43g Fiber 1g Sugars 10g Added sugars 6g Sodium 347mg Calcium 0% DV Potassium 2% DV

179. AIR-FRIED CALZONES

INGREDIENTS

- 1 teaspoon olive oil
- 1/4 cup finely chopped red onion (from 1 small onion)
- 3 ounces baby spinach leaves (about 3 cups)
- 1/3 cup lower-sodium marinara sauce
- 2 ounces shredded rotisserie chicken breast (about 1/3 cup)
- 6 ounces fresh prepared whole-wheat pizza dough
- 1 1/2 ounces pre-shredded part-skim mozzarella cheese (about 6 Tbsp.) Cooking spray

INSTRUCTIONS

Heat the oil over medium-high in a medium nonstick skillet. Add onion, and cook for 2 minutes, stirring occasionally, until tender. Add spinach; cover, and cook for 1 1/2 minutes until wilted. Remove pan from heat; stir in chicken and marinara sauce.

Divide the dough into four pieces equal to each. Roll each piece into a6-inch circle onto a lightly floured surface. Place one-fourth of each dough circle over half the spinach mixture. Top each with a quarter of the cheese. Fold dough to form half-moons over filling, crimping edges to seal off. Coat the calzones with spray to cook well.

Place the calzones in the air fryer basket and cook at 325 ° F for 12 minutes until the dough is golden brown, turning the calzones over after 8 minutes.

NUTRITIONAL INFORMATION

Calories 348 Fat 12g Satfat 3g Unsatfat 7g Protein 21g Carbohydrate 44g Fiber 5g Sugars 3g Added sugars 0g Sodium 710mg Calcium 21% DV Potassium 3% DV

180. WHOLE-WHEAT PIZZAS

INGREDIENTS

- 1/4 cup lower-sodium marinara sauce
- 2 whole-wheat pita rounds
- 1 cup baby spinach leaves (1 oz.)
- 1 small plum tomato, cut into 8 slices
- 1 small garlic clove, thinly sliced
- 1 ounce pre-shredded part-skim mozzarella cheese (about 1/4 cup)
- 1/4 ounce shaved Parmigiano-Reggiano cheese (about 1 Tbsp.)

INSTRUCTIONS

Spread the marinara sauce uniformly around 1 side of each pita. Cover the spinach leaves with half, tomato slices, onions, and cheeses.

Place 1 pita in air fryer basket and cook at 350 ° F for 4 to 5 minutes until cheese is melted and pita is crisp. Repeat with pita left over.

NUTRITIONAL INFORMATION

Calories 229 Fat 5g Satfat 2g Unsatfat 2g Protein 11g Carbohydrate 37g Fiber 5g Sugars 4g Added sugars 0g Sodium 510mg Calcium 18% DV Potassium 4% DV

181. DOUBLE-GLAZED CINNAMON BISCUIT BITES

INGREDIENTS

- 2/3 cup (about 2 7/8 oz.) all-purpose flour
- 2/3 cup (about 2 2/3 oz.) whole-wheat flour
- 2 tablespoons granulated sugar
- 1 teaspoon baking powder
- 1/4 teaspoon ground cinnamon
- 1/4 teaspoon kosher salt
- 4 tablespoons cold salted butter, cut into small pieces
- 1/3 cup whole milk Cooking spray
- 2 cups (about 8 oz.) powdered sugar
- 3 tablespoons water

INSTRUCTIONS

In a medium bowl, whisk the flours together, granulated sugar, baking powder, cinnamon and salt. Attach butter; use 2 knives or a pastry cutter to cut into mixture until butter is well mixed with flour and mixture resembles coarse cornmeal. Add milk, then stir until dough forms a ball. Place the dough on a floured surface and knead for about 30 seconds until the dough is smooth, forming a compact ball. Cut the dough into 16 bits equal to each other. Wrap each piece gently into a smooth ball.

Coat air fryer basket with spray to cook well. Place 8 balls in a bowl, leave room between each; spray the donut balls with the spray for cooking. Cook for 10 to 12 minutes, at 350 ° F until browned and puffed. Extract the donuts balls gently from the tub, and put over foil on a wire rack. Let it cool for 5 minutes. Repeat with balls remaining on the donuts.

Whisk powdered sugar and water together, until smooth in a medium bowl. Gently spoon half of the glaze onto balls of donuts. Let cool for 5 minutes; glaze again, making excess dripping away.

NUTRITIONAL INFORMATION

Calories 325 Fat 7g Satfat 4g Unsatfat 3g Protein 8g Carbohydrate 60g Fiber 5g Sugars 18g Added sugars 17g Sodium 67mg Calcium 10% DV Potassium 4% DV

182. SPANAKOPITA BITES

INGREDIENTS

- 1 (10-oz.) pkg. baby spinach leaves
- 2 tablespoons water
- 1/4 cup 1% low-fat cottage cheese
- 1 ounce feta cheese, crumbled (about 1/4 cup)
- 2 tablespoons finely grated Parmesan cheese
- 1 large egg white
- 1 teaspoon lemon zest (from 1 lemon)
- 1 teaspoon dried oregano
- 1/4 teaspoon black pepper
- 1/4 teaspoon kosher salt
- 1/8 teaspoon cayenne pepper 4 (13- x 18-inch) sheets frozen phyllo dough, thawed
- 1 tablespoon olive oil
- Cooking spray

INSTRUCTIONS

Place the spinach and water in a large pot; cook over warm, stirring frequently for 5 minutes until wilted. Spinach drain; cool for about 10 minutes. Press firmly with a paper towel to absorb the full amount of moisture.

In a medium bowl, mix spinach, cottage cheese, feta cheese, Parmesan cheese, white egg, zest, oregano, black pepper, garlic, and cayenne pepper.

Place one sheet of phyllo on a surface for work. Use a pastry brush to brown lightly with butter. Top with phyllo's second sheet; brush with oil. Continue to lay a stack of 4 oiled sheets to shape. Cut the stack of phyllo sheets into 8 (2 1/4-inch wide) strips when operating from the long side. Spoon about 1 tablespoon filling each strip to 1 short end. Fold one corner over the filling to make a triangle; continue folding back and forth to the end of the strip, forming a phyllo packet in a triangle shape.

Coat the air fryer basket lightly with spray for cooking. Place 8 packets in the basket, seam side downwards; spray the tops lightly. Cook at 375 ° F until deep golden brown and crispy, 12 minutes, rotating the packets over cooking halfway. Repeat with the remaining packets of phyllo. Serve warm, or at ambient temperature.

NUTRITIONAL INFORMATION

Calories 82 Fat 4g Satfat 1g Unsatfat 2g Protein 4g Carbohydrate 7g Fiber 1g Sugars 0g Added sugars 0g Sodium 232mg Calcium 8% DV Potassium 0% DV

183. SWEET POTATO CHIPS

INGREDIENTS

- 1 medium sweet potato, unpeeled, cut into 1/8-inch-thick slices
- 1 tablespoon canola oil
- 1/4 teaspoon sea salt
- 1/4 teaspoon freshly ground black pepper
- 1 teaspoon chopped fresh rosemary (optional) Cooking spray

INSTRUCTIONS

Soak sweet potato slices in a big bowl of cold water for 20 minutes. Drain sweet potatoes; dry pat with towels of paper.

Dry the bowl and add oil, salt, pepper and rosemary (if used). Remove sweet potatoes; toss to coat gently.

Coat the air fryer basket lightly with spray for cooking. Place half of the sweet potatoes in the basket and cook at 350 ° F for about 15 minutes in two lots until cooked and crispy.

Carefully remove sweet potatoes from air fryer to plate, using a pair of tongs. Let cool; immediately serve or place in a plastic container that is airtight.

NUTRITIONAL   INFORMATION

Calories 60 Fat 3.5g Satfat 0g Unsatfat 3g Protein 1g Carbohydrate 7g Fiber 1g Sugars 1g Added sugars 0g Sodium 160mg Calcium 0% DV Potassium 2% DV

184. CRISPY TOASTED SESAME TOFU

INGREDIENTS

- 2 (14-oz.) pkg. extra-firm tofu, drained and cut into 1-inch cubes Cooking spray
- 1/4 cup fresh orange juice (from 1 orange)
- 2 tablespoons lower-sodium soy sauce
- 1 tablespoon plus
- 1 tsp. honey
- 1 tablespoon plus
- 1 tsp. toasted sesame oil
- 1 teaspoon rice vinegar
- 1/2 teaspoon cornstarch
- 2 pkg. boil-in-bag brown rice (such as Uncle Bens)
- 1/2 teaspoon kosher salt
- 2 tablespoons chopped scallions
- 1 tablespoon toasted sesame seeds

INSTRUCTIONS

Preheat air fryerb to 200°F.

Place tofu on a sheet lined with several layers of paper towels; cover with additional towels of paper and a second sheet. Place up a weight. Let there be 30 minutes standing. Coat tofu with spray for cooking.

In air fryer tray, put half of the tofu in a single layer and cook at 375 ° F until crispy and golden brown, about 15 minutes, turning tofu cubes over halfway through the cooking process. Keep the remaining tofu warm in the preheated oven when cooking.

In a small casserole over warm, whisk together orange juice, soy sauce, butter, sesame oil, rice vinegar, and cornstarch. Bring to a boil, whisking constantly, for 2 to 3 minutes before sauce thickens. Off heat removes; set aside.

Prepare rice as directed by the package. Stir the saltwater.

Toss tofu with condensed soy sauce. Break the rice into 4 bowls; cover with tofu. Sprinkle with the sesame seeds and scallions.

NUTRITIONAL INFORMATION

Calories 445 Fat 20g Satfat 3g Unsatfat 15g Protein 23g Carbohydrate 46g Fiber 3g Sugars 8g Added sugars 6g Sodium 541mg Calcium 17% DV Potassium 3% DV

185. FLAX SEED FRENCH TOAST STICKS WITH BERRIES

INGREDIENTS

- 4 (1 1/2-oz.) whole-grain bread slices
- 2 large eggs
- 1/4 cup 2% reduced-fat milk
- 1 teaspoon vanilla extract
- 1/2 teaspoon ground cinnamon
- 1/4 cup packed light brown sugar, divided
- 2/3 cup flax seed meal Cooking spray
- 2 cups sliced fresh strawberries
- 8 teaspoons pure maple syrup, divided
- 1 teaspoon powdered sugar

INSTRUCTIONS

Slice each slice of bread into four long sticks. In a shallow dish, whisk together eggs, milk, cocoa, cinnamon and 1 tablespoon brown sugar. In a second, shallow dish, add flaxseed meal and remaining 3 tablespoons of brown sugar. Dip the pieces of bread in a mixture of eggs, soak them slightly and allow any excess to drip away. Dredge each piece in a mixture of flax seeds and cover on all sides. Coat the pieces of bread with cooking spray.

Place pieces of bread in a single layer in the air fryer basket, leave room between each slice and cook at 375 ° F in batches until golden brown and crunchy, 10 minutes, turn pieces over halfway through cooking.

Put 4 sticks of French toast on each plate to serve. Finish with 1/2 cup of strawberries, 2 teaspoons of maple syrup and a powdered sugar layer. Serve straight away.

NUTRITIONAL INFORMATION

Calories 361 Fat 10g Satfat 1g Unsatfat 7g Protein 14g Carbohydrate 56g Fiber 10g Sugars 30g Added sugars 22g Sodium 218mg Calcium 15% DV Potassium 7% DV

186. CRISPY, SWEET BEET CHIPS

INGREDIENTS

- 3 medium-size red beets (about 1 1/2 lb.), peeled and cut into 1/8-inch thick slices (about 3 cups slices)
- 2 teaspoons canola oil
- 3/4 teaspoon kosher salt
- 1/4 teaspoon black pepper

INSTRUCTIONS

Place the sliced beets, butter, salt, and pepper in a large bowl.

Put half of the beets in the air fryer basket and cook at 320 ° F until dry and crisp, 25 to 30 minutes, shaking the basket every 5 minutes. Repeat with left-over beets.

NUTRITIONAL INFORMATION

Calories 47 Fat 2g Satfat 0g Unsatfat 2g Protein 1g Carbohydrate 6g Fiber 2g Sugars 4g Added sugars 0g Sodium 48mg Calcium 1% DV Potassium 4% DV

187. CRISPY VEGGIE QUESADILLAS

INGREDIENTS

- 4 (6-in.) sprouted whole-grain flour tortillas
- 4 ounces reduced-fat sharp Cheddar cheese, shredded (about 1 cup)
- 1 cup sliced red bell pepper
- 1 cup sliced zucchini
- 1 cup no-salt-added canned black beans, drained and rinsed Cooking spray
- 2 ounces plain
- 2% reduced-fat Greek yogurt
- 1 teaspoon lime zest plus
- 1 Tbsp. fresh juice (from 1 lime)
- 1/4 teaspoon ground cumin
- 2 tablespoons chopped fresh cilantro
- 1/2 cup drained refrigerated pico de gallo

INSTRUCTIONS

Place the tortillas on a surface for work. Sprinkle over half of each tortilla with 2 table spoons of shredded cheese. Top cheese with 1/4 cup per red pepper slices, zucchini slices, and black beans on each tortilla. Remaining 1/2 cup cheese, sprinkle evenly. Fold tortillas to form quesadillas in the shape of a half-moon. Coat the quesadillas lightly with spray for frying, and protect with toothpicks.

Sprinkle the air fryer basket gently with a cooking spray. Carefully place 2 quesadillas in the basket and cook at 400 ° F until the tortillas are golden brown and slightly crispy, the cheese is melted and the vegetables are slightly softened. for 10 minutes, turning quesadillas over halfway through cooking. For remaining quesadillas, repeat for Stir yogurt, lime zest, lime juice, and cumin in a small bowl while the quesadillas cook. To serve, cut into wedges each quesadilla and sprinkle with coriander. Serve 1 spoonful of cumin cream and 2 spoonfuls of pico de gallo each.

NUTRITIONAL INFORMATION

Calories 291 Fat 8g Satfat 4g Unsatfat 3g Protein 17g Carbohydrate 36g Fiber 8g Sugars 3g Added sugars 0g Sodium 518mg Calcium 30% DV Potassium 6% DV

188. LOADED GREEK FETA FRIES

INGREDIENTS

- Cooking spray 2 (7-oz.) Yukon Gold or russet potatoes, scrubbed and dried
- 1 tablespoon olive oil
- 2 teaspoons lemon zest
- 1/2 teaspoon dried oregano
- 1/4 teaspoon kosher salt
- 1/4 teaspoon garlic powder
- 1/4 teaspoon onion powder
- 1/4 teaspoon paprika
- 1/4 teaspoon black pepper
- 2 ounces feta cheese, finely grated (about 1/2 cup)
- 2 ounces shredded skinless rotisserie chicken breast
- 1/4 cup prepared tzatziki
- 1/4 cup seeded and diced plum tomato
- 2 tablespoons chopped red onion
- 1 tablespoon chopped fresh flat-leaf parsley and oregano

INSTRUCTIONS

Preheat your air fryer up to 380 ° F. Coat with cooking spray on the pot.

Cut each potato in 1/4-inch-thick slices lengthwise; cut each slice into 1/4-inch fries.

In a large bowl, add the potatoes and oil.. Season with zest, dried oregano, salt, powdered garlic, onion powder, paprika, and pepper; shake to cover.

Cook the seasoned potatoes in 2 batches until they are crisp, about 15 minutes, tossing fries halfway through cooking time.

Return to basketball the first batch of fries, and cook for 1 to 2 minutes until moist. Cut fryer from air. Top fries with half the feta, ham, tzatziki, feta remaining, tomato, red onion and fresh herbs.

NUTRITIONAL INFORMATION

Calories 383 Fat 16g Satfat 7g Unsatfat 8g Protein 19g Carbohydrate 42g Fiber 4g Sugars 5g Added sugars 0g Sodium 654mg Calcium 21% DV Potassium 29% DV

189. BREAKFAST BOMBS

INGREDIENTS

- 3 center-cut bacon slices
- 3 large eggs, lightly beaten
- 1 ounce
- 1/3-less-fat cream cheese, softened
- 1 tablespoon chopped fresh chives
- 4 ounces fresh prepared whole-wheat pizza dough Cooking spray

INSTRUCTIONS

Cook the bacon over medium to very crisp in a medium skillet, around 10 minutes. Take bacon off the pan; crumble. Attach eggs to bacon drippings in pan; cook for about 1 minute, stirring frequently, until almost set, but still loose. Move eggs to a bowl; add cream cheese, chives and crumbled bacon to taste.

Divide the dough into four pieces equal to each. Roll each piece into a 5-inch circle on a lightly floured surface. Place one-fourth of each dough circle in the middle of the egg mixture. Brush with water outside the edge of the dough; wrap the dough around the mixture of the eggs to form a container, pinching the dough at the seams.

Place dough bags in the air fryer basket in a single layer; coat well with spray for cooking. Cook for 5 to 6 minutes at 350 ° F until golden brown, then test for 4 minutes.

NUTRITIONAL INFORMATION

Calories 305 Fat 15g Satfat 5g Unsatfat 8g Protein 19g Carbohydrate 26g Fiber 2g Sugars 1g Added sugars 0g Sodium 548mg Calcium 5% DV Potassium 2% DV

190. PORK DUMPLINGS WITH DIPPING SAUCE

INGREDIENTS

- 1 teaspoon canola oil
- 4 cups chopped bok choy (about 12 oz.)
- 1 tablespoon chopped fresh ginger
- 1 tablespoon chopped garlic (3 garlic cloves)
- 4 ounces ground pork
- 1/4 teaspoon crushed red pepper
- 18 (3 1/2-inch-square) dumpling wrappers or wonton wrappers Cooking spray
- 2 tablespoons rice vinegar
- 2 teaspoons lower-sodium soy sauce
- 1 teaspoon toasted sesame oil
- 1/2 teaspoon packed light brown sugar
- 1 tablespoon finely chopped scallions

INSTRUCTIONS

Steam the canola oil in a large nonstick skillet over medium-high. Add bok choy and cook, stirring frequently, for 6 to 8 minutes, until wilted and mostly dry. Cook for 1 minute, stirring constantly, add garlic and ginger. Move choy bok mixture to a plate for 5 minutes to cool. Clean the dry mixture with a paper towel.

In a medium bowl, combine ground pork, bok choy mixture, and crushed red pepper.

Place a dumpling wrapper on the work surface, and spoon in the center of the wrapper around 1 tablespoon fill. The edges of the wrapper are gently moistened with water using a pastry brush or your fingertips. Fold the wrapper over to form a half-moon shape, pushing the sealing edges. Repeat process with remaining fillers and wrappers.

Coat light air fryer basket with spray for cooking. Place 6 dumplings in a basket, leave room between each; spray the dumplings lightly with a spray for cooking. Cook at 375 ° F until lightly browned, for 12 minutes, turning dumplings by cooking over halfway. Repeat with remaining dumplings, keeping the dumplings cooked warm.

Meanwhile, in a small bowl, add rice vinegar, soy sauce, sesame oil, brown sugar, and scallions until the sugar is dissolved. To serve, place 3 dumplings with 2 spoonfuls of sauce on each plate.

Calories 140 Fat 5g Satfat 2g Unsatfat 3g Protein 7g Carbohydrate 16g Fiber 1g Sugars 1g Added sugars 0g Sodium 244mg Calcium 7% DV Potassium 5% DV

191. CURRY CHICKPEAS

INGREDIENTS

- 1 (15-oz.) can no-salt-added chickpeas (garbanzo beans), drained and rinsed (about 1 1/2 cups)
- 2 tablespoons red wine vinegar
- 2 tablespoons olive oil
- 2 teaspoons curry powder
- 1/2 teaspoon ground turmeric
- 1/4 teaspoon ground coriander
- 1/4 teaspoon ground cumin
- 1/4 teaspoon plus
- 1/8 tsp. ground cinnamon
- 1/4 teaspoon kosher salt
- 1/2 teaspoon Aleppo pepper Thinly sliced fresh cilantro

INSTRUCTIONS

Squeeze chickpea gently in a medium bowl with your hands (do not crush); remove chickpea skins.

Replace the chickpeas with vinegar and oil, and toss to coat. Stir gently to mix curry powder, turmeric, coriander, cumin, and cinnamon.

In air fryer tray, put the chickpeas in a single layer and cook at 400 ° F until crispy, about 15 minutes, shaking the chickpeas halfway through the cooking.

Pass chickpeas to a saucepan. Sprinkle with salt, pepper and coriander; toss to coat.

NUTRITIONAL INFORMATION

Calories 173 Fat 8g Satfat 1g Unsatfat 6g Protein 7g Carbohydrate 18g Fiber 5g Sugars 1g Added sugars 0g Sodium 146mg Calcium 6% DV Potassium 4% DV

192. BAGEL KALE CHIPS

INGREDIENTS

- 6 cups packed torn Lacinato kale leaves, stems and ribs removed
- 1 tablespoon olive oil
- 1 teaspoon lower-sodium soy sauce
- 1 teaspoon white or black sesame seeds
- 1/2 teaspoon dried minced garlic
- 1/4 teaspoon poppy seeds

INSTRUCTIONS

Wash the kale leaves completely dry and cut them into bits of 1 1/2 inch. In a medium bowl, blend the kale, olive oil, and soy sauce together, rubbing the leaves gently to make sure they are well coated with the mixture.

In the air fryer basket, put one-third of the kale leaves and cook at 375 ° F until crisp, 6 minutes, shaking the basket halfway through the cooking process. Place kale chips on a baking sheet, and sprinkle evenly while still hot with sesame seeds, garlic and poppy seeds. Continue with leaves remaining to the kale.

NUTRITIONAL INFORMATION

Calories 159 Fat 8g Satfat 1g Unsatfat 6g Protein 7g Carbohydrate 20g Fiber 5g Sugars 0g Added sugars 0g Sodium 182mg Calcium 34% DV Potassium 0% DV

193. SHRIMP SPRING ROLLS WITH SWEET CHILI SAUCE

INGREDIENTS

- 2 1/2 tablespoons sesame oil, divided
- 2 cups pre-shredded cabbage
- 1 cup matchstick carrots
- 1 cup julienne-cut red bell pepper
- 4 ounces peeled, deveined raw shrimp, chopped
- 3/4 cup julienne-cut snow peas
- 1/4 cup chopped fresh cilantro
- 1 tablespoon fresh lime juice
- 2 teaspoons fish sauce
- 1/4 teaspoon crushed red pepper
- 8 (8-inch-square) spring roll wrappers
- 1/2 cup sweet chili sauce

INSTRUCTIONS

Heat 1 1/2 teaspoons of the oil over high in large skillet until it smokes slightly. Add the cabbage, carrots, and bell pepper; cook for 1 to 1 1/2 minutes, stirring constantly until lightly wilted. Spread over a rimmed baking sheet; cool down for 5 minutes.

Place in a large bowl cabbage mixture, shrimp, snow peas, coriander, lime juice, fish sauce, and crushed red pepper; toss together.

Place spring roll wrappers on the work surface and face 1 corner. Spoon 1/4 cup filling in the center of each spring roll wrapper, spreading over a 3-inch long strip from left to right.

Fold rising wrapper bottom corner over filling, tucking corner tip under filling. Fold corners left and right over full.

Brush the remaining corner softly with water; roll tightly to the remaining corner; press gently to seal. Spring brush rolls with 2 table spoons of oil left.

Place 4 spring rolls in the air fryer basket and cook for 6 to 7 minutes at 390 ° F until crispy, turning the spring rolls after 5 min. Continue with spring rolls left. Serve with chili sweet sauce.

NUTRITIONAL INFORMATION

Calories 180 Fat 9g Satfat 1g Unsatfat 7g Protein 7g Carbohydrate 19g Fiber 3g Sugars 5g Added sugars 0g Sodium 318mg Calcium 7% DV Potassium 8% DV

194. FISH AND CHIPS

INGREDIENTS

- 2 (10-oz.) russet potatoes, scrubbed Cooking spray
- 1 1/4 teaspoons kosher salt, divided
- 1 cup (about 4 1/4 oz.) all-purpose flour
- 2 large eggs 2 tablespoons water
- 1 cup whole-wheat panko (Japanese-style breadcrumbs)
- 4 (6-oz.) skinless tilapia fillets
- 1/2 cup malt vinegar

INSTRUCTIONS

Use the manufacturer's instructions to cut potatoes into spirals on a spiralizer. In lots, put in the air fryer basket in a single layer; spray with cooking spray, tossing to make sure they are completely covered. Cook at 375 ° F until the outside is golden brown and crispy, 10 minutes, turning halfway through cooking. To keep warm, remove the potatoes from the basket and cover. Sprinkle with 1/4 teaspoon salt evenly when all potatoes are baked.

While the potatoes are cooking, stir in a shallow dish flour and 1/2 teaspoon salt together. In a second shallow dish, whisk gently eggs and water together. In a final, shallow dish, add panko and remaining 1/2 teaspoon salt. Lengthwise cut each fish filet into 2 long strips. Dredge in a mixture of flour, shake off the waste. Dip in a mixture of eggs, allowing any excess to trickle free. Dredge in a mixture of panko and push to stick. Coat fish with cooking spray on both sides.

Place fish in a single layer in the air fryer tray and cook at 375 ° F in lots until golden brown, 10 minutes, turning the fish halfway through cooking.

To serve, put on each plate 2 pieces of fish and equal amounts of potato spirals with 2 tablespoons of malt vinegar to dip in.

NUTRITIONAL   INFORMATION

Calories 415 Fat 7g Satfat 2g Unsatfat 3g Protein 44g Carbohydrate 46g Fiber 4g Sugars 2g Added sugars 0g Sodium 754mg Calcium 5% DV Potassium 24% DV

195. BACON AVOCADO FRIES

INGREDIENTS

- 3 avocados
- 24 thin strips of bacon
- 1/4 c. ranch dressing, for serving

INSTRUCTIONS

Slice each avocado into eight wedges of equal size. The wrap should wedge with a bacon strip, and cut bacon if necessary.

Operating in hundreds, create a single layer of air fryer rack. Cook for 8 minutes at a temperature of 400° until bacon is cooked and crispy.

The ranch serves dry.

NUTRITIONAL INFORMATION

(per serving): 120 calories, 4 g protein, 3 g carbohydrates, 2 g fiber, 0 g sugar, 11 g fat, 2 g saturated fat, 190 mg sodium

196. ANTIPASTO EGG ROLLS

INGREDIENTS

- 12 egg roll wrappers
- 12 slices provolone
- 12 slices deli ham
- 36 slices pepperoni
- 1 c. shredded mozzarella
- 1 c. sliced pepperoncini
- Vegetable oil, for frying on stovetop
- 1/4 c. freshly grated Parmesan
- 1 tbsp. Italian dressing, for serving

INSTRUCTIONS

Put an egg roll wrapper in a diamond shape on a clean surface placing a slice of provolone in the middle. Finish with one slice of ham, 3 slices of pepperoni and a large pinch of both pepperoncini and mozzarella. Fold in half at the edge and fold tightly in hands. Roll gently, then seal with a few drops of water to fold.

Cook egg rolls in batches at 390 ° until golden, about 12 minutes, flipping over halfway through.

197. CHEESY BEEF EMPANADAS

INGREDIENTS

FOR THE DOUGH

- 3 c. all-purpose flour, plus more for surface
- 1 tsp. kosher salt
- 1 tsp. baking powder
- 1/2 c. cold butter, cut into cubes
- 3/4 c. water
- 1 large egg
- FOR THE BEEF FILLING
- 1 tbsp. extra-virgin olive oil
- 1 yellow onion, chopped
- 2 cloves garlic, minced
- 1 lb. ground beef
- 1 tbsp. tomato paste
- 1 tsp. oregano
- 1 tsp. cumin
- 1/2 tsp. paprika
- Kosher salt
- Freshly ground black pepper
- 1/2 c. chopped tomatoes
- 1/2 c. chopped pickled jalapeños
- 1 1/4 c. shredded Cheddar
- 1 1/4 c. Shredded Monterey Jack
- Egg wash, for brushing
- Freshly chopped cilantro, for garnish
- Sour cream, for serving

INSTRUCTIONS

MAKE DOUGH

In a large container or bowl, mix together salt, flour, and baking powder. Use your hands or a pastry cutter to cut butter into the flour until pea-sized. Add water and egg, and combine until it forms a dough. Place the dough on a lightly floured surface and knead for about 5 minutes until smooth.

Wrap in plastic wrap, and cool for at least 1 hour.

FOR AIR FRYER

Heat oil in a large saucepan over medium heat. Add onion and cook for about 5 minutes until tender, then add the garlic and cook until fragrant, 1 minute longer. Attach the ground beef and cook for 5 minutes, breaking meat with a wooden spoon, until no more orange. Drain out the fat.

Return the saucepan to medium heat, and paste the tomato into the beef. Season with salt and pepper and add oregano, cumin, and paprika. Add tomatoes and jalapeños and cook for about 3 minutes, until hot. Remove from heat and slightly allow to cool.

Place dough on a surface that is lightly floured and divide in half. Half roll out to 1/4 "wide. Cut out circles by using a 4.5 "circular cookie cutter. Replace the rest of the dough. Reroll scraps for taking out more rounds once.

Moisten gently the outer edge of a dough round with water and place about 2 tablespoons in the middle and top filling with cheddar and Monterey. Fold dough overfill in half. Use a fork together to crimp tops, then brush with wash the shell. Repeat with dough and remaining filling.

Put empanadas in a parchment-lined Air Fryer bowl, ensure that they do not strike, and cook for 10 minutes in 400 ° batches.

Serve with sour cream and garnish with cilantro.

198. HOMEMADE CANNOLI

INGREDIENTS

FOR THE FILLING:

- 1 (16-oz.) container ricotta
- 1/2 c. mascarpone cheese
- 1/2 c. powdered sugar, divided
- 1 c. heavy cream
- 1 tsp. pure vanilla extract
- 1 tsp. orange zest
- 1/4 tsp. kosher salt
- 1/2 c. mini chocolate chips, for garnish

FOR THE SHELLS:

- 2 c. all-purpose flour, plus more for surface
- 1/4 c. granulated sugar
- 1 tsp. kosher salt
- 1/2 tsp. cinnamon
- 4 tbsp. cold butter, cut into cubes
- 6 tbsp. white wine
- 1 large egg
- 1 egg white, for brushing
- Vegetable oil, for frying

INSTRUCTIONS

MAKE FILLING: Drain ricotta by positioning it over a large bowl with a fine-mesh strainer. Let drain in the fridge for at least one hour and until overnight.

Beat heavy cream and 1/4 cup powdered sugar in a large bowl using a hand blender until stiff peaks develop.

Combine the ricotta, mascarpone and remaining 1/4 cup powdered sugar, cinnamon, orange zest and salt in another large bowl. Fold into the milk with whipping. Refrigerate for at least 1 hour, until ready to fill with cannoli.

MAKE SHELLS: Whisk flour, sugar, salt, and cinnamon together in a large bowl. Cut the butter with your hands or pastry cutter into a flour mixture until pea-sized. Add wine and egg, and combine until it forms a dough. Knead the dough in a bowl a few times to help it come together. Put in a flat circle, then cover in plastic wrap and refrigerate for a minimum of 1 hour and up to overnight.

Divide the dough into half on a lightly floured surface. Roll out half to?"And dense. Use a cookie cutter with 4 "circle to cut dough out. Repeat with extra flour. Re-roll scraps to take out some additional circles.

Wrap dough around cannoli molds and brush egg whites to tie the dough together.

FOR AIR FRYER: Work in lots, put molds in air fryer basket and cook at 350 ° for 12 minutes, or until golden.

Gently remove twist shells off molds when cool enough to handle or use a kitchen towel to stay on.

Place filling with an open star tip in a pastry bag. Filling the pipe into tubes, then dipping ends in mini chocolate chips.

199. BROWNIES

INGREDIENTS

- 1/2 c. granulated sugar
- 1/3 c. cocoa powder
- 1/4 c. all-purpose flour
- 1/4 tsp. baking powder
- Pinch kosher salt
- 1/4 c. butter, melted and cooled slightly
- 1 large egg

INSTRUCTIONS

Grease a 6-casserole saucepan with cooking spray. In a medium bowl, whisk to mix sugar, cocoa powder, flour, baking powder, and salt. In a small bowl, whisk butter and egg until mixed. Attach to dry wet ingredients and stir until mixed. Move brownie batter to the prepared cake pan and smooth top. Bake in an air fryer for 16-18 minutes.

200. BRUSSELS SPROUTS CHIPS

INGREDIENTS

- 1/2 lb. brussels sprouts, thinly sliced
- 1 tbsp. extra-virgin olive oil
- 2 tbsp. freshly grated Parmesan, plus more for garnish
- 1 tsp. garlic powder
- Kosher salt
- Freshly ground black pepper
- Caesar dressing, for dipping

INSTRUCTIONS

Sprinkle Brussels with butter, parmesan and garlic powder in a large bowl, then season with salt and pepper. Arrange in air fryer also plate.

Bake at 350 ° for 8 minutes, toss and bake for an additional 8 minutes, until golden and crisp.

Garnish with more Parmesan, and serve dipping with a caesar dressing.

201. CHEESE BURGER

INGREDIENTS

- 1 lb. ground beef
- 2 cloves garlic, minced
- 1 tbsp. low-sodium soy sauce
- Kosher salt
- Freshly ground black pepper
- 4 slices American cheese
- 4 hamburger buns
- Mayonnaise
- Lettuce
- Sliced tomatoes
- Thinly sliced red onion

INSTRUCTIONS

Combine the beef, garlic, and soy sauce into a large bowl. Form into 4 patties and flatten to a circle of 4. Season salt and pepper to both sides.

Put 2 patties in the air fryer, cook for medium at 375 ° for 4 minutes per side. Remove and top with a slice of cheese with immediate effect. Repeat with 2 patts left.

Using mayo to cover hamburger buns, then top with lettuce, patties, tomatoes, and onions.

202. BLOOMING ONION

INGREDIENTS

- FOR THE ONION
- 1 large yellow onion
- 3 large eggs
- 1 c. breadcrumbs
- 2 tsp. paprika
- 1 tsp. garlic powder
- 1 tsp. onion powder
- 1 tsp. kosher salt
- FOR THE SAUCE
- 2/3 c. mayonnaise
- 2 tbsp. ketchup
- 1 tsp. horseradish
- 1/2 tsp. paprika
- 1/2 tsp. garlic powder
- 1/4 tsp. dried oregano
- Kosher salt

INSTRUCTIONS

Slice off the stem of the onion and set the onion to the flat side. Cut down an inch from the root into 12 to 16 sections, being careful not to cut through all the way. Flip over and drag sections of onion gently to separate petals.

Whisk together eggs and 1 table cubit of water in a shallow bowl. Whisk together the breadcrumbs and spices in yet another shallow bowl. Dip the onion into the wash of the eggs, then dredge in the mixture of the breadcrumb with a spoon to cover fully.

Put in an air fryer basket and cook for 20 minutes at 375 ° C.

Meanwhile, make the sauce: Whisk mayonnaise, ketchup, horseradish, paprika, garlic powder, and dried oregano together in a medium bowl. Season to salt.

Serve the onion with the sauce, to dip.

203. MOZZARELLA STICKS

INGREDIENTS

- 6 mozzarella sticks
- 1 c. panko bread crumbs
- Kosher salt
- Freshly cracked black pepper
- 2 large eggs, well-beaten
- 3 tbsp. all-purpose flour
- Warm marinara, for serving

INSTRUCTIONS

FOR AIR FRYER

Freeze mozzarella sticks for at least 2 hours, until frozen solid.

Set up a breading station after 3 hours: placed panko, eggs, and flour in three separate shallow bowls. Broadly season the panko with salt and pepper.

Coat frozen mozzarella sticks in flour, then dip into milk, then panko, back into the egg, and then back into the panko.

Arrange frozen breaded mozzarella sticks in the basket of your air fryer in one even row. Cook on 400 ° for 6 minutes, or on the outside until golden and crisp and melt in the center.

Serve it for dipping with moist marinara sauce.

204. GARLIC HERB TURKEY BREAST

INGREDIENTS

- 2 lb. turkey breast
- Kosher salt
- Freshly ground black pepper
- 4 tbsp. melted butter
- 3 cloves garlic, minced
- 1 tsp. freshly chopped thyme
- 1 tsp. freshly chopped rosemary

INSTRUCTIONS

Pat turkey breast dry, and season with salt and pepper on both sides.

Blend melted butter, garlic, thyme and rosemary in a small bowl. All over the turkey breast, brush the butter.

Place in the air fryer basket, skin side up, and cook for 40 minutes at 375 °, or until the internal temperature reaches 160 °, flipping through halfway.

Let it rest 5 minutes before you slice.

205. CINNAMON ROLLS

INGREDIENTS

- FOR THE ROLLS
- 2 tbsp. melted butter, plus more for brushing
- 1/3 c. packed brown sugar
- 1/2 tsp. ground cinnamon
- Kosher salt
- All-purpose flour, for surface
- 1 (8-oz.) tube refrigerated Crescent rolls
- FOR THE GLAZE
- 2 oz. cream cheese, softened
- 1/2 c. powdered sugar
- 1 tbsp. whole milk, plus more if needed

INSTRUCTIONS

Make rolls: Line air fryer bottom with parchment paper, and butter brush. Combine butter, brown sugar, cinnamon, and a big pinch of salt in a medium bowl, until smooth and fluffy.

Roll out crescent rolls in one piece, on a lightly floured surface. Pinch seams and fold in half. Roll into a rectangle of 9"-x-7 Spread the butter mixture over the dough and leave a 1/4 "border. Starting at a long edge, roll up the dough like a roll of jelly, then break it into 6 parts crosswise.

Arrange pieces, cut-side up, evenly spaced, in a prepared air fryer.

Set air fryer to 350 °, and cook for about 10 minutes until golden and cooked through.

Create the glaze: Whisky cream cheese in a medium bowl, powdered sugar, And milk. Add more milk to thin glaze by the teaspoonful if necessary.

Spread glaze and serve over moist cinnamon rolls.

206. PARMESAN FRIED TORTELLINI

INGREDIENTS

- 1 (9-oz.) package cheese tortellini
- 1 c. Panko breadcrumbs
- 1/3 c. freshly grated Parmesan
- 1 tsp. dried oregano
- 1/2 tsp. garlic powder
- 1/2 tsp. crushed red pepper flakes
- Kosher salt
- Freshly ground black pepper
- 1 c. all-purpose flour
- 2 large eggs
- Marinara, for serving

INSTRUCTIONS

Cook tortellini in a large pot of boiling salted water until al dente, in line with package instructions. Drain and drain.

Mix the Panko, Parmesan, oregano, garlic powder, and red pepper flakes together in a shallow bowl. Mix with pepper and salt. Beat the eggs in another shallow bowl, then add the flour in a third shallow bowl.

Coat tortellini in flour, then dredge in eggs, and mixture with Panko. Start until it covers all tortellini.

Place in air fryer and fry at 370 ° for 10 minutes, until crispy.

Serve on marinara.

207. FRIED PICKLES

INGREDIENTS

- 2 c. dill pickle slices
- 1 egg, whisked with 1 tbsp. water
- 1/2 c. bread crumbs
- 1/4 c. freshly grated Parmesan
- 1 tsp. dried oregano
- 1 tsp. garlic powder
- Ranch, for dipping

INSTRUCTIONS

Pat pickle chips dry, using paper towels. Stir bread crumbs, Parmesan, oregano, and garlic powder together in a medium bowl.

First in the egg and then in the bread crumb mixture, the dredge pickle bits. Operating in groups, putting the air fryer basket in a single layer. Cook for 10 minutes, at 400 °.

With ranch serve warm.

208. S'MORES

INGREDIENTS

- FOR CAMPFIRE
- 4 whole graham crackers
- 4 marshmallows
- 4 pieces chocolate (such as Hershey's)
- FOR AIR FRYER
- 4 whole graham crackers
- 2 marshmallows
- 4 pieces chocolate (such as Hershey's)

INSTRUCTIONS

FOR AIR FRYER:

To create 8 squares break all graham crackers in half. Using a pair of scissors, cut marshmallows in half crosswise.

Place the marshmallows on 4 graham squares cut side down. Place marshmallow side up in air fryer basket and cook for 4 to 5 minutes at 390 °, or until golden.

Remove from air fryer and place on top of each toasted marshmallow a piece of chocolate and graham square and serve.

209. MOLTEN LAVA CAKE

INGREDIENTS:

- 1.5 TBS Self Rising Flour
- 3.5 TBS Baker's Sugar (Not Powdered)
- 3.5 OZ Unsalted Butter
- 3.5 OZ Dark Chocolate (Pieces or Chopped)
- 2 Eggs

INSTRUCTIONS:

Preheat your Air Fryer to 375F Grease and flour 4 regular ramekins in healthy oven.

Melt dark chocolate and butter for 3 minutes in a clean, microwave bowl at level 7, stirring all over. Remove from microwave, and stir until consistency is reached.

Whisk / Beat the eggs and sugar until smooth and pale.

Pour the melted chocolate into a mixture of eggs. Remove flour. Use a spatula for an even combination of everything.

Fill the ramekins about 3/4 full with cake mixture and bake in the preheated air fryer at 375F for 10 minutes.

Remove from the air fryer and allow it to cool in a ramekin for 2 minutes. Flip the ramekins gently upside down onto the serving plate, scraping the bottom with a butter knife to loosen edges.

210. CRUSTLESS CHEESECAKE

INGREDIENTS

- 16 oz cream cheese softened to room temperature
- 3/4 cup zero calorie sweetener make sure it measures the same as sugar
- 2 eggs
- 1 tsp vanilla extract
- 1/2 tsp lemon juice
- 2 tbsp sour cream

INSTRUCTIONS

Preheat the fryer on air to 350 degrees.

Mix the eggs, sweetener, vanilla and lemon juice together in a blender until smooth. Add the sour cream and cream cheese and mix free and silky until lumpy. The more you whip it out, the more it will be creamier.

Pour batter into two spring pans of 4-inch shape and cook for 8-10 minutes or until set.

Allow the spring-form pan to cool completely. Refrigerator overnight, or for 2-3 hours minimum.

211. VEGAN BEIGNETS

NGREDIENTS

- For the powdered baking blend:
- 1 cup Whole Earth Sweetener Baking Blend
- 1 teaspoon organic corn starch
- For the proofing:
- 1 cup full-fat coconut milk from a can
- 3 tablespoons powdered baking blend
- 1 1/2 teaspoons active baking yeast
- For the dough:
- 2 tablespoons melted coconut oil
- 2 tablespoons aquafaba, the drained water from a can of chickpeas
- 2 teaspoons vanilla
- 3 cups unbleached white flour, with a little extra to sprinkle on the cutting board for later

INSTRUCTIONS

Attach the Whole Earth Baking Blend and the corn starch to your mixer and blend until smooth. The cornstarch will keep it from clumping so if you don't use all of it in the recipe you can store it.

(Or you can add normal powdered sugar later in the recipe.) Heat the coconut milk until it's warm but cool enough to stick your

finger inside without burning. If it's too hot you are going to kill the yeast. Remove it with the sugar and leaven to your mixer. Let sit for 10 minutes, until the yeast starts foaming.

Mix in the coconut oil, aquafaba, and cinnamon using the paddle attachment. Then, add a cup at a time to the flour.

The dough is going to be wetter than if you made a loaf of bread, but you should be able to scrape the dough out and form a ball without it being on your hands.

Place the dough in a mixing bowl and cover with the towel of a clean dish and allow to rise for 1 hour.

Scatter some flour over a large cutting board and scatter the dough in a rectangle? Thick inches. Cut into 24 squares and allow for 30 minutes of proof before cooking.

Preheat your air fryer to 390 degrees.

You can bring 3 to 6 beignets in at a time, depending on the size of your air fryer.

Cook them on one side for 3 minutes. Flip them, then take another 2 minutes to cook. Because the air fryers differ, you might need to cook yours for another minute or two to get golden brown.

Sprinkle liberally and enjoy the powdered baking mix you made at the beginning!

Continue to cook in the lots until all are finished.

Preheat the oven to 350 ° C. Place the beignets on a parchment-paper-lined baking sheet.

Bake until golden brown, or for about 15 minutes. Sprinkle liberally and enjoy the powdered baking mix you made at the beginning!

NUTRITIONAL INFORMATION

Yield 24 Serving Size 1 Amount Per Serving Calories 102 Total Fat 3g Saturated Fat 3g Trans Fat 0g

Unsaturated Fat 0g Cholesterol 0mg Sodium 2mg Carbohydrates 15g Fiber 1g Sugar 1g Protein 3g

212. BLUEBERRY HAND PIES

INGREDIENTS

- 1 cup (128g) blueberries
- 2.5 tbsp caster sugar
- 1 tsp lemon juice
- 1 pinch salt
- 14 ounces (320g) refrigerated pie crust or shortcrust pastry roll
- water
- vanilla sugar to sprinkle on top (optional)

INSTRUCTIONS

AIR FRYER VERSION:

Mix together the blueberries, sugar, lemon juice, and salt in a medium bowl.

Roll out the piecrusts (or shortcrust pastry roll) and cut out the individual circles 6-8(4-inch).

In the center of each circle place about 1 tablespoon of blueberry filling.

Moisten the edges of the dough with water, fold the dough over the filling to form the shape of a half-moon.

The piecrust edges are gently crimped together using a fork. And cut the top of the hand pies into three slits.

Spray the cooking spray on the hand pies and sprinkle with the vanilla sugar (if used).

The air fryer is preheated to 350F/180C.

Inside the air-fryer basket, place 3-4 hand pies in a single layer.

Cook for 9-12 minutes, or until brown is golden.

Let the pastries cool down for at least 10 minutes before serving.

NUTRITIONAL INFORMATION

Calories: 251kcal , Carbohydrates: 30g , Protein: 3g , Fat: 12g , Saturated Fat: 4g , Sodium: 207mg , Potassium: 62mg , Fiber: 1g , Sugar: 5g , Vitamin A: 10IU , Vitamin C: 2.1mg , Calcium: 9mg , Iron: 1.4mg

213. SPICED APPLES

INGREDIENTS

- 4 small apples, sliced
- 2 tablespoons ghee or coconut oil, melted
- 2 tablespoons sugar
- 1 teaspoon apple pie spice

INSTRUCTIONS

Layer apples in a saucepan. Sprinkle with ghee or coconut oil, and sprinkle with the flavor of sugar and apple pie. Stir in the apples to coat evenly.

Place the apples in a small pan for air fryers, and place them inside the bowl. Set the fryer to air for 10 minutes at 350 °. Perforate the apples with a fork to make sure they are tender. Place in an air fryer for an additional 3-5 minutes if necessary.

Serve with ice cream or whipped topping.

214. FLOURLESS KEY LIME CUPCAKES

INGREDIENTS

- Philips Airfryer
- 250 g Greek Yoghurt
- 200 g Soft Cheese
- 2 Large Eggs
- 1 Large Egg yolk only
- ¼ Cup Caster Sugar
- 1 Tsp Vanilla Essence
- 2 Limes juice and rind
- Metric - Imperial

INSTRUCTIONS

Mix the Greek yogurt and the soft cheese together with a wooden spoon or a hand mixer until they are smooth and fluffy and look like mayonnaise.

Stir in the eggs and mix. add the sugar, the vanilla essence, and the limes, then combine.

You'll now have a nice chocolate mix and you'll need to fill in the contents of 6 cupcake cases. Put the rest in later on to one side.

Bake the Airfryer cupcakes for 10 minutes at 160c then another 10 minutes at 180c.

When cooking, the cupcakes extract the bowl's contents into a cupcake nozzle and put it in the refrigerator for 10 minutes.

Once the cupcakes are finished allow them to cool down on a baking tray for 10 minutes.

Creating the top layer of your cupcakes when they are cool using the nozzle. Fridge for 4 hours, so your cupcake topping has time to set properly and decorate with spare limes afterward.

NUTRITIONAL INFORMATION

Calories: 218kcal , Carbohydrates: 13g , Protein: 9g , Fat: 14g , Saturated Fat: 7g , Cholesterol: 120mg , Sodium: 155mg , Potassium: 99mg , Fiber: 0g , Sugar: 11g , Vitamin A: 600IU , Vitamin C: 6.5mg , Calcium: 101mg , Iron: 0.6mg

215. BANANA S'MORES

INGREDIENTS

- 4 bananas
- 3 TABLESPOONS mini semi-sweet chocolate chips
- 3 TABLESPOONS mini peanut butter chips
- 3 TABLESPOONS mini marshmallows
- 3 TABLESPOONS graham cracker cereal

INSTRUCTIONS

Air fryer preheats to 400oF.

Slice lengthwise along the inside of the curve into unpeeled bananas but do not slice through the bottom of the peel. Slightly open up the banana to form a bag.

Chocolate chips, peanut butter chips, and marshmallows fill every pocket shape. Poke cereal with the graham cracker into the filling.

Place the bananas into the basket of the air fryer, lean on each other to hold them upright with the filling facing up. Air-fry for 6 minutes, or until the banana is soft to the touch, blackened the peel and melted and toasted the chocolate and marshmallows.

Allow them cool for a few minutes, and then simply serve the filling out with a spoon.

216. CHURROS WITH MEXICAN CHOCOLATE

INGREDIENTS

- Churros
- 1 8 oz can refrigerated crescent rolls
- 2 TBSP sugar
- 1 TBSP cinnamon
- 2 TBSP melted butter
- Mexican Chocolate Sauce for Dipping
- 1/2 cup dark chocolate chips
- 1 tsp cinnamon
- 1/8 tsp cayenne pepper, (more or less depending on preference)
- 1/4 cup heavy cream

INSTRUCTIONS

Churros Air Fryer Preheat air fryer to 330 degrees.

you will Whisk together the sugar and the cinnamon in a small bowl.

Unroll the crescent dough in a well-floured surface and divide it into 4 rectangles, pressing to close the perforations.

Brush with melted butter on each rectangle.

Sprinkle just 2 rectangles of cinnamon-sugar with about 2 teaspoons Cover the sugar sprinkled rectangles with the other two rectangles, butter side up.

Cut each rectangle stack into 4 strips Twist each stripe with a pizza cutter or a sharp knife and place it on a baking sheet. Place each churro gently in the preheated air fryer and cook for 5 to 6 minutes or until golden brown and crisp.

Put the remaining melted butter on the churros and sprinkle the remaining cinnamon-sugar mixture.

217. BRAZILIAN GRILLED PINEAPPLE

INGREDIENTS

- 1 pineapple peeled, cored and cut into spears
- 1/2 cup Brown Sugar
- 2 teaspoons ground cinnamon
- 3 tablespoons melted butter

INSTRUCTIONS

In a small bowl, add the brown sugar and the cinnamon.

Brush the melted butter to the pineapple spears. Sprinkle cinnamon sugar over the spears and press gently to ensure that it sticks well.

Place the spears in a single layer of the air-fryer basket. This may have to be done in batches, depending on the size of your air fryer. Set the fryer for the first batch to 400 ° F for 10 minutes (6-8 minutes for the next batch as it preheats your air fryer). Brush with any remaining butter on halfway through.

When pineapples are heated through, and the sugar bubbles.

NUTRITIONAL INFORMATION

Calories: 295kcal , Carbohydrates: 57g , Protein: 1g , Fat: 8g , Saturated Fat: 5g , Fiber: 3g , Sugar: 48g

218. FRUIT CRUMBLE MUG CAKES

INGREDIENTS

- Philips Airfryer
- 110 g Plain Flour
- 50 g Butter
- 30 g Caster Sugar
- 30 g Gluten Free Oats
- 25 g Brown Sugar
- 4 Plums
- 1 Small Apple
- 1 Small Pear
- 1 Small Peach
- Handful Blueberries
- 1 Tbsp Honey
- Metric - Imperial

INSTRUCTIONS

Air Fryer preheat to 160c.

Using the corer remove from the fruit the cores and the stones and dice into very small pieces of squares.

-the fruit in the bottom of the mugs between the four mugs and spread them out. Sprinkle with brown sugar and sprinkle with honey until well coated. The place to one side.

In a mixing bowl, put the flour, butter and caster sugar and rub the fat into the flour. You may then add the oats when it resembles fine breadcrumbs. Blend well.

Protect a portion of your crumble with the tops of the mugs.

Set in the Air Fryer at 160c for 10 minutes. So cook at 200c for another 5 minutes after 10 minutes, so you can get a lovely crunch to the top of your crumble.

Notes We used gluten-free oats and this really balanced it out as the flour can be rather heavy. For whatever fruit you have in, you can also change it a bit as we think rhubarb works really well too.

NUTRITIONAL INFORMATION

Calories: 380kcal , Carbohydrates: 68g , Protein: 5g , Fat: 11g , Saturated Fat: 6g , Cholesterol: 26mg , Sodium: 93mg , Potassium: 331mg , Fiber: 5g , Sugar: 36g , Vitamin A: 685IU , Vitamin C: 12.8mg , Calcium: 27mg , Iron: 1.9mg

219. SOFT CHOCOLATE BROWNIES

INGREDIENTS

- Philips Airfryer
- 125 g Caster Sugar
- 2 Tbsp Water
- 142 ml Milk
- 125 g Butter
- 50 g Chocolate
- 175 g Brown Sugar
- 2 Medium Eggs beaten
- 100 g Self Raising Flour
- 2 Tsp Vanilla Essence
- Metric - Imperial

INSTRUCTIONS

Preheat your fridge to 180c.

Start by baking brownies of chocolate–melt 100 g of butter and chocolate in a bowl above a pan over medium heat. Remove the brown sugar, the medium eggs and then the vanilla essence. Add the flour that raises itself and mix well.

Pour the mixture into a greased dish of a suitable size for your refrigerator.

Cook on a 180c in your refrigerator for 15 minutes.

It is time to make the caramel sauce while the brownies are cooking–Mix the caster sugar and the water in a pan over medium heat until the sugar is melted. Then turn it up and cook for another three minutes, until a light brown color has turned.

Take off the heat and then add your butter after 2 minutes and continue to stir until all is melted. Then add the milk, slowly.

Set one side of the caramel sauce so it cools down.

Chop them into squares when the brownies are ready and place them on a plate with some sliced banana, and cover them with some caramel sauce.

Service!

Notes if you are in nuts and have no allergies then add 50 g of walnuts to your brownie mix at the same time as it is moved to a jar before going into the air fryer.

NUTRITIONAL INFORMATION

Calories: 482kcal , Carbohydrates: 67g , Protein: 5g , Fat: 22g , Saturated Fat: 13g , Cholesterol: 101mg , Sodium: 190mg , Potassium: 131mg , Fiber: 0g , Sugar: 54g , Vitamin A: 640IU , Calcium: 69mg , Iron: 0.8mg

220. OVEN APPLE PIE

INGREDIENTS

- Kitchen Gadgets:
- Air Fryer
- Pie Pan
- Air Fryer Apple Pie Ingredients:
- 400 g Air Fryer Pie Crust
- 325 g Small Apple Chunks
- 50 g Caster Sugar
- 1 Small Lemon zest and juice
- 2 Tsp Cinnamon
- ½ Tsp Nutmeg
- 1 Small Egg for egg wash

- Metric – Imperial

INSTRUCTIONS

Roll out the pie crust, and place it inside the pie pan bottom.

Take your peeled and diced apples and your lemon, cinnamon, and nutmeg in the pie pan and push them down and make sure there are no apple gaps.

Remove the pie crust's second layer, and press over your apples. Stab with a knife in the middle to allow the pie room to breathe, then add a layer of egg wash using a pastry brush.

Put the middle shelf in the air fryer oven, and cook for 30 minutes at 180c/360f.

Serve with milk, custard and ice cream.

NUTRITIONAL INFORMATION

Calories: 288kcal, Carbohydrates: 38g, Protein: 4g, Fat: 14g, Saturated Fat: 4g, Cholesterol: 20mg, Sodium: 213mg, Potassium: 118mg, Fiber: 3g, Sugar: 11g, Vitamin A: 52IU, Vitamin C: 9mg, Calcium: 25mg, Iron: 2mg

221. CHOCOLATE ECLAIRS

INGREDIENTS

- Philips Airfryer
- Eclair Dough:
- 50 g Butter
- 100 g Plain Flour
- 3 Medium Eggs
- 150 ml Water
- Cream Filling:
- 1 Tsp Vanilla Essence
- 1 Tsp Icing Sugar
- 150 ml Whipped Cream
- Chocolate Topping:
- 50 g Milk Chocolate chopped into chunks
- 1 Tbsp Whipped Cream
- 25 g Butter
- Metric - Imperial

INSTRUCTIONS

Airfryer preheats to 180c.

When heating up, put fat in the water and melt in a wide pan over medium heat, then bring to boil.

Remove from heat and pour in a meal.

Return the pan to heat and stir it into the center of the pan forming a medium ball.

Turn the dough onto a cold plate to cool down. When it is in the eggs cool beat until you have a smooth blend.

Then form the Airfryer into éclair and place it in it. Cook on 180 for 10 minutes, then on 160 for another 8 minutes.

When cooking the dough make your cream filling–combine the vanilla essence with a whisk, whipped cream, and icing sugar until it is nice and thick.

Allow the eclairs to cool and make your chocolate topping while they are cooling–place in a glass bowl the milk chocolate, whipped cream, and butter. Place it over a pan of hot water and mix well until the chocolate has melted.

Cover with melted chocolate on the eclair tops and then serve!

NUTRITIONAL INFORMATION

Calories: 195kcal, Carbohydrates: 14g, Protein: 3g, Fat: 13g, Saturated Fat: 8g, Cholesterol: 85mg, Sodium: 83mg, Potassium: 72mg, Fiber: 0g, Sugar: 4g, Vitamin A: 400IU, Calcium: 29mg, Iron: 0.9mg

222. PINEAPPLE CAKE

INGREDIENTS

- Philips Airfryer
- 225 g Self Raising Flour
- 100 g Butter
- 100 g Caster Sugar
- 200 g Pineapple chopped into chunks
- 100 ml Pineapple Juice
- 50 g Dark Chocolate grated
- 1 Medium Eggs
- 2 Tbsp Whole Milk
- Metric - Imperial

INSTRUCTIONS

Preheat the air fryer to 200c, and grate a tin of cake.

Blend the butter into the flour in a tub. Mix it in until the mixture is breadcrumbs-like.

Add the sugar, the chunks of pineapple and the juice and remove the dark chocolate. Place on one foot.

Beat the egg and the milk in a jug together.

Mix the liquid into the mixture of the breadcrumbs until you have a smooth cake mix.

Cook for 40 minutes on a 200c heat in the Airfryer.

Rest, and serve for 10 minutes.

NUTRITIONAL INFORMATION

Calories: 612kcal , Carbohydrates: 81g , Protein: 9g , Fat: 27g , Saturated Fat: 16g , Cholesterol: 95mg , Sodium: 202mg , Potassium: 257mg , Fiber: 3g , Sugar: 35g , Vitamin A: 715IU , Vitamin C: 26.4mg , Calcium: 48mg , Iron: 2.4mg

223. BRITISH LEMON TARTS

INGREDIENTS

- Philips Airfryer
- 100 g Butter
- 225 g Plain Flour
- 30 g Caster Sugar
- 1 Large Lemon zest and juice
- 4 Tsp Mrs Darlington's Lemon Curd
- Pinch Nutmeg
- Metric - Imperial

INSTRUCTIONS

In a large mixing bowl make your shortcrust pastry. Mix together the butter, flour and sugar using the rubbing in INSTRUCTIONS. When it resembles fine breadcrumbs add the lemon rind and juice, nutmeg, then mix again. Add water a little at the time using the water to combine the ingredients until you have lovely soft dough.

Roll out your pastry with a little flour.

Using small ramekins or little pastry cases rub a little flour around them to stop them sticking and then add your pastry. Please make sure your pastry is nice and thin otherwise when cooked it will end up way too thick.

Add ½ teaspoon into each of your mini tart containers and then cook your lemon tarts for 15 minutes on 180c.

Put on for a few minutes to cool and then serve.

NUTRITIONAL INFORMATION

Calories: 218kcal , Carbohydrates: 27g , Protein: 3g , Fat: 10g , Saturated Fat: 6g , Cholesterol: 26mg , Sodium: 100mg , Potassium: 30mg , Fiber: 0g , Sugar: 5g , Vitamin A: 310IU , Vitamin C: 1mg , Calcium: 7mg , Iron: 1.3mg

224. BAKED OATMEAL

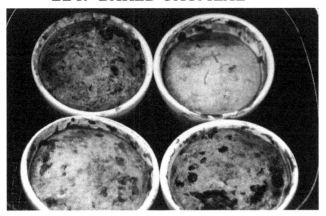

INGREDIENTS

- Kitchen Gadgets:
- Air Fryer
- 4 Ramekins
- Air Fryer Baked Oatmeal Ingredients:
- 200 g Banana
- 120 g Gluten Free Quick Oats
- 1 Tbsp Vanilla Essence
- 2 Tbsp Honey
- 2 Large Eggs
- 2 Tbsp Greek Yoghurt
- 75 ml Skimmed Milk
- Extra Baked Oatmeal Ingredients:
- Handful Fresh Blueberries
- 2 Tbsp Fresh Raspberries
- 2 Tbsp Mixed Berries
- Metric – Imperial

INSTRUCTIONS

Mash your banana, with a fork, into your cup. Stir in the essence of cocoa, sugar, oats, and eggs. Blend well. Apply a little milk and Greek yogurt at a time until you have a batter in pancake form.

Attach any additional ingredients, then combine.

Put in ramekins, cups, mugs, etc. and put your basket in the air fryer.

Cook at 200c/400f, for 8 minutes.

Serving hot.

NUTRITIONAL INFORMATION

Calories: 225kcal , Carbohydrates: 43g , Protein: 8g , Fat: 3g , Saturated Fat: 1g , Cholesterol: 83mg , Sodium: 44mg , Potassium: 250mg , Fiber: 5g , Sugar: 18g , Vitamin A: 189IU , Vitamin C: 6mg , Calcium: 62mg , Iron: 2mg

225. WONTONS APPETIZER

INGREDIENTS

- 1 package won ton wrappers
- 1 package coleslaw mix
- 2 tbsp soy sauce
- 2 tbsp butter

INSTRUCTIONS

How To Make The Mixture

Melt the butter in a large, cast iron pan.

Stir in coleslaw mixture and cook for about 5 minutes.

Stir in the soy sauce, then cook for another minute.

Where applicable, season with salt and pepper.

Remove from heat and allow the mixture to cool before the wontons are placed together.

How To Assemble The Wontons

On top of a sheet of parchment paper, lie the wonton wrappers.

In one corner of the wonton wrapper, put about a spoonful of the cooled coleslaw mixture.

Dip your finger in a small bowl filled with water and scatter a very small amount of water over the wonton edges.

Fold one corner of the catty-corner wonton wrapper to the opposite corner making a triangle shape that pushes the sides together tightly to squeeze out any air bubbles.

Place on a baking tray covered with parchment paper and cover with a damp paper towel while continuing to shape the rest of the wontons, add them to the tray and cover with the dampened paper as well.

INSTRUCTIONS

Preheat the air fryer with a temperature setting for 10 minutes at 375 degrees.

Sprinkle the basket with non-stick cooking spray once the air fryer is preheated and add a few wontons to the basket and let it cook for 3 to 4 minutes or until the wontons are golden brown.

Repeat the process until they cook all the wontons.

Extract from the basket once cooked and allow it to cool before enjoying it.

NUTRITIONAL INFORMATION Yield: 60 Serving Size: 1, Amount Per Serving: Calories: 7 Total Fat: 1g Saturated Fat: 0g Trans Fat: 0g Unsaturated Fat: 0g Cholesterol: 1mg Sodium: 37mg Carbohydrates: 0g Fiber: 0g Sugar: 0g Protein: 0g

226. TOASTED RAVIOLI

INGREDIENTS

- 1 (10 ounce) package refrigerated ravioli
- 1 cup Italian Seasoned Bread Crumbs
- 3 eggs, beaten
- 1/2 teaspoon garlic salt
- 3/4 cup Parmesan cheese, divided
- Marinara and fresh parsley for serving

INSTRUCTIONS

Microwave a medium sized bowl water until boiling. Drop ravioli in for about 5 minutes. Drain.

In a bowl combine bread crumbs with 1/2 cup or Parmesan cheese. I gave the shredded cheese a bit of a rough chop.

Beat eggs in a small bowl with the garlic salt.

Dip ravioli in egg then press into bread crumbs, coating both sides.

Fill the basket of your air fryer with a single layer of ravioli.

Set to 350 degrees and 9 minutes.

Remove from fryer and serve hot with marinara for dipping, with a nice dusting of fresh parsley and shredded Parmesan cheese

NUTRITIONAL INFORMATION:

Yield: 15 Serving Size: 1 Amount Per Serving: Calories: 73 Total Fat: 3g Saturated Fat: 1g Trans Fat: 0g Unsaturated Fat: 1g Cholesterol: 42mg Sodium: 307mg Carbohydrates: 7g Fiber: 1g Sugar: 1g Protein: 4g

227. BREADED MUSHROOMS

INGREDIENTS

- 250 grams Button mushrooms
- flour
- 1 egg
- Breadcrumbs
- 80 grams Finely grated Parmigiano Reggiano cheese
- salt and pepper

INSTRUCTIONS

In a cup, mix the Parmigiano cheese with the breadcrumbs and put it to one side.

Beat an egg in a separate bowl, and put it on one side.

Pat with kitchen paper to dry the mushrooms.

Roll up the flour with the mushrooms.

Dip the egg chestnuts.

Dip the breadcrumbs/cheese mixture into the mushrooms to ensure even coating.

Cook for 7 minutes on 180 degrees in the Airfryer. When shake when cooking.

Serve warm with a dipping sauce of your choosing.

228. CARROTS WITH HONEY

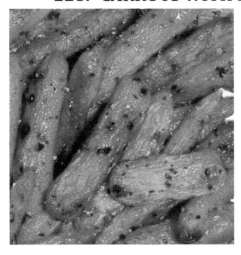

INGREDIENTS

- 2 to 3 cups of carrots, cut in 1/2 inch pieces
- 1 tablespoon olive oil
- 1 tablespoon honey
- tiny drizzle of soy sauce
- salt and pepper to taste

DIRECTION

Air-fryer set to 390 F.

Put the cut carrots in a cup, add olive oil, honey and soy, toss to coat gently and try a bit of oil to cover all surfaces. Season with salt and ground carrots to black pepper. Place your air-fryer in the basket and cook for about 12 minutes, shaking the pan each time. Serve forthwith.

229. CHUNKY CRAB CAKE

INGREDIENTS:

- 2 large eggs
- 2 tablespoons mayonnaise
- 1 teaspoon Dijon mustard
- 1 teaspoon Worcestershire sauce
- 1 ½ teaspoon Old Bay seasoning
- Fresh pepper to taste
- ¼ cup finely chopped green onion
- 1 pound lump crab meat
- ½ cup panko

INSTRUCTIONS:

In a medium bowl, add the milk, mayonnaise, Dijon mustard, Worcestershire, Old Bay and blend well. Attach the finely chopped green onion to the mixture of mayonnaise, and blend well.

Remove the crab until all are mixed into the mayonnaise mix. Attach the panko to the crab/mayonnaise mix and fold together until mixed, keeping the crab pieces intact and being cautious not to overmix.

Cover the mixture of crabs and put them in the refrigerator for about 1 hour.

Form into roughly 8 1 inch thick crab cakes, make sure the cakes are not packed too tightly.

Air-fryer preheats to 350F. Once the air-fryer reaches the desired temperature, put 4 crab cakes gently in the basket and set for 10 minutes to air fry, the crab cake should be set and with a light crust. After 5 minutes make sure to rotate the crab cakes to achieve even cooking.

Turn gently onto a plate when finished. Serve with wedges of Lemon.

230. COUNTRY FRIED STEAK

INGREDIENTS

- Air Fryer Steak
- 1 Pound Bottom Round Steak or Cube Steak
- 1/2 Cup Flour
- 1/2 teaspoon Garlic Powder
- 1/2 teaspoon Onion Powder
- 1/2 teaspoon Paprika
- 1 Egg
- 1 teaspoon Cayenne OR your favorite spice blend. This is OPTIONAL!!! Only if you want it spicy
- Salt and Pepper for Steak

INSTRUCTIONS

Air Fryer Steak Beat Egg Mix flour, garlic powder, onion powder, and (if you want spice) Cayenne pepper or other favorite SPICY seasonings Lightly salt and pepper steak on both sides (APPX: 1/8 teaspoon per side) Dip steak into egg Sprinkle the flour mixture on the steak. Shake off excess flour Dip back into the egg Sprinkle on extra flour and press the flour gently to ensure that it sticks to steak Spray one side of steak with cooking spray (this is what causes it to brown) Position sprayed steak sided in Air Fryer Spray steak top with cooking spray Cook at 360 degrees for 10 minutes

Flip Steak Over Cook for additional 7 minutes Cooking spray with spray. Switch Air Fryer and cook for another 5 minutes up to

390 degrees Serve with potatoes and Gravy.

NUTRITIONAL INFORMATION

Calories: 230kcal , Carbohydrates: 13g , Protein: 28g , Fat: 7g , Saturated Fat: 2g , Cholesterol: 110mg , Sodium: 372mg , Potassium: 432mg , Fiber: 1g , Sugar: 1g , Vitamin A: 443IU , Vitamin C: 1mg , Calcium: 38mg , Iron: 3mg

231. MONTE CRISTO SANDWICH

INGREDIENTS

- 1 egg
- 3 tablespoons half and half
- ¼ teaspoon vanilla extract
- 2 slices sourdough white or multigrain bread
- 2½ ounces sliced swiss cheese
- 2 ounces slices deli ham
- 2 ounces sliced deli turkey
- 1 teaspoon butter melted
- powdered sugar
- raspberry jam for serving

INSTRUCTIONS

In a shallow bowl, mix the egg, half, and half, with vanilla extract.

Put the bread on the table. Create a sandwich with one slice of Swiss cheese, bacon, turkey and then another slice of Swiss cheese on a slice of bread. Top with the other bread slice, then gently press down to flatten.

Air fryer preheats to 350oF.

Cut out a piece of aluminum foil about the same size as the bread and melted butter to smooth the foil. Dip the egg batter on both sides of the sandwich. Let each side of the batter soak in bread for about 30 seconds. Then place the sandwich on the aluminum foil, and move it to the basket of the air fryer.

Brush the top of the sandwich with melted butter to give extra browning. 10-minute air-fry at 350oF. Flip the sandwich over, add butter and air-fry for another 8 minutes.

Sprinkle with powdered sugar and pass the sandwich to a serving plate. Serve with preserved raspberry or blackberry on the side.

232. BLUEBERRY LEMON MUFFIN

INGREDIENTS

- 2 1/2 cups self rising flour
- 1/2 cup Monk Fruit (or use your preferred sugar)
- 1/2 cup cream
- 1/4 cup avocado oil (any light cooking oil)
- 2 eggs
- 1 cup blueberries
- zest from 1 lemon
- juice from 1 lemon
- 1 tsp. vanilla
- brown sugar for topping (a little sprinkling on top of each muffin-less than a teaspoon)

INSTRUCTIONS

Mix the self-growing flour and sugar in a small bowl. Deposit back.

The milk, sugar, lemon juice, eggs, and vanilla are mixed in a medium bowl.

Add the flour mixture to the water, and stir until mixed. Blueberries blend in.

In silicone cupcake plates, spoon the batter, sprinkle with 1/2 tsp. Brown sugar over each muffin.

Bake for 10 minutes at 320 degrees, test the muffins for 6 minutes to make sure they do not cook too quickly. Place a toothpick in the middle of the muffin and it is finished when the toothpick comes out clean and the muffins have browned. No need to over-bake the muffins; after they are removed from the air fryer, they can continue to cook for another minute or two. remove and let cool.

233. MEXICAN-STYLE STUFFED CHICKEN BREASTS

INGREDIENTS

- 4 extra-long toothpicks
- 4 teaspoons chili powder, divided
- 4 teaspoons ground cumin, divided
- 1 skinless, boneless chicken breast
- 2 teaspoons chipotle flakes
- 2 teaspoons Mexican oregano
- salt and ground black pepper to taste
- ½ red bell pepper, sliced into thin strips
- ½ onion, sliced into thin strips
- 1 fresh jalapeno pepper, sliced into thin strips
- 2 teaspoons corn oil
- ½ lime, juiced

INSTRUCTIONS

Place the toothpicks in a small bowl and cover with water; let them soak when cooking to prevent them from burning.

In a shallow dish, bring together 2 teaspoons of chili powder and 2 teaspoons of cumin.

you will preheat the air fryer to 400 F (200 C).

Place the breast on a flat working surface. Horizontally slice through the heart. Pound up to around 1/4-inch thickness per half using a kitchen bracelet or rolling pin.

Sprinkle with remaining chili powder, remaining cumin, chipotle flakes, oregano, salt, and pepper evenly on each breast portion. In the center of 1 half of the breast, position 1/2 of the bell pepper, onion, and jalapeno.

Roll the chicken upwards from the tapered end and use 2 toothpicks to protect it. Repeat with other breasts, spices, and vegetables and keep the remaining toothpicks safe. In the shallow dish, roll each roll-up into the chili-cumin mixture while drizzling with olive oil until coated evenly.

Put roll-ups with the toothpick side facing up, in the air-fryer bowl. Set a 6-minute timer.

Switch over roll-ups. Continue cooking in the air fryer until the juices run clear and at least 165 degrees F (74 degrees C) reads an instant-read thermometer inserted into the middle, around 5 minutes more.

Drizzle the lime juice generously before serving onto roll-ups.

NUTRITIONAL INFORMATION FACTS

Per Serving:

185 calories; 8.5 g total fat; 32 mg cholesterol; 171 mg sodium. 15.2 g carbohydrates; 14.8 g protein

234. MEATLOAF

INGREDIENTS

- 1 pound lean ground beef
- 1 egg, lightly beaten
- 3 tablespoons dry bread crumbs
- 1 small onion, finely chopped
- 1 tablespoon chopped fresh thyme
- 1 teaspoon saltground black pepper to taste
- 2 mushrooms, thickly sliced
- 1 tablespoon olive oil, or as needed

INSTRUCTIONS

you will preheat an air fryer to 392 degrees F (200 degrees C).

In a cup, add ground beef, milk, bread crumbs, ointment, thyme, salt, and pepper. Knead and combine well.

Move the mixture of beef into a baking pan and smooth the rim. Press chestnuts into the top and coat with olive oil. Place the saucepan in the basket of the air fryer and slide into the air fryer.

Set 25-minute air fryer timer and roast meatloaf until well browned.

Let the meatloaf rest for at least 10 minutes before slicing and serving into wedges.

NUTRITIONAL INFORMATION FACTS

Per Serving: 297 calories; 18.8 g fat; 5.9 g carbohydrates; 24.8 g protein; 126 mg cholesterol; 706 mg sodium.

235. SHRIMP A LA BANG BANG

INGREDIENTS

- 1/2 cup mayonnaise
- 1/4 cup sweet chili sauce
- 1 tablespoon sriracha sauce
- 1/4 cup all-purpose flour
- 1 cup panko bread crumbs
- 1 pound raw shrimp, peeled and deveined
- 1 head loose leaf lettuce
- 2 green onions, chopped, or to taste (optional)

INSTRUCTIONS

Set 400 degrees F (200 degrees C) air-fryer.

In a bowl, stir in mayonnaise, chili sauce, and sriracha sauce until smooth. Book some bang bang sauce, if needed, in a separate bowl for dipping.

Layer flour on a saucepan. Bring the panko onto a separate plate.

Then coat the shrimp with flour, then mayonnaise mixture, then panko. Place shrimp wrapped on a baking sheet.

Place shrimp, without overcrowding, in the air fryer basket.

Cook for a further 12 minutes. Repeat with shrimp leftover.

Serve in green onions garnished with lettuce wraps.

NUTRITIONAL INFORMATION

Per Serving: 415 calories; 23.9 g fat; 32.7 g carbohydrates; 23.9 g protein; 183 mg cholesterol; 894 mg sodium.

236. SHRIMP A LA BANG BANG

INGREDIENTS

- 1/2 cup mayonnaise
- 1/4 cup sweet chili sauce
- 1 tablespoon sriracha sauce
- 1/4 cup all-purpose flour
- 1 cup panko bread crumbs
- 1 pound raw shrimp, peeled and deveined
- 1 head loose leaf lettuce
- 2 green onions, chopped, or to taste (optional)

INSTRUCTIONS

Set 400 degrees F (200 degrees C) air-fryer.

In a bowl, stir in mayonnaise, chili sauce, and sriracha sauce until smooth. Book some bang bang sauce, if needed, in a separate bowl for dipping.

Layer flour on a saucepan. Bring the panko onto a separate plate.

Then coat the shrimp with flour, then mayonnaise mixture, then panko. Place shrimp wrapped on a baking sheet.

Place shrimp, without overcrowding, in the air fryer basket.

Cook for a further 12 minutes. Repeat with shrimp leftover.

Serve in green onions garnished with lettuce wraps.

NUTRITIONAL INFORMATION

Per Serving: 415 calories; 23.9 g fat; 32.7 g carbohydrates; 23.9 g protein; 183 mg cholesterol; 894 mg sodium.

237. ROSEMARY POTATO WEDGES

INGREDIENTS

- 2 russet potatoes, sliced into 12 wedges each with skin on
- 1 tablespoon extra-virgin olive oil
- 2 teaspoons seasoned salt
- 1 tablespoon finely chopped fresh rosemary

INSTRUCTIONS

Preheat an air fryer to 380 F (190 C).

Place the potatoes in a wide bowl and add olive oil to roll. Sprinkle with the dried rosemary and salt and shake to mix.

Once the air fryer is dry, put the potatoes in an even layer in the fryer basket; you may need to cook them in batches.

For 10 minutes, air fried potatoes and then turn the wedges with tongs. Continue frying the air until the potato wedges reach the desired doneness, about ten more minutes.

NUTRITIONAL INFORMATION

Per Serving: 115 calories; 3.5 g fat; 19.2 g carbohydrates; 2.2 g protein; 0 mg cholesterol; 465 mg sodium.

238. POTATO HAY

INGREDIENTS

- 2 russet potatoes
- 1 tablespoon canola oil
- kosher salt and ground black pepper to taste

INSTRUCTIONS

Cut the potatoes into spirals using the medium grating attachment on a spiralizer and cut the spirals after 4 or 5 rotations with the cooking shears.

In a bowl of water soak the potato spirals for 20 minutes. Rinse well and drain. Pat potatoes dry with paper towels and remove as much humidity as possible.

Place the potato spirals into a large plastic resealable bag. Incorporate olive oil, salt, and pepper; mix to coat.

Preheat an air fryer to 360 F (180 C).

Place half the spirals of potato in the fry basket and insert them into the air fryer. Cook for about 5 minutes, until golden.

Rising to 390 degrees F (200 degrees C). Take out the fry basket and use tongs to toss potato spirals. Return container to air fryer and continue to cook, tossing regularly for 10 to 12 minutes, till turn golden brown. Lower the heat to 360 degrees F (180 degrees C) and repeat with left spirals of potato.

NUTRITIONAL INFORMATION

Per Serving: 113 calories; 3.6 g fat; 18.6 g carbohydrates; 2.2 g protein; 0 mg cholesterol; 106 mg sodium

239. ROASTED CAULIFLOWER

INGREDIENTS

- 3 cloves garlic
- 1 tablespoon peanut oil
- 1/2 teaspoon salt
- 1/2 teaspoon smoked paprika
- 4 cups cauliflower florets

INSTRUCTIONS

Preheat an air fryer up to 400 F (200 C).

Cut the garlic in half, and break a knife's tip. Put the oil, salt, and paprika in a cup. Apply cauliflower to coat and turn.

Put the coated cauliflower in the air fryer pot, and cook to ideal crispiness for about 15 minutes, stirring every 5 minutes.

Cook's Note: The cauliflower will still have some crunch after 15 minutes; if you want it crispier, cook for another 5 minutes. The timing really depends on the cauliflower's size so test regularly.

NUTRITIONAL INFORMATION

Per Serving: 118 calories; 7 g fat; 12.4 g carbohydrates; 4.3 g protein; 0 mg cholesterol; 642 mg sodium.

240. DONUTS

INGREDIENTS

- 1/2 cup granulated sugar
- 1 tablespoon ground cinnamon
- 1 (16.3-ounce) can flaky large biscuits, such as Pillsbury Grands! Flaky Biscuits
- Olive oil spray or coconut oil spray
- 4 tablespoons unsalted butter, melted

INSTRUCTIONS

Line a parchment-papered baking sheet. Mix the sugar and cinnamon into a shallow bowl; set aside.

Remove the biscuits from the can, break them apart and put them on the baking sheet. To cut holes out of the middle of each biscuit, use an a1-inch diameter biscuit cutter (or similarly sized bottle cap).

Coat an air fryer basket lightly with olive or coconut oil spray (do not use a non-stick cooking spray such as Pam which can harm the basket cover).

In the air Freyer, put 3 to 4 donuts in a single layer (they shouldn't touch). Open the fryer to air and set to 350 ° F. Cook, flipping through halfway, until the golden-brown donuts, max 5 to 6 minutes. Put donuts onto the baking sheet. Repeat with leftover biscuits. You should cook the donut holes too they should take a total of around 3 minutes.

Brush with melted butter on both sides of the warm donuts put them in the cinnamon sugar and flip to cover on both sides. Serving hot.

NUTRITIONAL INFORMATION

Per serving, based on 10 servings. Calories 248 Fat 12.6 g (19.4%) Saturated 5.0 g (24.9%) Carbs 31.2 g (10.4%) Fiber 1.1 g (4.4%) Sugars 11.0 g Protein 3.3 g (6.6%) Sodium 268.8 mg (11.2%)

241. SWEET AND SPICY BRUSSELS SPROUTS

INGREDIENTS

- 1 lb brussels sprouts cut in half
- 2 tbsp honey
- 1 1/2 tbsp vegetable oil
- 1 tbsp gochujang
- 1/2 tsp salt

INSTRUCTIONS

Line a parchment-papered baking sheet. Mix the sugar and cinnamon into a shallow bowl; set aside.

Remove the biscuits from the can, break them apart and put them on the baking sheet. To cut holes out of the middle of each biscuit, use an a1-inch diameter biscuit cutter (or similarly sized bottle cap).

Coat an air fryer basket lightly with olive or coconut oil spray (do not use a non-stick cooking spray such as Pam which can harm the basket cover).

In the air Freyer, put 3 to 4 donuts in a single layer (they shouldn't touch). Open the fryer to air and set to 350 ° F. Cook, flipping through halfway, until the golden-brown donuts, max 5 to 6 minutes.

Put donuts onto the baking sheet. Repeat with leftover biscuits. You should cook the donut holes too they should take a total of around 3 minutes.

Brush with melted butter on both sides of the warm donuts put them in the cinnamon sugar and flip to cover on both sides. Serving hot. Cooking time and temperature for different air-fryer brands may need to be slightly changed.

NUTRITIONAL INFORMATION

Calories: 128kcal, Carbohydrates: 20g, Protein: 3g, Fat: 5g, Saturated Fat: 4g, Sodium: 320mg, Potassium: 456mg, Fiber: 4g, Sugar: 11g, Vitamin A: 855IU, Vitamin C: 97.1mg, Calcium: 48mg, Iron: 1.6mg

242. TURKEY BREASTS

INGREDIENTS

- 4 pound turkey breast, on the bone with skin (ribs removed)
- 1 tablespoon olive oil
- 2 teaspoons kosher
- 1/2 tablespoon dry turkey or poultry seasoning, I used Bell's which has not salt

INSTRUCTIONS

Brush 1/2 spoonful of oil over the whole turkey breast. Rub with salt and turkey seasoning on both sides then rub over the skin side in the remaining half tablespoon of oil.

Preheat the air fryer 350F and cook skin side down for 20 minutes, turn over and cook until the internal temperature is 160F using an instant-read thermometer about 30 to 40 minutes higher depending on your breast size. Let's rest 10 minutes before they carve.

NUTRITIONAL INFORMATION

Serving: 4ounces, Calories: 226kcal, Protein: 32.5g, Fat: 10g, Saturated Fat: 2.5g, Cholesterol: 84mg, Sodium: 296mgBlue Smart Points:4Green Smart Points:5Purple Smart Points:5Points +:4

243. SWEET POTATO DESSERT FRIES

INGREDIENTS

- 2 medium sweet potatoes and/or yams peeled (see notes for low carb option)
- Half a tablespoon of coconut oil.
- 1 tablespoon arrowroot starch or cornstarch
- Optional 2 tsp melted butter (for coating)
- 1/4 cup coconut sugar or raw sugar
- 1 to 2 tablespoons cinnamon
- Optional powdered sugar for dusting
- Dipping Sauces
- Dessert Hummus
- Honey or Vanilla Greek Yogurt
- Maple Frosting {vegan}

INSTRUCTIONS

AIR FRYER INSTRUCTIONS:

Peel and wash your sweet potatoes with clean water then rinse.

Lengthwise slice of peeled sweet potatoes, 1/2 inch thick.

Place the sweet potato slices in 1/2 tbsp of coconut oil and arrowroot starch (or cornstarch) in air fryer at 370F for 18 minutes. Shake at 8-9 minutes on halfway.

Remove the fries and place them in a large bowl from the air fryer. Drizzle 2 tsp of optional butter over the fries. Then add in the sugar and cinnamon and throw the fries together again.

Sprinkle with powdered sugar and put on a plate to eat.

Serve fries of choice with a dipping sauce. Hold fries wrapped in foil and in the refrigerator for cooling. Then reheat to warm before serving again in the oven. Should keep for 2-3 days.

NUTRTIONAL INFORMATION

Calories Per Serving: 130% DAILY VALUE 3%Total Fat 2.3g Saturated Fat 1.7g 0%Cholesterol 1.3mg

2% Sodium 45.5mg 9% Total Carbohydrate 26.9g 12% Dietary Fiber 3g Sugars 14.8g 2% Protein 1.2g 3% Vitamin C 1.7mg 3% Iron 0.6mg

244. ZESTY RANCH FISH FILLETS

INGREDIENTS

- 3/4 cup bread crumbs or Panko or crushed cornflakes
- 1 30g packet dry ranch-style dressing mix
- 2 1/2 tablespoons vegetable oil
- 2 eggs beaten
- 4 tilapia salmon or other fish fillets
- lemon wedges to garnish

INSTRUCTIONS

Preheat your fryer until 180 degrees C.

Combine panko/breadcrumbs with ranch dressing blend. Add the oil and continue to stir until the mixture is crumbly and loose.

Dip the fish filets into the shell, letting the excess drip away.

Dip the fish fillets into the crumb mixture, ensuring they are uniformly and thoroughly coated.

Place your fryer carefully into the sun.

Cook for 12-13 minutes, depending on fillet thickness.

Quit and work. Squeeze the wedges of the lemon over the fish if you wish.

NUTRITIONAL INFORMATION

Calories: 315kcal, Carbohydrates: 8g, Protein: 38g, Fat: 14g, Saturated Fat: 8g, Cholesterol: 166mg, Sodium: 220mg, Potassium: 565mg, Vitamin A: 120IU, Calcium: 50mg, Iron: 1.9mg

245. CHURRO BITES

INGREDIENTS

- 1 cup water
- 8 tablespoons (1 stick) unsalted butter, cut into 8 pieces
- 1/2 cup plus 1 tablespoon granulated sugar, divided
- 1 cup all-purpose flour
- 1 teaspoon vanilla extract
- 3 large eggs
- 2 teaspoons ground cinnamon
- 4 ounces finely chopped dark chocolate
- 1/4 cup sour cream or Greek yogurt

INSTRUCTIONS

In a small saucepan over medium-high heat, bring the water, butter and 1 tablespoon of sugar to a simmer. Add the flour, and mix it easily with a sturdy wooden spoon.

Continue to cook, stirring constantly, for about 3 minutes, until the flour smells toasted and the mixture thickens. Transfer to a big bowl.

Beat the flour mixture with the same wooden spoon until it cools slightly but still warm, around 1 minute of steady stirring. Throw in the raspberry.

Stir the eggs one by one, ensuring each egg is added before adding the next.

Move the dough into a zip-top piping bag or gallon jar. Let the dough repose for 1 hour at room temperature.

While mix the chocolate sauce and cinnamon sugar.

A large bowl, adds the cinnamon and the remaining 1/2 cup sugar. Microwave the chocolate in a medium microwave-safe mixing bowl at intervals of 30 seconds, stirring 1 1/2 to 2 minutes between each, until the chocolate is melted.

Remove the yogurt or sour cream, and whisk until smooth. Cover and hold.

Preheat the air-fryer at 375 ° F for 10 minutes. Pip the batter directly into the preheated air fryer, making 6 (3-inch) bits and piping at least 1/2-inch apart from each.

Fry air for about 10 minutes, until golden brown. Move the churros to the cinnamon-sugar bowl immediately, and toss to coat. Repeat and fry the remaining batter with air.

NUTRITIONAL   INFORMATION

Per serving, based on 10 servings. (% daily value) Calories 253 Fat 14.4 g (22.2%) Saturated 8.3 g (41.5%) Carbs 26.8 g (8.9%) Fiber 1.8 g (7.4%) Sugars 14.3 g Protein 4.3 g (8.5%) Sodium 28.6 mg (1.2%)

246. CRISPY BREADED PORK CHOPS

INGREDIENTS

- olive oil spray
- 6 3/4-inch thick center cut boneless pork chops, fat trimmed (5 oz each)
- kosher salt
- 1 large egg, beaten
- 1/2 cup panko crumbs, check labels for GF
- 1/3 cup crushed cornflakes crumbs
- 2 tbsp grated parmesan cheese, omit for dairy free
- 1 1/4 tsp sweet paprika
- 1/2 tsp garlic powder
- 1/2 tsp onion powder
- 1/4 tsp chili powder
- 1/8 tsp black pepper

INSTRUCTIONS

Preheat the air fryer for 12 minutes to 400F, and sprinkle the basket lightly with oil.

Coat the pork chops on both sides with 1/2 tsp. kosher salt.

Place the panko, cornflake crumbs, parmesan cheese, 3/4 tsp of kosher salt, paprika, garlic powder, onion powder, chili powder and black pepper in a large shallow cup.

Drop the beaten egg into another. Dip the pork into the egg and then add in the crumbs.

Place 3 of the chops in the prepared basket and spritz with oil on top, once the air fryer is set.

Cook halfway spinning for 12 minutes, spritzing oil on both sides. Set aside, and repeat with the rest.

NUTRITIONAL FACTS

Serving: 1pork chop, Calories: 378kcal, Carbohydrates: 8g, Protein: 33g, Fat: 13g, Cholesterol: 121mg, Sodium: 373mg, Sugar: 1gBlue Smart Points:7Green Smart Points:7Purple Smart Points:7Points +:7

247. COCONUT SHRIMP WITH PIÑA COLADA DIP

INGREDIENTS

- For the shrimp:
- 1 1/2 pounds jumbo shrimp
- 1/2 cup cornstarch
- 2/3 cup light coconut milk
- 2 tablespoons honey
- 1 cup unsweetened shredded coconut
- 3/4 cup panko bread crumbs
- For the sauce:
- 1/3 cup light coconut milk
- 1/3 cup plain nonfat Greek yogurt
- 1/4 cup pineapple chunks drained
- 1/4 teaspoon salt more to taste
- 1/4 teaspoon pepper more to taste
- Toasted coconut for garnish

INSTRUCTIONS

Remove the shell from the shrimp, and if needed, keep the tail intact.

Place the cornstarch and add the shrimp in a gallon-sized bag. Toss to shirk.

Whisk coconut milk and honey in a medium bowl, until mixed. Combine coconut and panko in yet another medium bowl.

Remove shrimp from the jar, and knock off any excess cornstarch gently. Dunk shrimp in a mixture of milk, then dredge in a mixture of coconut.

You might need to gently press loose coconut and panko onto the shrimp.

Pass coated shrimp to your air-fryer bowl. Warm your fryer to 350 degrees F, and cook for 6-8 minutes, flipping shrimp once, until the coconut is golden brown and the shrimp are cooked through.

Meanwhile, get the sauce ready. Combine the coconut milk, butter, pineapple, salt, and pepper in a mix in a medium bowl. Complete with polished coconut.

248. ZUCCHINI CORN FRITTERS

INGREDIENTS

- 2 medium zucchini
- 1 cup corn kernels
- 1 medium potato cooked
- 2 tbsp chickpea flour
- 2-3 garlic finely minced
- 1-2 tsp olive oil
- salt and pepper
- For Serving:
- Ketchup or Yogurt tahini sauce

INSTRUCTIONS

Use a grater or food processor to cook the zucchini. Mix the grated zucchini and little salt in a mixing bowl and leave for 10-15 minutes. Then use clean hands or using a cheesecloth to suck out excess water from the zucchinis.

Even grate the cooked potato or mash it.

In a mixing bowl, add the courgette, potato, corn, chickpea flour, garlic, salt, and pepper.

Take 2 tbsp of batter roughly, make it a patty shape, and place it on parchment paper.

Brush the oil gently on each fritter's surface. Air Fryer is preheated to 360F.

Place the fritters onto the Air Fryer preheated mesh without touching each other. Cook for 8 min.

Then turn the fritters around and cook for another 3-4 minutes, or until well done or until you get the color you want.

Serve warm with tahini ketchup or yogurt sauce (see the preparation notes)

Notes

Cooking potato in a microwave oven-cook the potato for 3 min. Then, place for a few minutes in cold water. Peel and then mash or grate.

Until cooking, put the prepared patties onto the parchment paper. It really will help clean the oil and then pull it out without cracking or holding down.

(Please do not insert the parchment paper inside the Fryer. Simply keep the raw fritters before loading them into the Air Fryer) Add more flour if necessary. Instead of chickpea meal, you can also use all-purpose flour.

Yogurt tahini sauce-mix 1/2 cup yogurt with 1 tsp tahini, and sauté according to taste with salt.

249. FRENCH FRIES

INGREDIENTS

- 3 medium russet potatoes
- 2 tbsp parmesan cheese
- 2 tbsp finely chopped fresh parsley
- 1 tbsp olive oil plus more to brush wire basket
- salt

INSTRUCTIONS

Cut potatoes into 1/4 "thick fries. Use a kitchen towel, pat dry to remove the remaining humidity. Add parmesan cheese, fresh parsley, salt, and oil. Stir or gently mix together to coat cheese, herbs, and oil evenly. you will Preheat the Air Fryer at 360 F for two to three minutes. Spray some oil lightly on the base of the wire basket. Then spread the seasoned fries evenly on the mesh. Cook for a total of 20 min.

NUTRITIONAL INFORMATION

Serves 4 Amount Per Serving Calories   189% Daily Value Total Fat 4.4g 7% Saturated Fat 0.9g   Sodium   346.2mg 14% Total Carbohydrate 34.3g   11% Dietary Fiber 2.5g   10% Sugars 1.2g Protein 4.8g

250. KOREAN FRIED CAULIFLOWER

INGREDIENTS

- 1 cauliflower cut up into smaller pieces
- For the batter
- 1 cup flour
- 1/2 cup cornstarch
- 2 tsp baking soda
- 1 tbsp garlic powder
- 1 tbsp paprika
- 1 cup water
- For the sauce
- 6 tbsp Gochujang (pepper paste)
- 4 tbsp soy sauce
- 2 tbsp honey
- 4 tbsp water

INSTRUCTIONS

Combine the food, cornstarch, baking soda, garlic powder, and paprika into a large bowl. Give it a mix, and then add the batter to the surface.

Dip the cauliflower into the batter and ensure it is thoroughly coated. Let it sit on a rack and let extra batter dip off for a minute.

When ready, put it in a single layer in the air fryer and set it to 350 for 12 minutes (no preheating required!) While the cauliflower is "frying" in the air fryer, prepare your sauce by mixing all the ingredients in the sauce into a saucepan. Mix it well, and then turn off the heat to a simmer on low heat. Once the cauliflower is done in the air fryer, put it in the saucepan before setting aside to cover the cauliflower.

Keep until all of the cauliflower is fried.

Optional: serve snacks like celery and sweet potato fries with other balanced game days (which can also be made in the air fryer)

251. TOASTED COCONUT FRENCH TOAST

INGREDIENTS

- Per 1 Serving:
- 2 Slices of Gluten-Free Bread (use your favorite)
- 1/2 Cup Lite Culinary Coconut Milk
- 1 Tsp Baking Powder
- 1/2 Cup Unsweetened Shredded Coconut

INSTRUCTIONS

Mix the coconut milk and baking powder together in a large, rimmed dish.

Spread the coconut shredded onto a platter.

Take each slice of bread and soak in the coconut milk mixture for the first time, and a few seconds before moving to the shredded coconut plate and cover the slice in the coconut completely.

Place both the coated bread slices in your air fryer, close them and set the temperature to 350 ° F and 4 minutes.

Remove and top with maple syrup, or your favorite French toast toppings until finished!

252. SALMON

INGREDIENTS

- 1 lb salmon Alaska king (fresh, not frozen)
- 1/2 teaspoon chili powder
- 1/4 teaspoon pepper
- 1/4 teaspoon salt
- 2 whole limes
- parsley fresh garnish

INSTRUCTIONS

Spice the salmon with some powder, chili pepper, and salt.

Slice one of the limes after the salmon has been seasoned, and place on top of the salmon.

Once you've got the lime on the salmon put the salmon in the air fryer.

Set the air fryer at 375 degrees F and cook for approximately 8 minutes.

You will know that the salmon is ready with a meat thermometer, once it hits 145 degrees F in the thickest part.

Slice the remaining lime open and squeeze the juice over the salmon as it comes out of the air fryer and garnishes with chopped parsley afterward.

NUTRITIONAL INFORMATION

Calories: 324kcal Protein: 45g Fat: 14g Saturated Fat: 2g Cholesterol: 124mg Sodium: 398mg Potassium: 1111mg Vitamin A: 240IU Calcium: 27mg Iron: 1.8mg

253. ZUCCHINI ENCHILADAS

INGREDIENTS

- 1 large Zucchini
- 1 cup of shredded Chicken
- 1 small Onion diced
- 1 teaspoon of ground Cumin
- 1 teaspoon of Chili Powder
- 1 teaspoon of Garlic Powder
- 1 teaspoon of Smoked Paprika
- 1 cup of red Enchilada Sauce
- ¼ cup of shredded Mexican Blend Cheese
- 2 tablespoon of Olive Oil
- Salt and pepper to taste
- Drizzle of Sour Cream and Green Onion to garnish

INSTRUCTIONS

Heat up the olive oil in a large frying pan over medium heat and brown the diced onion until translucent.

Attach and blend well the seasoning–garlic powder, ground cumin, chili powder, smoked paprika, salt, and pepper.

Add the shredded chicken next, and blend well.

Add the enchilada sauce 3/4 cup and let it simmer for 2 minutes until the chicken is covered by the sauce. Test any seasoning and change it if necessary. Hold on cool aside.

Cut the zucchini in half while the chicken cools, in a lengthwise direction. Render thin strips of the zucchini, using a Y-shaped vegetable peeler. Of each half, you can easily get 6 to 8 slices.

Layout three slices of zucchini, each overlapping.

Place on one end of the zucchini strips about a tablespoon of the chicken mixture. Roll it up and place it on a greased baking dish that can fit in a basket with an air fryer.

Repeat with remaining strips of zucchini and a mixture of chicken.

Add the remaining 1/4 cup enchilada sauce over the strips of rolled zucchini.

Sprinkle with scrambled cheese.

Air to cook for 10 minutes at 330 F.

Serve hot with sour cream chips and a sprinkle of sliced green onion.

254. EGG AND CORN SALAD

INGREDIENTS

- 6 large Eggs
- 3 ears of Corn cut into smaller pieces
- 2 teaspoon of Canola or Vegetable Oil
- Salt and Pepper to taste
- ¼ cup of sliced Red Onion
- ½ cup of julienned Carrots
- ½ cup of julienned Red Bell Pepper
- ½ cup of julienned Green Pepper
- Dressing
- 1 cup of Mayonnaise
- 1 tablespoon of Yellow or Dijon Mustard
- 1 teaspoon of Maple Syrup or Honey
- Salt and Pepper to taste

INSTRUCTIONS

Place the trivet in the basket of your air fryer. Stir the eggs in.

Air-fry at 250 F for 20 minutes.

To avoid the cooking process, submerge the eggs in an ice bath as soon as the fryer beeps, using tongs.

Then, cut and dice them into large chunks.

Cut the corn cobs into small pieces in the air fryer to fit them in.

Coat the corns in vegetable oil and sprinkle salt and pepper over them.

Fry air for 10 minutes at 400, then flip once.

Once the corn is finished and slightly cooled, the kernels are carefully cut out from the cob using a knife.

Combine the air-fried corn kernels, the diced eggs, sliced onions, and julienned carrots, red and green peppers, in a large bowl. Good shoot it. The mayonnaise, mustard, maple syrup, salt, and pepper are mixed in a small bowl. Whisk to merge.

Attach egg and corn salad to the dressing and toss to blend properly.

Cover and let the flavors evolve for about an hour chill.

Serve with grilled meat as a hand.

Refrigerate the leftovers right away.

NOTES Air fries at 400 F for 20 minutes when using frozen corn on the cob, rotating the corn cobs every 5 to 6 minutes after each.

255. PARMESAN SHRIMP

INGREDIENTS

- 2 pounds jumbo cooked shrimp, peeled and deveined
- 4 cloves garlic, minced
- 2/3 cup parmesan cheese, grated
- 1 teaspoon pepper
- 1/2 teaspoon oregano
- 1 teaspoon basil
- 1 teaspoon onion powder
- 2 tablespoons olive oil
- Lemon, quartered

INSTRUCTIONS

Combine the garlic, parmesan cheese, pepper, oregano, basil, onion powder and olive oil in a large cup.

Toss shrimp gently in the mixture until coated evenly.

Sprinkle with non-stick spray air fryer basket and put shrimp in a bowl.

Cook 8-10 minutes at 350 degrees, or until shrimp seasoning is browned.

Squeeze the shrimp over the lemon, before eating.

NOTES Bake at 400 degrees for 6-8 minutes, when using an oven.

256. HONEY CHIPOTLE BACON WRAPPED TATER TOT BOMBS

INGREDIENTS:

- 8 slices of bacon
- 3 tablespoons honey
- 1/2 tablespoon chipotle chile powder
- 16 frozen Tater Tots

INSTRUCTIONS:

Preheat your air fryer to 400 degrees F.

Split the slices of bacon in half, widthwise. Place the bacon slices out next to each other onto a tray.

Warm up the honey about 15 seconds in the microwave. Brush it over slices of bacon.

Sprinkle with the chipotle powder uniformly on the honey brushed bacon.

Wrap single Tater Tot with the seasoned bacon and place every side of the seam down on the plate. Don't tie yourself too closely. Seal each with a toothpick at its edge.

Place 8 of the wrapped tots in the basket of the air fryer and cook for 8 to 14 minutes, then test for doneness after 8 minutes. Repeat with wrapped tots in the second half.

Remove the toothpicks, and immediately drink. The leftover residue can be reheated in the oven or toaster.

257. HOT DOGS

INGREDIENTS

- 2 hot dogs
- 2 hot dog buns
- 2 tablespoons grated cheese if desired

INSTRUCTIONS

Preheat your air fryer for about 4 minutes, to 390 degrees. Put two hot dogs in the air fryer and cook for 5 minutes. Take the hot dog off the air fryer. Place the hot dog on a bun, then add the cheese if you wish. Place the dressed hot dog in the air fryer, then cook for another 2 minutes.

NUTRITIONAL INFORMATION

Calories: 289kcal, Carbohydrates: 29g, Protein: 12g, Fat: 13g, Saturated Fat: 5g, Cholesterol: 36mg, Sodium: 613mg, Potassium: 119mg, Fiber: 0g, Sugar: 2g, Vitamin A: 150IU, Vitamin C: 0.6mg, Calcium: 193mg, Iron: 2.6mg

258. JALAPENO POPPERS

INGREDIENTS

- 10 jalapeno peppers halved and deseeded
- 8 oz of cream cheese I used a dairy-free cream cheese
- 1/4 c fresh parsley
- 3/4 c gluten-free tortilla or bread crumbs

INSTRUCTIONS

Mix 1/2 crumbs and cream cheese together. In the parsley add until combined.

Stuff with that mixture single pepper.

To build the top coating, gently press the tops of the peppers into the remaining 1/4 c of crumbs.

Cook in the air fryer for 6-8 minutes at 370 degrees F OR in a conventional oven for 20 minutes at 375 degrees F.

Let's get cool and have fun!

Notes

Wear gloves or be vigilant after cutting and desiring these jalapenos. Remove both seeds and white membrane (unless you like things spicy!)

Scoop out the seeds and the membrane using a knife.

NUTRITIONAL INFORMATION

Calories: 951kcal , Carbohydrates: 83g , Protein: 23g , Fat: 69g , Saturated Fat: 22g , Sodium: 890mg , Potassium: 430mg , Fiber: 21g , Sugar: 14g , Vitamin A: 2773IU , Vitamin C: 186mg , Calcium: 184mg , Iron: 4mg

259. BAKED THAI PEANUT CHICKEN EGG ROLLS

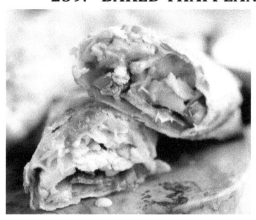

INGREDIENTS

- 4 egg roll wrappers
- 2 c. rotisserie chicken shredded
- 1/4 c. Thai peanut sauce
- 1 medium carrot very thinly sliced or ribboned
- 3 green onions chopped
- 1/4 red bell pepper julienned
- non-stick cooking spray or sesame oil

INSTRUCTIONS

Airfryer preheats to 390 ° or oven to 425 ° C.

Toss the chicken in a tiny bowl with the Thai peanut sauce.

Place the wrappers of the egg roll out onto a dry surface. Arrange 1/4 of the carrot, bell pepper, and onions over the bottom third of an egg roll wrapper. Spoon 1/2 cup of mixed chicken over the vegetables.

Moisture the wrapper's outer edges with sweat. Fold the wrapper's sides toward the middle and roll straight.

Repeat with wrappers leftover. (Until ready to use, keep the remaining wrappers covered with a damp paper towel.)

Spray non-stick cooking spray on assembled egg rolls. Flip them over, and also spray on the backsides.

Place the egg rolls in the Airfryer and bake for 6-8 minutes at 390 °, or until crispy and golden brown.

(When the egg rolls are cooked in an oven, put the seam side down on a baking sheet filled with cooking spray. Bake for 15-20 minutes at 425 degrees.) Slice in half, then serve with additional Thai Peanut Sauce to dip.

260. GARLIC MUSHROOMS

INGREDIENTS

- 8 oz. mushrooms , washed and dried
- 1-2 Tablespoons olive oil
- 1/2 teaspoon garlic powder
- 1 teaspoon Worcestershire or soy sauce
- Kosher salt , to taste
- black pepper , to taste
- lemon wedges (optional)
- 1 Tablespoon chopped parsley

INSTRUCTIONS

Cut the mushrooms in half or quarters (depending on the size you prefer). Add to the bowl then mix for 10-12 minutes with butter, garlic powder, Worcestershire / soy sauce, salt and pepper Air fry at 380 ° F, tossing and shaking half way through. Squeeze the lemon and chopped parsley on top.

261. PERSONAL PIZZA

INGREDIENTS

- 1 Stonegate Mini Naan Round
- 2 tbsp jarred pizza sauce
- 2 tbsp shredded pizza cheese or shredded Mozzarella
- 6 or 7 mini Pepperoni

INSTRUCTIONS

Top the mini naan round with the pizza sauce, shredded pizza cheese and mini pepperoni.

Place the topped personal pizza into the basket of an air fryer.

Set the air fryer to about 375 degrees F. "Fry" the pizza for between 5 to 7 minutes- or until cheese is completely melted and starting to brown. Serve immediately.

262. GARLIC PARMESAN ZUCCHINI

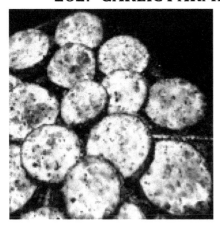

INGREDIENTS

- 2 small to medium size zucchini
- 1 Tbsp olive oil
- 2 Tbsps grated parmesan cheese (plus more to sprinkle over top)
- 3/4 Tbsp garlic powder
- 1/2 Tbsp Italian seasoning
- kosher salt, pepper

INSTRUCTIONS

Slice the courgettes into 1/4 "slices. Garnish with olive oil, parmesan cheese, garlic powder, Italian seasoning, and kosher salt and pepper.

Toss until the coating is even. Place it in the basket of the air fryer, it's ok if they overlap a little. Sprinkle on top with some more parmesan.

Note: You may need to do these in two lots, depending on the size of your air fryer.

Set air-fryer at 400 degrees for 12 minutes.

263. HAMBURGERS

INGREDIENTS

- 1 pound ground beef, lean
- salt & pepper, to taste

INSTRUCTIONS

Preheat Air Fryer for 2-3 minutes, at 400 degrees F.

Break the ground beef into four even portions and form round patties. Season to taste, on both sides.

In Air Fryer basket put the hamburger patties in a single layer.

Cook them for 10 minutes at 400 degrees F. Flip the patties and then cook for another 2-3 minutes until completely cooked.

264. CHEESY TACO CRESCENTS

INGREDIENTS

- 1 can Pillsbury refrigerated crescent sheets
- 4 monterey jack cheese sticks
- 1/2 lb ground beef, browned
- 1/2 envelope taco seasoning mix

INSTRUCTIONS

Preheat Air Fryer to 400 ° F.

Combine ground beef and 1/2 envelope of taco seasoning in a small, microwave-safe dish. Microwave for 1-2 minutes on strong, until dry.

Slice the crescent sheets into eight equal squares. Cut a single piece of cheese in half.

Place 1/2 stick of cheese and 1-2 tablespoons of meat mixture on each crescent square to secure. Roll up each square and crimp ends.

Layer Air Fryer box, with a foil rectangle. Grease the foil and put a single layer of crescents on top.

Cook on for 5 minutes. Turn over and continue cooking for 2-3 minutes until browned.

265. SAUSAGE BALLS

INGREDIENTS

- 1 lb Jimmy Dean pork sausage
- 1 lb Velveeta cheese
- 1 1/2 cups Bisquick baking mix

INSTRUCTIONS

preheats Air Fryer to 320 degrees F.

In the food processor, combine the sausage and Velveeta cheese. (The mixture isn't going to be completely smooth.) Apply Bisquick and pump until all ingredients are mixed.

Roll in walnut-sized balls and at one-time place 10-12 Sausage Balls in Air Fryer basketball or shallow baking dish.

Cook for 5 minutes. Turn the balls over and bake for another 5 minutes, until the Sausage Balls are golden brown.

266. WHOLE WHEAT CHICKEN NUGGETS

INGREDIENTS

- 16 oz 2 large skinless boneless chicken breasts, cut into even 1-inch bite sized pieces
- 1/2 teaspoon kosher salt and black pepper, to taste
- 2 teaspoons olive oil
- 6 tablespoons whole wheat Italian seasoned breadcrumbs
- 2 tablespoons panko
- 2 tablespoons grated parmesan cheese
- olive oil spray

INSTRUCTIONS

Preheat the fryer with air for 8 minutes to 400 ° F.

Place the olive oil in one bowl and breadcrumbs, parmesan cheese and panko cheese in another.

Spice the chicken with salt and pepper, then add the olive oil into the bowl and mix well so that the olive oil covers all the chicken evenly.

Bring in the breadcrumb mixture a few chunks of chicken at a time to cover, then onto the bowl.

Spray the top lightly with a spray of olive oil then fry for 8 minutes, turning halfway. Back to white.

NUTRITIONAL INFORMATION

Serving: 4oz chicken, Calories: 188kcal, Carbohydrates: 8g, Protein: 25g, Fat: 4.5g, Saturated Fat: 1g, Cholesterol: 57mg, Sodium: 427mg, Sugar: 0.5g

267. CAJUN BREAKFAST SAUSAGE

INGREDIENTS

- 1.5 lbs ground sausage (chicken sausage or lean pork).
- 1 tsp chili flakes
- Fresh thyme 2 tsp fresh leaves only or 1/2 tsp to 1 tsp dried thyme
- 1 tsp onion powder
- 1/2 tsp each paprika and cayenne
- 1/4 tsp or to taste Sea Salt: black pepper each
- Chopped sage (optional)
- 2 tsp brown sugar, coconut palm sugar, or maple syrup for paleo option
- 3 tsp minced garlic
- Tabasco 2 tsp plus extra for serving
- Herbs to garnish optional

INSTRUCTIONS

Place ground sausage in large bowl. Make sure it's chilled. Add your additional spices and herbs. Mix together with hands. Add Tabasco sauce or omit for less spicy option.

Shape into patties about 3 to 3 1/2 in width and 1 to 1.5 inch thick. They will shrink when cooked or air fried .

In large bowl place ground sausage. Make sure they're chilled. Add the extra spices and herbs. Lock hands and lock. For less spicy alternative add Tabasco sauce or remove.

Shape into patties roughly 3 to 3 1/2 in width and 1 to 1.5 inch thick. When cooked or air fried, they can shrink.

Place patties on a parchment paper-lined baking tray to avoid sticking.

Put 4-5 patties at a time in an air fryer.

On manual or chicken configuration at 370F, air fryer 20 min. Halfway through cooking take the tray out to flip the patties. When you reinsert the tray, the cooking will begin.

Remove sausage from air-fryers as soon as the timer is off. Put on and cover with a clean plate. Repeat on extra patties.

Serve with your option of extra Tabasco sauce or gravy.

NUTRITIONAL INFORMATION

Total Fat 4.4g Saturated Fat 1.2g, 15% Cholesterol 45.2mg, 4% Sodium 84.6mg, 4% Total Carbohydrate 11.3g, 3% Dietary Fiber 0.8g, Sugars 1g 22%, Protein 11.2g, 17% Vitamin C 10.1mg, 6% Iron 1mg

268. WHOLE SALMON CAKES

INGREDIENTS

- 1 lb ALDI Fresh Atlantic Salmon Side (half a side)
- 1/4 Cup Avocado, mashed
- 1/4 Cup Cilantro, diced + additional for garnish
- 1 1/2 tsp Yellow curry powder
- 1/2 tsp Stonemill Sea Salt Grinder
- 1/4 Cup + 4 tsp Tapioca Starch, divided (40g)
- 2 SimplyNature Organic Cage Free Brown Eggs
- 1/2 Cup SimplyNature Organic Coconut Flakes (30g)
- SimplyNature Organic Coconut Oil, melted (for brushing)

For The Greens:

- 2 tsp SimplyNature Organic Coconut Oil, melted
- 6 Cups SimplyNature Organic Arugula & Spinach Mix, tightly packed
- Pinch of Stonemill Sea Salt Grinder

INSTRUCTIONS

Cut the salmon skin, dice the flesh and place in a large bowl.

Add the avocado, coriander, curry powder, sea salt and whisk until well combined. Then, whisk the tapioca starch in 4 tsp until well absorbed.

Line a parchment-papered baking sheet. Forme the salmon into 8, 1/4 cup-sized patties, slightly over 1/2 inch thick, and put on the plate. Freeze for 20 minutes so they can work with more quickly.

While the patties freeze, preheat your Air Fryer 10 minutes to 400 degrees and rub the basket with coconut oil. Whisk the eggs in addition, and growing them in a shallow dish. In separate shallow dishes, put the remaining 1/4 cup of Tapioca starch and the coconut flakes as well.

Dip one into the tapioca starch once the patties have cooled, ensuring it is fully covered. Then dip it into the shell, completely cover it and gently brush off any excess. Finally, just push the cake's top and sides into the coconut flakes and place it in the air fryer, coconut flake-side up. Repeat with all those cookies.

Brush the tops gently with a bit of melted coconut oil (optional but recommended) and cook until golden brown and crispy on the outside, and the inside is juicy and tender around 15 minutes. Note: The patties will stick a little bit to the basked Air Fryer, so use a sharp-edged spatula to extract them.

Heat the coconut oil up in a large pan over medium heat when the cakes have about 5 minutes left to cook. Add a pinch of salt and cook in the Arugula and Spinach Mix, stirring constantly until the greens start to wilt, just 30 seconds-1 minute.

Divide the greens into 4 bowls, then the salmon cakes. Garnish with DEVOUR and extra cilantro!

269. TWICE AIR FRIED POTATOES

INGREDIENTS

- 2 large Idaho Russet Baking Potatoes
- 1 to 2 teaspoons olive oil leave out to make oil free
- 1/4 cup unsweetened vegan yogurt
- 1/4 cup unsweetened nondairy milk
- 2 tablespoons nutritional   yeast
- 1/2 teaspoon salt sub your favorite salt free substitute to make salt free
- 1/4 teaspoon pepper
- 1 cup chopped spinach or kale
- Optional Topping Ingredients:
- 1/4 cup unsweetened vegan yogurt
- Smoked salt and pepper
- Chopped chives parsley or other favorite fresh herb

INSTRUCTIONS

Fry each potato on all sides with oil.

If your model does not need it, preheat your air fryer to 390 °. Remove the potatoes to your air-fryer basket once it's dry.

Set the cooking time to 30 minutes, then turn over the potatoes and cook for another 30 minutes when the time is up.

Note: You may need to cook another 10 to 20 minutes, depending on the size of your potatoes. You should know when you can quickly pierce it with a fork, they're full.

Let the potatoes cool enough to touch them without getting yourself burnt.

Cut each potato in half lengthwise and scoop out the center of the potato carefully, thus leaving enough to create a stable shell of the potato skin and a thin layer of the white part.

For smooth, mash the scooped potato, vegan yogurt, nondairy milk, NUTRITIONAL yeast, salt, and pepper.

Remove the chopped spinach, and fill the mixture with the potato shells.

You may be able to cook all 4 halves simultaneously, or you may have to cook 2 of them at a time, depending on the size of your air fryer.

Cook for 5 minutes at 350 degrees (or as close as you can set your air-fryer to that).

Serve with your list of top options, and enjoy!

270. TEX MEX CAULIFLOWER RICE

INGREDIENTS

- 1 medium cauliflower
- 1 tbsp oil
- 400 g tin black beans, drained (240g, or 1 1/4 cups, when drained)
- 100 g (2/3 cup) tinned sweetcorn
- 3 spring onions, sliced
- 1 tsp smoked paprika
- 1/2 tsp ground cumin
- 1/4 tsp hot chilli powder

- Salt
- Black pepper
- 50 g cheddar cheese, grated (~ 1/2 cup when grated)
- Toppings, to serve: your choice of sliced avocado, fresh coriander (cilantro), spring onions, sour cream, salsa, etc.

INSTRUCTIONS

Cut the leaves from the cauliflower, and break the cauliflower into florets by itself. Place it in a food processor, and blast until it looks like rice.

Place the cauliflower rice with a drizzle of oil into the Actifry. Cook, until softly golden brown, for 20 minutes.

Scrape the Actifry sides, then add the black beans, sweetcorn, spring onions, spices, and seasoning. Cook for another 10 minutes, then add the cheese and cook for an additional 5 minutes. Scrape the Actifry sides again, and serve with the toppings you want.

NUTRITIONAL INFORMATION

Amount Per Serving (1 portion) Calories 436 Calories from Fat 154% Daily Value, Fat 17.1g26% Saturated Fat 6.5g33%, Cholesterol 26mg9%, Sodium 336mg14%, Potassium 1536mg44%, Carbohydrates 55g18%, Fiber 18.6g74%, Sugar 10.2g11%, Protein 23.5g47%, Calcium 220mg22%, Iron 6.3mg35%

271. CRISPY AVOCADO TACOS

INGREDIENTS

- Salsa (can sub your favorite store bought)
- 1 cup finely chopped or crushed pineapple 240 g
- 1 roma tomato finely chopped
- 1/2 red bell pepper finely chopped
- 1/2 of a medium red onion 1/2 cup, finely chopped
- 1 clove garlic minced
- 1/2 jalapeno finely chopped
- Pinch each cumin and salt
- Avocado Tacos
- 1 avocado
- 1/4 cup all-purpose flour 35 g
- 1 large egg whisked
- 1/2 cup panko crumbs 65 g
- Pinch each salt and pepper
- 4 flour tortillas click for recipe
- Adobo Sauce
- 1/4 cup plain yogurt 60 g
- 2 Tbsp mayonnaise 30 g
- 1/4 tsp lime juice
- 1 Tbsp adobo sauce from a jar of chipotle peppers

INSTRUCTIONS

Salsa: Mix all the Salsa ingredients (in the food processor, finely chop by hand or blitz), cover, and put in the refrigerator.

Prep Avocado: Lengthwise cut an avocado in half, and remove the pit. Place the skin side of the avocado down and cut each half into 4 parts of equal size, then gently peel the skin off each.

Prep Station: Preheat oven to 450 F (230 C) or 375 F (190 C) air fryer. Arrange your workspace so that you have a bowl of flour, a bowl of whisked egg, a bowl of panko mixed in with S&P, and a baking sheet filled with parchments at the top.

Coat: Dip every slice of avocado into the flour first, then the egg and then the panko. Place onto the prepared baking sheet, bake or fry for 10 minutes, Flipping over cooking halfway, until finely browned.

Sauce: Mix all of the sauce ingredients while the avocados are cooking.

Serve: spoon salsa on a tortilla, top with 2 bits of avocado and sauce to drizzle over. Serve straight away, and enjoy!

NUTRITIONAL INFORMATION

Serving: 2tacos, Calories: 624kcal, Carbohydrates: 70.7g, Protein: 14.1g, Fat: 34.7g, Saturated Fat: 7.1g, Cholesterol: 100mg, Sodium: 281mg, Potassium: 1110mg, Fiber: 13.7g, Sugar: 17.1g, Calcium: 130mg, Iron: 4.9mg

272. TORTILLA CHISP

INGREDIENTS

3 Mission Yellow corn extra thin tortillas (or tortillas of choice) Cooking Spray Salt

INSTRUCTIONS

Air fryer preheat to 400 degrees. Cut the tortillas from the corn into triangles. I stacked up the tortillas, cut them all in half and then split them into nine triangles. Place the tortilla chips in the basket of your air fryer and sprinkle them with spray. Sprinkle with salt, then cook for 5 minutes. Take out the basket and flip it over to them. Sprinkle them once more, and continue to cook for 3 minutes.

273. CRUMBLE WITH BLUEBERRIES AND APPLE

INGREDIENTS

- 1 medium apple finely diced
- 1/2 cup frozen blueberries strawberries, or peaches
- 1/4 cup plus 1 tablespoon brown rice flour
- 2 tablespoons sugar
- 1/2 teaspoon ground cinnamon
- 2 tablespoons nondairy butter

INSTRUCTIONS

Preheat the air fryer for 5 minutes until 350 ° F. In an air fryer, mix the apple and the frozen blueberries–safe baking pan or ramekin.

Combine the flour, sugar, cinnamon, and butter in a small bowl. Spoon the mixture of flour over the fruit. Sprinkle some extra flour overall to cover any exposed fruit. Cook for 15 minutes, at 350 ° F.

NUTRITIONAL INFORMATION

Calories: 310kcal, Carbohydrates: 50g, Protein: 2g, Fat: 12g, Saturated Fat: 7g, Cholesterol: 31mg, Sodium: 5mg, Fiber: 5g, Sugar: 26g

274. MADAGASCAN BEAN STEW

INGREDIENTS

- 200 g (7 oz) baby new potatoes
- 1 tbsp oil
- 1/2 onion, finely diced
- 400 g tin black beans, drained but not rinsed (240g, or 1 1/4 cups, when drained)
- 400 g tin kidney beans, drained but not rinsed (240g, or 1 1/4 cups, when drained)
- 3 cloves garlic, minced
- 1 tbsp pureed ginger
- 2 large tomatoes, chopped
- 1 tbsp tomato puree
- Salt
- Black pepper
- 250 ml (1 cup) vegetable stock
- 1/2 tbsp cornstarch
- 1 tbsp water
- 1 large handful rocket (arugula)
- Cooked rice, to serve (optional)

INSTRUCTIONS

Cut the new baby potatoes into quarters, then add a dash of oil to the ActiFry. Set to 220 ° the ActiFry and cook for 10 minutes. Attach the chopped onion, then cook for another four minutes.

Then add the beans, garlic, ginger, tomatoes, puree tomatoes, and seasoning. Put the vegetable stock over.

Mix the cornstarch in a small bowl with a tiny dash of water, until smooth. Add that to the ActiFry too. Cook 15 more minutes.

Add the rocket, then cook for another 4 minutes, until wilted. add few extra tomato wedges with the rocket too, just for a slightly different look!

When needed serve hot with rice.

275. EGGPLANT BACON

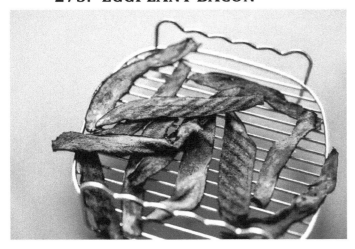

INGREDIENTS

- 1 medium eggplant
- 2 Tbsp soy sauce 30 mL, or tamari for GF option
- 1 Tbsp toasted sesame oil 15 mL
- 1 Tbsp olive oil 15 mL
- 1 tsp maple syrup 5 mL
- 1 tsp lemon juice 5 mL
- 1 tsp smoked paprika
- 1/2 tsp each salt, black pepper, and cumin
- 1/4 tsp vegan Worcestershire sauce

INSTRUCTIONS

Prep: Preheat oven or air fryer to 300 degrees F (150 C). Cut eggplant lengthwise into pieces, then slice thinly into long strips that resemble bacon (about 1/8 inch thick, a mandolin slicer makes this easier).

Flavor: Mix the remaining ingredients into a small bowl to mix. Liberally rub the eggplant slices onto both sides.

Cook: If the air is frying, place the bacon in your air frying pan in a single layer and cook for 10 to 15 minutes until dry and browned. When baking, place in a single layer on a parchment-lined baking sheet, and bake for 30 to 40 minutes, until dry and brown.

NUTRITIONAL INFORMATION

Serving: 1 serving Calories: 99kcal, Carbohydrates: 8.9g, Protein: 1.7g, Fat: 7.2g, Saturated Fat: 1g, Sodium: 748mg, Potassium: 297mg, Fiber: 4.3g, Sugar: 4.7g, Calcium: 10mg, Iron: 0.5mg

276. RIBEYE WITH COFFEE AND SPICE

INGREDIENTS

- 1 lb. ribeye steak
- 1 1/2 tsp. course sea salt
- 1 tsp. brown sugar
- 1/2 tsp. ground coffee
- 1/2 tsp. black pepper
- 1/4 tsp. chili powder
- 1/4 tsp. garlic powder
- 1/4 tsp. onion powder
- 1/4 tsp. paprika
- 1/4 tsp. chipotle powder
- 1/8 tsp. coriander
- 1/8 tsp. cocoa powder

INSTRUCTIONS

In a small bowl add the spices all over. Using a whisk-combine spice, make sure the brown sugar breaks down.

Sprinkle a large amount of spice mixture onto a platter. Lay one steak over spices. Steak liberally with spice mix then season and rub evenly into beef. Flip to ensure that the other hand always gets trained properly.

Pick up steak and force both sides into the remaining spice mix on the plate to avoid wasting any of the spices.

Let the steak sit for a minimum of 20 minutes to reach room temperature. It helps cook the steak evenly.

Meanwhile-Prepare air fryer tray to prevent sticking by coating it with oil. Preheat air fryer for at least 3 minutes, to 390 degrees.

Cook steak for 9 minutes, without disturbance. Do not open, and do not flip.

Once you have finished cooking time, remove from the air fryer and let rest for at least 5 minutes before slicing.

NUTRITIONAL INFORMATION

Calories: 495kcal, Carbohydrates: 5g, Protein: 46g, Fat: 32g, Saturated Fat: 14g, Cholesterol: 138mg, Sodium: 1573mg, Potassium: 607mg, Sugar: 2g, Vitamin A: 705IU, Vitamin C: 1.7mg, Calcium: 21mg, Iron: 4.5mg

277. BULGOGI BURGERS

INGREDIENTS

- For the Bulgogi Burgers:
- 1 pound (453.59 g) Lean Ground Beef
- 2 tablespoon (2 tablespoon) gochujang
- 1 tablespoon (1 tablespoon) dark soy sauce
- 2 teaspoon (2 teaspoon) Minced Garlic
- 2 teaspoon (2 teaspoon) minced ginger
- 2 teaspoon (2 teaspoon) Sugar
- 1 tablespoon (1 tablespoon) Sesame Oil
- 1/4 cup (25 g) Green Onions
- 1/2 tsp (0.5 tsp) Salt
- For the Gochujang Mayonaisse
- 1/4 cup (56 g) Mayonnaise
- 1 tablespoon (1 tablespoon) gochujang
- 1 tablespoon (1 tablespoon) Sesame Oil
- 2 teaspoon (2 teaspoon) Sesame Seeds
- 1/4 cup (25 g) scallions, chopped
- 4 (4) hamburger buns for serving

INSTRUCTIONS

In a large bowl, mix the ground beef, gochujang, soy sauce, garlic, ginger, sugar, sesame oil, chopped onions, and salt and allow the mixture to rest in a fridge for 30 minutes or up to 24 hours.

Divide the meat into four portions and form round patties with a slight depression in the middle to prevent the burgers from blowing out in a dome-shaped cooking process.

Set your air fryer for 10 minutes at 360F, and put the patties in the air fryer basket in a single layer.

Make sure the Gochujang Mayonnaise: combines together the sesame oil, mayonnaise, gochujang, sesame seeds, and scallions when cooking the patties.

NUTRITIONAL INFORMATION

Calories: 392kcal, Carbohydrates: 7g, Protein: 24g, Fat: 29g, Saturated Fat: 7g, Sugar: 3g

278. BOURBON BACON BURGER

INGREDIENTS

- 1 tablespoon bourbon
- 2 tablespoons brown sugar
- 3 strips maple bacon cut in half
- ¾ pound ground beef 80% lean
- 1 tablespoon minced onion
- 2 tablespoons bbq sauce
- ½ teaspoon salt
- freshly ground black pepper
- 2 slices colby jack cheese or monterey jack
- 2 kaiser rolls
- lettuce and tomato for serving
- zesty burger sauce:
- 2 tablespoons bbq sauce
- 2 tablespoons mayonnaise
- ¼ teaspoon ground paprika
- freshly ground black pepper

INSTRUCTIONS

Preheat the air fryer to 390oF and pour a small amount of water into the bottom of the container. (This will help prevent the burning and oxidation of the grease that drips into the bottom drawer.) In a small bowl, mix bourbon and brown sugar. Place the strips of bacon in the basket of air fryer and brush with a brown sugar mix. 4 minute air-fry at 390oF. Flip the bacon over, brush with more brown sugar and 390oF air-fry for another 4 minutes, until crispy.

Build the burger patties whilst the bacon is frying. In a large bowl, add the ground beef, onion, BBQ sauce, salt, and pepper. Thoroughly mix with your hands and shape the meat into 2 patties.

Move the burger patties to the air fryer basket and deep-fry the burgers for 15 to 20 minutes at 370oF, depending on how cooked you like your burger (15 minutes for mild to medium-rare; 20 minutes for well-done). Flip the burgers halfway through the process of cooking.

While the burgers are air-frying, they make the burger sauce to taste in a bowl by mixing the BBQ sauce with mayonnaise, paprika and freshly ground black pepper.

Once the burgers are cooked to your taste, top each patty for another minute with a slice of Colby Jack cheese and air-fry, just to melt the cheese. (You might want to pin the cheese slice with a toothpick to the burger so it doesn't blow in your air fryer Layer the sauce inside the Kaiser rolls, place the burgers on the sheets, top with the bourbon bacon, lettuce, and tomatoes and enjoy!

279. , EGG, SAUSAGE AND CHEESE, BREAKFAST BURRITO

INGREDIENTS

- 4 eggs
- 1 pound ground sausage
- 1/2 cup red pepper, diced (into 1 inch cubes)
- 1/2 cup salsa (any type)
- 4 tortilla shells
- 1/2 cup shredded cheese any type (I used Colby Jack)

INSTRUCTIONS

Scramble the eggs in a frying pan then remove the eggs and set aside.

Brown the sausage in the same skillet, and diced red peppers. Keep breaking the sausage until it is cooked to the full.

Once the sausage is fully cooked, add the eggs and the salsa and mix everything together.

Scoop about 3 table cubits of filling in the middle of a tortilla.

Roll up with two toothpicks, and lock it. Spray the tortilla outside with a spray of olive oil.

Place the fryer, tray or basket in the air and see the temperature for 5 minutes at 400 degrees F. As soon as the tortilla starts crisping up. Stir in some cheese. Continue airbrushing until the cheese is melted.

280. CARNE ASADA

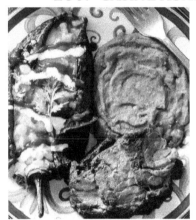

INGREDIENTS

- 2 medium (2 medium) limes, juiced
- 1 medium (1 medium) orange, peeled and seeded
- 1 cup (16 g) Cilantro
- 1 (1) Jalapeño pepper, diced
- 2 tablespoons (2 tablespoons) Vegetable Oil
- 2 tablespoons (2 tablespoons) White Vinegar
- 2 teaspoons (2 teaspoons) Ancho Chile Powder
- 1 teaspoons (2 teaspoons) splenda, or 2 teaspoon sugar
- 1 teaspoon (1 teaspoon) Salt
- 1 teaspoon (1 teaspoon) cumin seeds
- 1 teaspoon (1 teaspoon) Coriander Seeds
- 1.5 pounds (680.39 g) skirt steak

INSTRUCTIONS

Place all ingredients in a blender except the skirt steak, and combine until a smooth sauce is obtained.

Cut the steak of the skirt into four sections, and put it in a plastic zip-top bag.

Pour the marinade over the steak and allow the meat to marinate in the refrigerator for 30 minutes, or up to 24 hours.

Set your air fryer to 400F and put the steaks in the basket for the air fryer. It may need to be done in two parts, depending on the size of your air fryer.

Cook for 8 minutes, or until the internal temperature of your steak hits145F. It is essential not to overcook the skirt steak so that the meat is not toughened.

Let the steak take 10 minutes to rest. Don't rush the stage. Cut the steak against the grain (this part is essential) and serve.

281. LOW-CARB KETO BEEF SATAY

INGREDIENTS

- 1 pound beef flank steak, sliced thinly into long strips
- 2 tablespoons Oil
- 1 tablespoon Fish Sauce
- 1 tablespoon Soy Sauce
- 1 tablespoon minced ginger
- 1 tablespoon Minced Garlic
- 1 tablespoon Sugar
- 1 teaspoon Sriracha Sauce
- 1 teaspoon Ground Coriander
- 1/2 cup chopped cilantro, divided
- 1/4 cup chopped roasted peanuts

INSTRUCTION

Bring the strips of beef into a large bowl or a ziplock container.

Fill the beef with oil, fish sauce, soy sauce, ginger, garlic, sugar, Sriracha, coriander, and 1/4 cup cilantro and mix well. Marinate in the refrigerator for 30 minutes, or up to 24 hours.

Place the strips of beef in the air fryer basket using a pair of tongs, lay them side by side and eliminate overlap.

Place as much marinade as possible behind, and dump this marinade.

Set your air fryer to 8 minutes at 400F, flipping halfway once.

Remove the meat into a serving tray, top with the remaining 1/4 cup of chopped coriander and the chopped peanuts.

Easy Peanut Sauce to serve.

282. PALEO KETO CHICKEN COCONUT MEATBALLS

INGREDIENTS

- 1 pound (453.59 g) Ground Chicken
- 2 (2) Green Onions, finely chopped
- 1/2 cup (8 g) Cilantro, chopped
- 1 tablespoon (1 tablespoon) Hoisin Sauce
- 1 tablespoon (1 tablespoon) Soy Sauce
- 1 teaspoon (1 teaspoon) Sriracha Sauce
- 1 teaspoon (1 teaspoon) Sesame Oil
- 1/4 cup (23.25 g) Unsweetened Shredded Coconut
- Salt, to taste
- Ground Black Pepper, to taste

INSTRUCTIONS

Airfryer instructions

It turned out to be really good in an air fryer, the only problem is that It could fit only 6-8 at a time and you would have to do it in lots.

Cook for 10 minutes at 350F, flipping once before they hit 150-165F indoor temperature.

Brown on for 2-3 minutes at 400.

NUTRITIONAL INFORMATION

Serving: 1g, Calories: 223kcal, Carbohydrates: 3g, Protein: 20g, Fat: 14g, Saturated Fat: 6g, Fiber: 1g Sugar: 1g

283. CRUNCHY AVOCADO FRIES

INGREDIENTS

- 1 avocado
- 1 egg
- 1/2 cup panko bread crumbs
- 1/2 teaspoon salt

INSTRUCTIONS

Get a mature, yet firm, avocado. Cut in half, and carry the pit forward. Cut wedges into an avocado.

In one tub, suck the egg with salt. Remove panko to another saucepan.

Dip the wedges into the mixture of the eggs, then the crumbs in the panko.

Place the wedges in a single layer for 8-10 minutes in preheated to 400F air fryer. Halfway through shake.

When they are lightly brown, they're done.

NUTRITIONAL INFORMATION

Calories: 251kcal, Carbohydrates: 19g, Protein: 6g, Fat: 17g, Saturated Fat: 3g, Cholesterol: 81mg, Sodium: 729mg, Potassium: 547mg, Fiber: 7g, Sugar: 1g, Vitamin A: 265IU, Vitamin C: 10.1mg, Calcium: 52mg, Iron: 1.7mg

284. CORNISH HEN

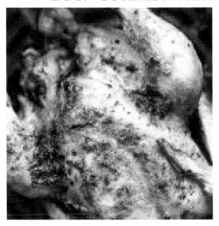

INGREDIENTS

- 1 cornish hen
- salt
- black pepper
- paprika
- coconut spray or olive oil spray

INSTRUCTIONS

Wash Corish hen with spices. Spray Olive oil or coconut oil spray basket with the air fryer. Place Cornish hen (390F for 25 minutes) in your Air Fryer. Turn over halfway. Take it carefully, and serve

NUTRITIONAL INFORMATION

Calories: 300kcal, Protein: 25g, Fat: 21g, Saturated Fat: 5g, Cholesterol: 151mg, Sodium: 91mg, Potassium: 354mg, Vitamin A: 160IU, Vitamin C: 0.7mg, Calcium: 17mg, Iron: 1.2mg

285. BRUSSEL SPROUTS

INGREDIENTS

- 2 cups Brussels sprouts – sliced lengthwise into 1/4 thick pieces
- 1 tablespoon olive oil OR maple syrup
- 1 tablespoon balsamic vinegar
- 1/4 teaspoon sea salt

INSTRUCTIONS

Toss the Brussels, oil, or maple syrup, vinegar and salt together in a bowl.

Cook for 8-10 minutes at 400F, shake (and check their progress) after 5 minutes and then at a mark of 8. You go for browned and crispy, but not burnt!

286. AIR-FRIED OKRA

INGREDIENTS:

- 7-8 ounces fresh okra
- 1 egg
- 1 cup skim milk
- 1 cup breadcrumbs
- 1/2 teaspoon sea salt
- oil for misting or cooking spray

INSTRUCTIONS

Cut the stem ends from the okra, and cut into slices of 1/2 inch.

Beat egg and milk together in a medium-sized bowl. Add slices of okra and then stir to coat.

Combine the breadcrumbs and salt together in a sealable plastic bag or jar with a lid.

Remove okra from egg mixture, letting excess drip off, and transfer into the bag with breadcrumbs. Be sure okra is well-drained before placing it in the breadcrumbs. You might want to use a slotted spoon to raise a little okra at a time and let drip off plenty of the egg wash before placing it in the breadcrumbs.

Shake the crumbs in okra to coat well.

Place all the coated okra in the air fryer basket and mist with oil or spray for cooking. Okra doesn't need to be in a single later time, and at this stage, it's not appropriate to spray both sides. A strong spritz is going to do on top.

Cook for 5 minutes, at 390 F. Shake basket to redistribute as you shake, and give it another oil spritz.

Cook for 5 minutes. Shake again, and dust. Cook longer for 2 to 5 minutes, or until golden brown and crispy.

287. EASY COCONUT PIE

INGREDIENTS

- 2 eggs
- 1 1/2 cups milk (you can use coconut milk or almond milk)
- 1/4 cup butter
- 1 1/2 tsp. vanilla extract
- 1 cup shredded coconut (I used sweetened)
- 1/2 cup Monk Fruit (or your preferred sugar)
- 1/2 cup coconut flour

INSTRUCTIONS

Coat a Six Non-stick spray pie plate and cover with batter. Continue to follow the INSTRUCTIONS set out above.

Cook on the Air Fryer for 10 to 12 minutes at 350 degrees. Check the pie halfway through the cooking time to make sure it isn't burning, give a turn to the plate, use a toothpick to check for doneness. Continue cooking accordingly. Cooking time for an air fryer can vary from one manufacturer to another.

288. GLUTEN-FREE LOW-CARB CHOCOLATE LAVA CAKE

INGREDIENTS

- 1 egg
- 2 tablespoons cocoa powder
- 2 tablespoons water
- 2 tablespoons non-GMO erythritol
- 1/8 teaspoon Now Brand Better Stevia
- 1 tablespoon golden flaxmeal
- 1 tablespoon coconut oil, melted
- 1/2 teaspoon aluminum-free baking powder
- dash of vanilla
- pinch of Himalayan salt

INSTRUCTIONS

Whisk all the ingredients into a Pyrex or ramekin 2-cup glass dish.

Preheat the air fryer just for a minute at 350 °.

Place glass dish in the air fryer with cake mixture and bake for 8-9 minutes at 350 ° C.

Take off the dish carefully with an oven mitt.

Let it cool for some minutes then enjoy it!

289. EASY OMELETTE

INGREDIENTS

- 2 eggs
- 1/4 cup milk
- Pinch of salt
- Fresh meat and veggies, diced (red bell pepper, green onions, ham and mushrooms)
- 1 teaspoon McCormick Good Morning Breakfast Seasoning – Garden Herb
- 1/4 cup shredded cheese (I used cheddar and mozzarella)

INSTRUCTIONS

Combine the eggs and milk in a small bowl, until well mixed.

Pour a pinch of salt into the mixture of the eggs.

Add the egg mixture to your veggies.

Pour the mixture of the eggs into a well grated 6 Then x3 Pan-pan.

Put the pan in the air fryer bowl.

Cook 8–10 minutes at 350 degrees Fahrenheit.

Sprinkle the breakfast seasoning onto the eggs halfway through the cooking, and sprinkle the cheese over the top.

To loosen the omelet from the sides of the pan, use a thin spatula and transfer it to a plate.

Add extra green onions to garnish, optional

290. PARMESAN DILL FRIED PICKLE CHIPS

INGREDIENTS

- 32 oz. jar whole large dill pickles
- 2 eggs
- 2/3 c. panko bread crumbs
- 1/3 c. grated Parmesan
- 1/4 tsp. dried dill weed

INSTRUCTIONS

Slice the pickles into 1/4 thick slices, diagonally. Place between paper towel layers, and pat dry. Beat the eggs, until smooth, in a shallow bowl. Add the Panko bread crumbs, Parmesan and dill weed into a resealable bag and shake until well combined. In 4-5 piece batches, dip the pickle slices into the egg mixture, be sure to remove any excess egg and then toss them in the Panko mix. Add half of the powdered pickle chips to the Airfryer and bake at the highest temperature for 8-10 minutes. Remove and add the remaining pickle chips from the Airfryer and bake for 8-10 minutes. Serve for dipping straight away with a zesty ranch.

NOTE: You can cook all of the chips in one batch if you own a bigger XL Airfryer.

291. FRIED CATFISH

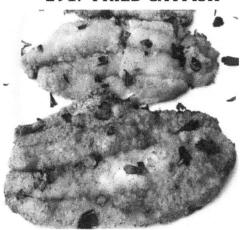

INGREDIENTS

- 4 catfish fillets
- 1/4 cup seasoned fish fry I used Louisiana
- 1 tbsp olive oil
- 1 tbsp chopped parsley optional

INSTRUCTIONS

Preheat Air Fryer to 400 ° C.

Rinse the catfish, and dry brush.

Pour the fried fish into a big Ziploc bag for seasoning.

Add catfish, one at a time, into the bag. Seal, and shake the jar. Ensure seasoning coats the entire filet.

Sprinkle the olive oil over each filet.

Place the filet in the basket at Air Fryer. (Because of the size of my filets I cooked each at a time). Open and simmer for 10 minutes.

Flip over the shrimp. Cook for 10 minutes.

Flip over the snake.

Cook for another 2-3 minutes or until crispness desired.

Top with some parsley.

292. GREEK SPANAKOPITA PIE

INGREDIENTS

- Philips Airfryer
- Leftover Turkey brown meat shredded
- Filo Pastry
- 2 Large Eggs
- 1 Small Egg reserved for pastry brushing
- 200 g Spinach
- 1 Large Onion
- 2 Large Eggs
- 250 g Cream Cheese
- 100 g Feta Cheese chopped into small cubes
- 1 Tsp Basil
- 1 Tbsp Oregano
- 1 Tbsp Thyme
- Salt & Pepper
- Metric - Imperial

INSTRUCTIONS

Get your remaining vegetables out of the refrigerator, and season well with salt and pepper.

Place your vegetables in a pillow or teatowel case, and ring out any excess moisture. Place them with your seasoning and the feta cheese in a mixing bowl.

Mix in your egg and soft cheese until you have a nice creamy blend.

Line a filo pastry dish and add it to your mixture so it's 3/4 full. Fill with the rest of the pastry, then brush with beaten egg. Air-fry on 180c for 20 minutes.

NUTRITIONAL INFORMATION

Calories: 385kcal, Carbohydrates: 9g, Protein: 16g, Fat: 32g, Saturated Fat: 17g, Cholesterol: 295mg, Sodium: 598mg, Potassium: 523mg, Fiber: 2g, Sugar: 4g, Vitamin A: 6035IU, Vitamin C: 18.9mg, Calcium: 298mg, Iron: 3.5mg

293. CRUNCHY BASIL CROUTONS

INGREDIENTS

- 2 heaping cups cubed baguette or your preferred bread, cut in 1 inch pieces
- 2 teaspoons extra virgin olive oil
- 2 teaspoons lemon juice
- 1/2 teaspoon dried oregano
- 1/2 teaspoon dried basil
- 1/2 teaspoon granulated garlic
- Pinch salt & pepper

INSTRUCTIONS

Place the baguette cubed into a large mixing bowl. Drizzle extra virgin olive oil and lemon juice over the bread uniformly. Sprinkle on dried oregano, dried basil, granulated garlic, salt, and pepper.

Toss the cubed bread with your hands, get everything evenly coated and make sure that the spices are on the bread instead of stuck on the sides of the bowl.

Put the bread into the basket for the air fryer. Cook for 5 minutes at 400 degrees, and stop once or twice to shake the basket.

Serve topped with your favorite salad.

NUTRITIONAL INFORMATION

Calories: 30kcal, Carbohydrates: 4g, Fat: 1g, Sodium: 46mg, Potassium: 8mg, Vitamin C: 0.5mg, Calcium: 9mg, Iron: 0.3mg

294. FRIED RAVIOLI

INGREDIENTS

- 1 (14-ounce) jar marinara sauce
- 1 (9-ounce) box cheese ravioli, store-bought or meat ravioli
- 1 teaspoon olive oil
- 2 cups Italian-style bread crumbs
- 1 cup buttermilk
- 1/4 cup Parmesan cheese

INSTRUCTIONS

Submerge ravioli into buttermilk. Add olive oil to the breadcrumbs and then press into the ravioli.

Place the breaded ravioli on baking paper into the heated air fryer and cook for about 5 minutes at 200 ° F. Serve warmly for dipping with marinara sauce.

295. ROSEMARY GARLIC GRILLED PRAWNS

INGREDIENTS

- 8 prawns (medium size will be ideal, mine were large prawns)
- 3-4 garlic cloves (minced)
- 1/2 tbsp melted butter
- 1 sprig rosemary leaves (chopped)
- salt & black pepper
- Green capsicum (prepare 8 slices)

INSTRUCTIONS

Marinate the prawns for an hour or more, with all the above seasoning.

Using 2 prawns per skewer, and 2 capsicum slices.

Preheat the fryer to air.

The prawns are grilled for 5-6 minutes with temperature 180 degrees C.

Raising the temperature to 200 degrees C and grilling for a min.

296. BEEF SCHNITZEL

INGREDIENTS

- 2 tablespoon vegetable oil
- 50g breadcrumbs
- 1 egg, whisked
- 1 thin beef schnitzel
- 1 lemon, to serve

INSTRUCTIONS

Preheat the Airfryer to 180 ° C.

Combine the oil and the breadcrumbs. Keep stirring until the mixture becomes crumbly and loose.

Sprinkle the schnitzel into the egg then shake any remaining.

Dip the schnitzel into the crumb mix to ensure it's covered evenly and completely.

Then, lie gently in the air fryer and cook for 12 minutes. (The period can vary with the thickness of the schnitzel).

Serve with lemon straight away.

297. VEGAN PECAN CRUSTED EGGPLANT

INGREDIENTS:

- 2 tablespoons egg replacer
- 4 tablespoons water
- 1 cup panko breadcrumbs
- 1/4 teaspoon salt
- 1/4 teaspoon pepper
- 1/4 teaspoon dry mustard
- 1/4 teaspoon marjoram
- 1/2 cup pecans
- 6 tablespoons almond milk
- 1 large eggplant, about 1 1/4 pounds
- salt and pepper to taste (for eggplant slices)
- oil for misting or cooking spray

INSTRUCTIONS

In a medium bowl, mix the egg replacer and water, and set aside.

In the food processor place the panko crumbs, 1/4 teaspoon salt, 1/4 teaspoon pepper, mustard, and marjoram. Clean until it finely crushes the crumbs. Remove the pecans and process them in short pulses until finely chopped nuts. Go fast, and don't overdo it!

Air fryer preheats to 390 F.

Move the food processor coating mixture into a shallow dish.

To blend well add almond milk to the egg replacer mixture and whisk.

Cut the eggplant into 1/2 inch slices and brush on to taste with salt and pepper.

Dip the slices of the eggplant into the milk mixture, then roll in the crumbs and press into coat well. Spray oil to both sides.

Place half of the eggplant in the air fryer basket, and cook for 6 to 8 minutes at 390 F or until turn to golden brown and crispy coating.

298. SPINACH FRITTATA

INGREDIENTS

- 1 small red onion - minced
- 1/3 pack of spinach
- 3 eggs
- Salt, pepper n mozzarella cheese

INSTRUCTIONS

Preheat Airfryer at 180deg C In the baking pan, add oil for a min Add minced onions to the pan for 2-3mins or until they have turned translucent Add spinach n fry for 3-5mins to about half cooked. They may have looked a little dry but that's okay, just keep frying with the oil.

Whisk the beaten eggs, add the cheese for 8 minutes or until cooked.

299. BROWNIES AFTER DARK

INGREDIENTS:

- 1 egg
- 1/2 cup granulated sugar
- 1/4 teaspoon salt
- 1/2 teaspoon vanilla
- 1/4 cup butter, melted
- 1/4 cup flour, plus 2 Tablespoons
- 1/4 cup cocoa
- cooking spray

Optional:

- vanilla ice cream
- caramel sauce
- whipped cream

INSTRUCTIONS

Beat the egg, sugar, salt, and vanilla all together until light.

Add the butter melted, and stir well. Stir in cocoa and rice.

Lightly spray 6 "x 6" baking pan with cooking spray.

Put batter in a saucepan and cook for 11 to 13 minutes at 330 ° F. Cool and cut into 4 squares, or 16 little brownie bites.

300. BANANA BREAD

INGREDIENTS

- 4 tablespoons plus 2 teaspoons unsalted butter, at room temperature
- ¾ cup all-purpose flour, plus more for dusting the pan
- ½ very ripe banana, peeled
- ¼ cup light brown sugar
- 2 large eggs
- ¼ cup granulated sugar
- ¾ teaspoon vanilla extract
- 1 teaspoon ground cinnamon
- ¼ teaspoon ground nutmeg
- ¼ teaspoon salt
- ¼ teaspoon baking soda
- teaspoon baking powder
- cup chopped pecans, lightly toasted

INSTRUCTIONS

Grease a loaf pan (or 2 cup capacity) of 5 3/4-inch X 3-inch X 2 1/8-inch, with 2 butter spoons. Slightly Staub the inside of the pan with flour, striking out any excess. Set aside as the batter prepares.

Combine the remaining 4 tablespoons of butter, one half of the banana and the light brown sugar in a medium bowl, and mash together using a spoon back. Apply to the bowl the milk, granulated sugar, vanilla extract, cinnamon, nutmeg and salt, and briskly whisk in to incorporate. Sift soda, baking powder and flour in the baking pan and stir until combined. Fold in the pecans and pour over the batter into the loaf pan. Place the loaf pan in the Air Fryer basket And the drawer closes. Set the temperature for 30 minutes to 320 degrees Fahrenheit and Timer. Set the timer for another 20 minutes, baking until a wooden skewer or a cake tester inserted in the center comes out clean when the timer goes off.

Use tongs to lift the loaf pan out of the basket when it is baked and let it cool for at least 20 minutes before turning the loaf pan over Plate and remove pan for bread release. Cut into slices, and warmly served.

301. BANANA MUFFINS

INGREDEINTS

- Wet Mix
- 4 ripe bananas (Cavendish size)
- 2 eggs
- 90g brown sugar (100g for white sugar)
- 1 tsp vanilla essence
- 3 tbsp milk (can substitute with unsweetened applesauce)
- 1 spoonful Nutella (optional)

Dry Mix

- 250g flour (whole wheat or plain)
- 1 tsp salt
- 1 tsp baking soda
- 1 tsp baking powder
- 1 tsp cinnamon
- 2 tbsp cocoa powder (optional)

Optional

- 1 handful chopped walnuts
- Chocolate sprinkles
- Dried fruits

INSTRUCTIONS

Mash ripened bananas in a bowl, then add the remaining "Wet Mix" Combine perfect.

Banana Bread Muffin-Mix flour Sift "Dry Blend" and add "Wet Mix." Do fold gently to mix, but do not rub vigorously.

Banana Bread Muffin-Walnuts Add chopped walnuts, dried fruits, or sprinkles of chocolate to any option. Sprinkles of chocolate should be available in TODAY.

Banana Bread Muffin-Mixture of cake If in the oven, preheat to 175 ° C. If you have an air fryer, preheat to 120 ° C.

Pour into the muffin cups with batter. Bake for 20-25mins in the oven and for 30mins in the air-fryer or until a toothpick in the middle of the muffin comes out clean.

Banana Bread Muffin-Airfryer Be excited about making delicious muffins! Yeah, I'm not making beautiful muffins but they sure tasted great! Now that I've done this successfully, I can pull back my baking ambitions.

302. CHEESY GARLIC BREAD IN

INGREDIENTS:

- Round Bread Slices-5
- Melted Butter-4 tbsp
- Chopped garlic cloves-3
- Sun Dried Tomato Pesto- 5 tsp
- Grated Mozzarella Cheese-1 cup

INSTRUCTIONS

use baguette bread for my cooking, and cut it into thick, round slices first.

Add some melted butter (in which cloves of garlic were added) to the slices of bread.

Apply each slice with a teaspoon of sun-dried tomato pesto.

A generous amount of grated cheese is added at the top of each slice.

Place these slices of bread in an air fryer and cook them for 6-8 minutes at 180-degree celsius. If you do not have an air fryer you can bake it at 180 degrees in convection mode.

303. PINEAPPLE STICKS WITH YOGHURT DIP

INGREDIENTS

- Pineapple Sticks
- 1/2 pineapple
- 1/4 cup desiccated coconut
- Yoghurt Dip
- 1 small sprig fresh mint
- 1 cup vanilla youghurt

INSTRUCTIONS

Pineapple Sticks: Preheat the fryer up to 200 degrees C.

Cut the pineapple into sticks, which are similar in size to chips.

Dip the pineapple into the desiccated coconut, the pineapple's moisture is sufficient to keep it sticking.

Lay the pineapple sticks gently in the basket and cook Yoghurt Dip for 10 minutes: finely dice the mint leaves, then stir in the vanilla yogurt.

To serve: place the dip in the center of a large plate, in a small bowl. The pineapple sticks are distributed around the bowl.

304. NUTELLA-BANANA SANDWICHES

- • **INGREDIENTS**
- • butter softened
- • 4 SLICES white bread
- • ¼ CUP chocolate hazelnut spread Nutella
- • 1 banana

INSTRUCTIONS

Air fryer preheat to 370oF.

Place the soft butter on one side of all bread slices, and put the slices on the table, buttered side down. Spread the chocolate hazelnut spread across the slices of bread. Cut the banana in half, and slice each half lengthwise into three slices. Place the banana slices on two bread slices, and top with the remaining bread slices to make two sandwiches. Cut the sandwiches in half (triangles or rectangles)-this will make all of them fit in the air fryer at once. The sandwiches are moved to the air fryer.

5-minute air-fry at 370oF. Flip over the sandwiches and air-fry for another 2 to 3 minutes or until the top slices of bread are nicely browned. Grab a glass of milk or a midnight cape while the sandwiches cool down slightly and enjoy

305. STRAWBERRY LEMONADE VEGAN POP TARTS

INGREDIENTS

Strawberry Chia Jam:

- 1 1/2 cups sliced strawberries fresh or frozen
- 1 1/2 cups pitted dark cherries
- 2 tbsp lemon juice or to taste
- 2 tsp maple syrup or to taste
- 3 tbsp chia seeds

Pop-tarts:

- 1 cup whole wheat pastry flour
- 1 cup all purpose flour
- ¼ tsp salt
- 2 tbsp light brown sugar
- 2/3 cup very cold coconut oil
- ½ tsp vanilla extract
- ½ cup (or so) ice cold water

Lemon Glaze:

- 1 1/4 cup powdered sugar
- 2 tbsp lemon juice
- zest of 1 lemon
- 1 tsp melted coconut oil
- ¼ tsp vanilla extract
- Colourful sprinkles to decorate

INSTRUCTIONS

Chia Jam: Heat the cherries and strawberries in a saucepot until they get syrupy and start bubbling. When super soft, pound them with a potato masher until the mixture is jammy, loose and with some clear bits of fruit inside.

Remove, and sample, lemon juice, and maple syrup. Adjust the lemon and maple syrup to suit your fruit's sweetness.

Take off the heat the mixture, move it to a jar and throw in the chia seeds. Allow the mixture to be set for a minimum of 20 minutes, or until it thickens. You will have plenty of extra jams so you can use it all week on toast or on oatmeal.

Pop-tarts: Mix the flours, salt, and sugar in a large bowl. Cut with a pastry cutter or fork into the cold coconut oil until you see tiny pea-shaped pieces on the dough.

Drizzle in the coffee and add one tablespoon in the ice-cold water at a bowl. It should be enough moist to form it into a ball without it flaking away but not sticky.

Cut the dough into your surface and rolling pin, half and lightly flour. Roll out the dough by 7 cm of rectangles to just a few millimeters thick then cut into 5 cm. Place the rectangles lined with a Silpat or parchment paper onto a baking sheet.

Place one heaping jam teaspoon on each of the centering dough rectangles. Then moisten your finger all around the edge (around the jam). Top with another circle, then crimp the edges to seal using your pick.

Poke three sets of 3 holes with your fork into the top of the pop tart. Continue with still pop-tarts. Place the baking sheet in the fridge for 20 minutes to set.

Heat up to 400 F on the Philips air fryer. Add the fryer basket with four pop-tarts, and set the timer for 10 minutes. Remove the remaining pop-tarts and repeat until they are all cooked. Allow for about 20 minutes to cool off.

Lemon Glaze: Blend the powdered sugar, lemon juice, lemon zest, coconut oil, and vanilla extract together in a dish.

Paste-on each pop-tarts about a tablespoon of icing and decorate with your favorite sprinkles and sugars. Let the icing set and enjoy!

306. MOZZARELLA STICKS

INGREDIENTS

- 6 mozzarella sticks
- 1 c. panko bread crumbs
- Kosher salt
- Freshly cracked black pepper
- 2 large eggs, well-beaten
- 3 tbsp. all-purpose flour
- Warm marinara, for serving

INSTRUCTIONS

FOR AIR FRYER

Freeze mozzarella sticks for at least 2 hours, until frozen solid.

Set up a breading station after 3 hours: placed panko, eggs, and flour in three separate shallow bowls. Broadly season the panko with salt and pepper.

Coat frozen mozzarella sticks in flour, then dip into milk, then panko, back into the egg, and then back into the panko.

Arrange frozen breaded mozzarella sticks in the basket of your air fryer in one even row. Cook on 400 ° for 6 minutes, or on the outside until golden and crisp and melt in the center.

Serve it for dipping with moist marinara sauce.

307. SUGARED DOUGH DIPPERS WITH CHOCOLATE AMARETTO SAUCE

INGREDIENTS

- 1 pound bread dough defrosted
- ½ cup butter melted
- 1 cup sugar
- 1 cup heavy cream
- 12 ounces good quality semi-sweet chocolate chips
- 2 tablespoons amaretto liqueur or almond extract

INSTRUCTIONS

Roll the dough into two fifteen-inch logs. Cut every single log into 20 slices. Cut each slice in half, then twist the dough halves 3 to 4 times together. Place the twisted dough on a sheet of cookies, brush with melted butter and sprinkle sugar over the twists of the dough.

Air fryer preheats to 350oF.

Blend melted butter to the bottom of the air fryer basket. Air-fry twists the dough in batches. Place 8 to 12 in the air fryer basket (depending on the size of your air fryer).

Five-minute air-fry. Turn the strips of dough over and brush butter to the other side. Air-fry another 3 minutes.

Build the chocolate amaretto sauce while cooking dough. Bring in the heavy cream over medium heat to a simmer. Place the chocolate chips in a large bowl, and pour over the chocolate chips the hot cream. Stir until the chocolate begins melting. So turn to a whisk and whisk until the chocolate has melted completely and the sauce is smooth. Stir the Amaretto in. Transfer to the serving platform.

Place them into a shallow dish as the batches of dough twists are complete. Brush with melted butter and brush generously with sugar, shaking the platter to cover the two sides.

Serve the sugary dough dippers on the side with the moist Amaretto chocolate sauce.

308. CHURRO DOUGHNUT HOLES

INGREDIENTS

- 1 cup white all purpose flour
- 1/4 cup organic sugar
- 1 teaspoon baking powder
- 1/4 teaspoon cinnamon
- 1/2 teaspoon salt
- 2 tablespoons aquafaba
- 1 tablespoon melted coconut oil
- 1/4 cup soy or almond milk
- 2 teaspoons cinnamon
- 2 tablespoons sugar

INSTRUCTIONS

Blend the flour, sugar, baking powder, cinnamon and salt in a large bowl. Blend well.

Stir aquafaba, coconut oil, and soy milk. Blend well. When I mixed with a fork, I had the best results, then went in with my hands and kneaded the dough together for a few seconds when it became too steep to beat with a fork. You should get a ball of slightly sticky dough when you're done.

Stick the dough bowl in the refrigerator for a total of one hour. You can even make the dough ahead the night. If you do so, store yourself in an airtight container.

Mix the cinnamon and the remaining 2 tablespoons of sugar in a shallow bowl. Put it aside. Cut a piece of parchment paper so that it covers some of the bottoms of your air fryer but does not fully cover it. I'm using a rectangle, and I cut around 1? Less than the edge, letting air flow in plenty.

Remove the dough from the refrigerator, then knead it quickly. Divide the pieces into 12 pieces, shaping them into balls. Dredge each cinnamon sugar ball and arrange on the parchment paper into a single layer, leaving at least 1? Out of space around every ball. I air-fried mine in 2 batches each with 6 Chonut Holes.

Air to fry for 6 minutes at 370F. Shaking these is a disaster. DO NOT SHAKE. Just trust me.

Let them cool off the basket for 5-10 minutes before removing. You want these fully cooled, and the total cooling period depends on how much you fried at once and the size of your bowl.

309. ZEBRA BUTTER CAKE

INGREDIENTS

- 115g butter
- 2 eggs
- 100g castor sugar
- 100g self raising flour, sifted
- 30ml milk
- 1tsp vanilla extract
- 1 tbsp of cocoa powder

INSTRUCTIONS

Airfryer preheats to 160C. Line the 6 "baking tin base and grease the surface of the tray Beat butter and sugar in a mixer until fluffy Add eggs one at a time and add vanilla extract and milk. Mix well in mixer Add sifted flour and mix until half batter is mixed and set aside Add cocoa powder to a mixer and mix well Scoop 2 tablespoons of plain batter in the center of a baking tin. Place the baking tin in the air fryer and bake for 30 minutes at 160C, or until skewer appears clean.

310. EASY CHOCOLATE SOUFFLE

INGREDIENTS

- 3 ounces semi-sweet chocolate, chopped
- 1/4 cup butter
- 2 eggs, separated
- 3 tablespoons sugar
- 1/2 teaspoon pure vanilla extract
- 2 tablespoons all-purpose flour
- powdered sugar for garnish
- whipped cream for topping (optional)

INSTRUCTIONS

Two 6-ounce ramekins with butter and sugar. (Butter the ramekins and then add sugar to the butter by shaking it in a ramekin and dumping any excess.) Melt the chocolate and butter in a double boiler put aside.

The egg yolks beat vigorously in a separate bowl. Stir in the sugar and vanilla extract and beat again well. Drizzle in butter and chocolate, then mix well.

Stir in the flour, mix until no lumps are present.

Pre-heat the air fryer to 330oF. Whisk the egg whites in a separate bowl to a soft peak level when they can "nearly" stand up at the end of the whisk.

Do you fold? Gently incorporate the whipped egg whites in the chocolate mixture until all the whites have been mixed with the chocolate mixture in the remaining egg whites.

Carefully transfer the batter to the buttered ramekins, leaving approximately 1/2-inch above. (You may have a little extra batter depending on how airy the batter is, so if you want, you might be able to squeeze out a third soufflé.) Place the ramekins in the air fryer basket and air-fry for 14 min.

The soufflés should have gotten up beautifully and brown on top. (Don't worry if the top turns a little dark in the next step you'll cover it with powdered sugar. Dust it with powdered sugar and serve immediately.

you can serve a slightly warm souffle and overlaid it with whipped cream.

311. THAI-STYLE FRIED BANANAS

INGREDIENTS

- 4 Ripe Bananas
- 2 tablespoons All Purpose Flour (Maida)
- 2 tablespoons Rice flour
- 2 tablespoons Corn flour
- 2 tablespoons Dessicated Coconut
- 1 pinch Salt
- 1/2 teaspoon Baking powder
- 1/2 teaspoon Cardamom Powder (Elaichi) , (optional)
- Cooking oil , to drizzle
- 1/4 cup Rice flour , for coating
- Sesame seeds (Til seeds) , for coating

INSTRUCTIONS

Get all the ingredients together to start making the Fried Bananas, and keep them handy. We'll start by making the fried banana batter for you. Add the maida, rice flour, cornflour, baking powder, salt, coconut and mix in a large bowl to combine properly. Next, add in small water to make a thick and almost smooth batter at a time. The batter should be so capable of covering a spoon's back. Maintain ready rice flour and sesame seeds. If you use mini bananas (almost a large size of your finger), then slice them in half lengthwise. Cut it in half if you are using a big banana, then slice it halfway through the duration. Keep it aloof. Next grease an 8x 8-inch foil or oil-filled butter paper and brush it with flour. This is so that they do not stick to the foil or the paper when we air fry the batter-dipped bananas. Use the foil or butter paper to pinch the ends so that air circulation leaves a little space.

Dip the banana slices into the wet batter, then roll into the dry rice flour with the wet batter-coated banana slices and then onto the sesame seeds. I like to add sesame seeds to the rim because it adds crunchiness to the fried bananas.

Place the bananas dipped by the batter in the greased foil or butter paper. At 200 ° C, air fry the bananas for 10 to 15 minutes, Flipping around halfway so it gets equally fried all around.

Serve the Thai Crispy Fried Bananas as a tea time snack, or even as a dessert served with vanilla ice cream, when available.

312. CHEESE SAMBOOSA

INGREDIENTS

- For the cheese
- ½ cup of raw cashews (pre-boiled for 10 mins)
- 3 tbsp of NUTRITIONAL yeast
- 3 tbsp + 2 tsp of Tapioca starch
- ¾ tsp sea salt
- 1 tsp apple cider vinegar
- 1¼ cup of water
- For the samboosa
- 1 package of samosa pastry sheets
- 1 tbsp olive oil
- ½ cup water

INSTRUCTIONS

Add all the ingredients of the cheese to a blender, and combine it until smooth.

Pour the blended mixture over medium heat into a small saucepan, then use a wooden spoon or spatula and stir continuously while cooking. You will see tiny clumps begin to form as you do and your mixture will turn into one big gooey mass of cheese at around the five-minute mark. Cook for another 30 seconds to one minute to ensure it's all firm.

Store in a glass container and allow for at least 30 minutes before handling to cool in the refrigerator.

Place a samosa pastry sheet vertically on a cutting board or plate, and start with a light water wash using a pastry brush It allows the edges to stay together better (you may be able to skip it step depending on how dry/humid your sheets are).

Add about 1-2 teaspoons of the cheese mixture to the far right corner, then fold the pastry over the filling in a triangle form using the bottom right "point." Then take the top right of that triangle and fold horizontally, repeating the two previous steps until you have a parcel shaped like a triangle, sealing down the final flap.

Keep until all sheets of samosa have been used up.

313. LEMON TOFU

INGREDIENTS

- 1 pound extra-firm tofu drained and pressed, or use super-firm tofu
- 1 Tablespoon tamari
- 1 Tablespoon cornstarch, or arrowroot powder
- For the sauce:
- 1 teaspoon lemon zest
- 1/3 cup lemon juice
- 1/2 cup water
- 2 Tablespoon organic sugar
- 2 teaspoons cornstarch, or arrowroot powder

INSTRUCTIONS

Place the cubes of tofu in a plastic quarter size storage bag. Put the tamari in and seal the bag. Shake the bag until the tamari is all filled with tofu.

Attach the cornstarch spoonful to the jar. Again shake until coated with tofu. Set the tofu aside to marinate for 15 minutes or more.

In the meantime add all the ingredients in the sauce to a small bowl and mix with a spoon. Deposit back.

Drop the tofu into a single layer in the air fryer. This is probably going to have to be done in two batches. Cook the tofu for 10 minutes at 390 degrees, and shake after 5 minutes.

Once the tofu batches have been cooked, add them all to a skillet over medium - high heat. Give a stir to the sauce, and pour over the tofu. Remove tofu and sauce until the sauce has thickened, and heat the tofu through.

Serve with rice and steamed vegetables immediately, if you so wish.

NUTRITIONAL INFORMATION

Calories: 112kcal , Carbohydrates: 13g , Protein: 8g , Fat: 3g , Sodium: 294mg , Potassium: 250mg , Sugar: 8g , Vitamin C: 8.5mg , Calcium: 36mg , Iron: 1.3mg

314. CLASSIC FALAFEL

INGREDIENTS

- 1 ½ cups dry garbanzo beans
- ½ cup chopped fresh parsley
- ½ cup chopped fresh cilantro
- ½ cup chopped white onion
- 7 cloves garlic
- 2 Tbsp. all purpose flour
- ½ tsp. sea salt
- 1 Tbsp. ground cumin
- tsp. ground cardamom
- 1 tsp. ground coriander
- tsp. cayenne pepper

INSTRUCTIONS

Overnight soak: In a large bowl, place dried garbanzo beans and cover with 1 inch of water. Let them stay for 20-24 hours, uncovered. Drain carefully. Quick soak: In a strainer, rinse garbanzo beans and add them to a large pot. Cover with two water and bring it to boil. Let boil, cover the pot and remove from heat for 1 minute. Let them stay for one hour. Drain carefully.

Add the parsley, cilantro, onion, and garlic in a food processor bowl. Mix well until combined.

To the food processor, add soaked garbanzo beans, rice, cinnamon, cumin, cardamom, cilantro, and cayenne. Pulse until the ingredients form a coarse, rough dish. Occasionally scrape downside of the food processor. Place the mixture in a bowl, cover for 1-2 hours and refrigerate to allow the flavors to come together.

When cooled, remove from the fridge and form into 11/2-inch balls, then slightly flatten the balls to form patties.

Air fryer preheats to 400 ° F. Sprinkle the fryer basket with oil, lightly.

Place falafel in a tub, be careful not to overload. Cook for 10 minutes, and turn through halfway. Repeat with left falafel.

NUTRITIONAL INFORMATION

Per Serving: Calories 150, Total Fat 2.5g (Saturated 0g, Trans 0g), Cholesterol 0mg, Sodium 160mg, Total Carbohydrate 25g (Dietary Fiber 7g, Total Sugars 4g, Includes 0g Added Sugars), Protein 8g, Vitamin D 0%, Calcium 4%, Iron 15%, Potassium 6%

315. VEGAN CORN FRITTERS

INGREDIENTS

- About 2 C of Fresh Frozen or Grilled WHOLE Corn Kernels
- 1 C of Corn + 2-3 Tbl Almond Milk plus salt/pepper for the creamed corn mixture, to taste
- 1/3 C Finely Ground Cornmeal
- 1/3 C Flour
- 1/2 tsp Salt
- 1/4 tsp Pepper
- 1/2 tsp Baking Powder
- Onion Powder to taste
- Garlic Powder to taste
- 1/4 tsp Paprika
- 2 Tbl Green Chiles with juices
- About 1/4 C Chopped Italian Parsley
- Vegetable Oil for frying

FOR THE TANGY DIPPING SAUCE:

- 4 Tbl Vegan Mayonnaise
- 4 tsp Dijon or to taste
- 2 tsp Grainy Mustard or to taste

INSTRUCTIONS

Combine with a whisk the dry ingredients (flour, cornmeal, baking powder, seasonings, and parsley)

Pulse 1 C of corn with 2-3 Tbl of Almond Milk together in a food processor. Season with pepper and salt.

Attach the corn mixture until well mixed into the flour mixture.

Remove 2 C kernels of whole grain, folding to blend. Do not work over, and do not add any more flour or cornmeal. If it appears loose but is going to be firm as they cook.

Preheat a skillet over medium heat, then add approximately 1 tbl of oil.

Pack the batter tightly with a cookie scoop, and place it in the oven. Quickly flatten with a spatula to form a patty shape.

Allow one side to cook until golden and flip, another side to cook. To remove any excess oil, remove to the paper towels. Season to salt. Stir the ingredients in the dipping sauce and serve immediately.

316. LOW CARB CRISPY SEASONED JICAMA FRIES

INGREDIENTS:

- 1 lb jicama
- 3 tbs butter or oil
- 1 tsp chili powder
- 1-2 tsp salt, to taste
- 1/2 tsp garlic powder
- 1/2 tsp onion powder
- dash of paprika
- dash of black pepper

INSTRUCTIONS

Preheat oven to 400 ° C.

Peel & slice the jicama into forms of a French fry. I like to buy Trader Joe's pre-sliced jicama, which lets me bypass most of that step! I'm still double-checking to make sure the fries I want are of the size.

Put jicama slices onto the stove to boil in a bowl. Let boil for 15 minutes. Then take off and dry pat.

Melt the butter/oil and seasonings together.

Toss jicama until evenly coated in seasoning mix.

Spread over a baking sheet in a single layer and bake for 40 mins, flipping through halfway.

When done remove from the oven. Let rest for three to four minutes before serving.

317. CRISPY BAKED ARTICHOKE FRIES

INGREDIENTS

- 1 14 oz can Artichoke Hearts, quartered
- For the Wet Mix:
- 1 cup All Purpose Flour
- 1/2 – 1 cup Unsweetened Plant-Based Milk (I used Almond)
- 1/2 tsp Garlic Powder
- 3/4 tsp Salt
- 1/4 tsp Black Pepper, or to taste

For the Dry Mix:

- 1 1/2 cup Panko Bread Crumbs
- 1/2 tsp Paprika
- 1/4 tsp Salt

INSTRUCTIONS

Preheat it to 500F, if you are using an Oven. Then, drain the Artichoke Hearts can and cut it into quarters.

Place the quartered Artichoke Hearts on half of a big, clean dishtowel on one side. Fold the other half of the towel over the quarters, then press gently to remove moisture. Let the Artichokes sit in the towel to dry further while the Wet and Dry mixes are being prepared.

Prepare the Wet Mix by adding all ingredients to a small bowl that has a wide rim. I suggest you start with 1/2 cup of Plant Milk and then work your way up in 1 tbsp increments. You want the pancake batter to be slightly thicker than the Mix.

Prepare the Dry Mix in a separate small, large rimmed bath.

Dip each Artichoke Quarter into the Wet Mix using separate hands for each mix, gently shake off the excess batter, then put it in the Dry Mix and coat well. Repeat with every piece of Artichoke.

In the oven: put on a grated or lined baking sheet and bake 10-13 minutes at 500F In the Air Fryer: bake 10-13 minutes at 340 F. I baked my Fries in 2 batches, so between the Fries, there was some "breathing space," and they didn't stick together.

Serve warm and with whatever Dipping Sauce you want.

318. BOW TIE PASTA CHIPS

INGREDIENTS

- 2 cups dry whole wheat bow tie pasta (use brown rice pasta to make it gluten-free)
- 1 tablespoon olive oil (or use aquafaba for oil-free option)
- 1 tablespoon yeast
- 1 1/2 teaspoon Italian Seasoning Blend
- 1/2 teaspoon salt

INSTRUCTIONS

Cook the pasta on the box for 1/2 the time it took. Toss with the olive oil or aquafaba, nutritional yeast, Italian seasoning, and salt the drained pasta.

If yours is small, put about half of the mixture in your air fryer basket; larger ones will cook in one pot.

Cook them for 5 minutes at 390 ° F. Shake the basket and cook for another 3 to 5 minutes, or until crunchy.

Note: When they cool down, these will crisp up more.

319. PORTOBELLO MUSHROOM PIZZAS WITH HUMMUS

INGREDIENTS

- 4 large portobello mushrooms
- balsamic vinegar
- salt and black pepper
- 4 tablespoons oil-free pasta sauce (such as 365 Organic)
- 1 clove garlic , minced
- 3 ounces zucchini , shredded, chopped, or julienned (about 1/2 medium)
- 2 tablespoons sweet red pepper , diced
- 4 olives kalamata olives , sliced
- 1 teaspoon dried basil
- 1/2 cups hummus (see notes for Kalamata version)
- fresh basil leaves or other herbs , minced

INSTRUCTIONS

Well, wash out the portobellos. Cut off the stems with a knife, and cut the gills. Pat dry on the insides and brush or spray balsamic vinegar on both sides. Sprinkle salt and pepper over the top.

Place 1 spoonful of pasta sauce within each mushroom and sprinkle with garlic.

Instructions for air fryers Preheat the Air Fryer to 330F. Place as many mushrooms as a single layer will fit, or use a rack to hold two layers. (You may need to do this in batches, depending on your size or air fryer and portobellos.) Air Fry 3 minutes long.

Cut the mushrooms and cover each with equal amounts of zucchini, peppers, and olives and sprinkle with dried basil, salt, and pepper. Returning 3 minutes to the Air Fryer. Inspect and rearrange the mushrooms if using a rack. Switch to the Air Fryer for another 3 minutes, or until tender mushrooms. Drizzle with hummus and sprinkle with basil or other herbs on a tray. You can briefly put the portobellos back in the air fryer to warm the hummus if you want.

320. RADISH HASH BROWNS

INGREDIENTS

- 1 pound Radishes washed
- 1 medium Yellow/Brown Onion
- 1 teaspoon Garlic Powder
- 1 teaspoon Granulated Onion Powder
- 3/4 teaspoon Pink Himalayan Salt (or Sea Salt)
- 1/2 teaspoon Paprika
- 1/4 teaspoon Freshly Ground Black Pepper
- 1 Tablespoon Pure Virgin Coconut Oil

INSTRUCTIONS

Well wash Radishes, and cut off the roots. Remove the steam, and leave 1/4-1/2 inch.

Use a food processor or mandolin, then slice the onions and radishes.

Coconut oil is added and blends well. Grease Basket Air Fryer.

Add Air Fryer Basket with Radishes and Onions.

Cook for 8 minutes at 360 degrees, then turn a few times.

Dump Radishes and Onions into Mixing Bowl again. Attach seasonings to the radishes and onions and cook for five minutes at 400 degrees, shaking halfway through.

NUTRITIONAL INFORMATION

Low Carb Air Fryer Radish Hash Browns Amount Per Serving Calories 62.81Calories from Fat 33% Daily Value Fat 3.68g6% Saturated Fat 3.09g19% Sodium 482mg21% Potassium 313.31mg9% Carbohydrates 7.18g2% Fiber 2.44g10% Sugar 3.32g4% Protein 1.24g2% Vitamin A 123.14IU2% Vitamin C 18.82mg23% Calcium 34.68mg3% Iron 0.49mg3%

321. SWEET SOUR PORK

INGREDIENTS

- 2 pounds Pork cut into chunks
- 2 large Eggs
- 1 teaspoon Pure Sesame Oil (optional)
- 1 cup Potato Starch (or cornstarch)
- 1/2 teaspoon Sea Salt
- 1/4 teaspoon Freshly Ground Black Pepper
- 1/16 teaspoon Chinese Five Spice
- 3 Tablespoons Canola Oil
- Other
- Oil Mister
- 1 prepared Simple Sweet and Sour Sauce Recipe

INSTRUCTIONS

Combine the potato starch, salt, pepper and Five Chinese Spice in one mixing bowl.

Beat the eggs in another mixing bowl, then add Sesame Oil.

Dredge the pieces of pork into Potato Starch and shake off any excesses. Dip each piece quickly into the mixture of the eggs, shake off excess and then return to the mixture of the Potato Starch.

Coat with oil from air fryer tub. Drop pieces of pork into a basket and sprinkle with oil.

Cook for about 8-12 minutes (or until pork is cooked), at 340 degrees, shaking the basket a few times.

Serve with my Simple Sweet Recipe and Sour Sauce.

322. COPYCAT TACO BELL CRUNCH WRAPS

INGREDIENTS

- 2 lbs ground beef
- 2 servings Homemade Taco Seasoning Recipe
- 1 1/3 c water
- 6 flour tortillas, 12 inch
- 3 roma tomatoes
- 12 oz nacho cheese
- 2 c lettuce, shredded
- 2 c Mexican blend cheese
- 2 c sour cream
- 6 tostadas
- Olive oil or butter spray

INSTRUCTIONS

Preheat air fryer to 400 Prepare ground beef according to taco seasoning packet 4 tbs of nacho cheese, 1 tostada, 1/3 c sour cream, 1/3 c lettuce in the middle of each flour tortilla. To cover, flood the edges up, over the top, it should look like a pinwheel Repeat 2 and 3 with remaining wraps Lay seam side down in your air fryer Spray with oil Fry for 2 minutes or until brown Use a spatula, turn carefully and spray again Cook another 2 minutes and repeat with remaining wraps Allow to cool for a few minutes and enjoy.

NUTRITIONAL INFORMATION

Amount Per Serving Calories 954 Saturated Fat 30g Cholesterol 187mg Sodium 1235mg Carbohydrates 34g Fiber 2g Sugar 7g Protein 42g

323. RANCH STYLE CHICK PEAS

INGREDIENTS

- 1 15 ounce can chickpeas - drained but not rinsed
- 2 tablespoons olive oil - divided
- 1 batch Homemade Ranch Seasoning
- 1 teaspoon sea salt
- 2 tablespoons lemon juice

INSTRUCTIONS

Toss the chickpeas and 1 tablespoon of the olive oil together in a small bowl. Air to fry for 15 minutes at 400F.

Transfer the chickpeas back to your small bowl, then toss in the remaining oil plus the ranch seasoning, salt, and lemon juice to make the beans nice and coat.

Transfer the chickpeas back to your air fryer basket and cook for another 5 minutes at 350F Serve now, or cool completely, and then store in an airtight container.

324. GLUTEN FREE ONION RINGS

INGREDIENTS

- 2 eggs
- 1/2 cup unsweetened almond or cashew milk
- 1 1/4 cup of Trim Healthy Mama Baking Blend
- 1/2 teaspoon Himalayan salt
- 1/2 teaspoon paprika (optional)
- 1/8 teaspoon cayenne
- 1 large sweet onion

INSTRUCTIONS

In a shallow bowl, add the eggs and milk together, which is easy to dip into. Mix the flour, salt, paprika, cayenne in a shallow bowl that's easy to dip into your rings. Slice the onion and carve rings in 1/4 to 1/2 inch circles.

Preheat air fryer for a minute or two on 350 °.

Dip slices of onion into a mixture of eggs and then dredge through a mixture of flour. Place onion slices in a single layer of air fryer bowl, may be slightly overlapped. Spark lightly with oil spray. Fry 5-8 minutes in air fryer, turn the onion slices over, spray lightly and fry for another 5-8 minutes. Frying time may depend on the thickness of the onions at one time and how many rings there are in the fryer.

325. ZUCCHINI PARMESAN CHIPS

INGREDIENTS

- 2 medium sized Zucchinis thinly sliced
- 1 Egg lightly beaten
- ½ cup Italian-seasoned Breadcrumbs
- ½ cup grated Parmesan Cheese
- ½ teaspoon of Smoked Paprika optional
- Cooking spray or mist
- Salt and freshly cracked pepper to taste

INSTRUCTIONS

Use a knife or mandolin slicer to cut the zucchinis as thinly as possible. To get rid of excess moisture, pat dry with a paper towel.

Beat the egg in a shallow bowl with a minute sprinkling of water, a pinch of salt and pepper. Combine the breadcrumbs, grated cheese, and smoked paprika into another shallow bowl.

Dip a slice of zucchini in the egg, then mix with the cheese-breadcrumbs. Press to paint. Place a wire rack over the crumb-coated slices. Repeat Spray the crumb-coated zucchini slices with cooking spray or mist with all the slices.

Place the slices in the air fryer's basket in a single layer, ensuring they do not overlap.

Spray fried for 8 minutes in batches at 350o F. Sprinkle with salt (if needed) and pepper with ketchup or salsa to taste, and serve hot.

NUTRITIONAL INFORMATION

YIELD: 4 SERVING SIZE: 1

Amount Per Serving: Calories: 588 Total Fat: 24g Saturated Fat: 10g Trans Fat: 0g Unsaturated Fat: 10g Cholesterol: 230mg Sodium: 2370mg Carbohydrates: 62g Fiber: 8g Sugar: 11g Protein: 34g

326. AIR FRYER VEGETABLES

INGREDIENTS

- Assorted Vegetables
- 3 Tbsp Olive Oil
- Salt and Pepper

INSTRUCTIONS

Preheat Air Fryer to 375 degrees Cut the vegetables to ensure that they are cooked quickly and evenly Place the vegetables in a bowl Sprinkle with olive oil and sprinkle with salt and pepper to taste.

327. PORK TAQUITOS

INGREDIENTS

- 30 oz. of cooked shredded pork tenderloin
- 2 1/2 cups fat free shredded mozzarella
- 10 small flour tortillas
- 1 lime, juiced
- Cooking spray
- Salsa for dipping (optional)
- Sour Cream (optional)

INSTRUCTIONS

Air fryer preheat to 380 degrees.

Sprinkle the lime juice over the bacon and stir gently.

Microwave 5 tortillas of 10 seconds at a time with a wet paper towel over it, to soften.

Then add 3 oz. Of pork, and 1/4 cup for tortilla cheese.

328. PORTABELLO MUSHROOM PIZZAS

INGREDIENTS

- 4 large portobello mushrooms
- balsamic vinegar
- salt and black pepper
- 4 tablespoons oil-free pasta sauce (such as 365 Organic)
- 1 clove garlic , minced
- 3 ounces zucchini , shredded, chopped, or julienned (about 1/2 medium)
- 2 tablespoons sweet red pepper , diced
- 4 olives kalamata olives , sliced
- 1 teaspoon dried basil
- 1/2 cups hummus
- fresh basil leaves or other herbs , minced

INSTRUCTIONS

Cut the mushrooms and cover each with equal amounts of zucchini, peppers, and olives and sprinkle with dried basil, salt, and pepper. Back 3 minutes to the Air Fryer. Inspect and rearrange the mushrooms if using a rack. Switch to the Air Fryer for another 3 minutes, or until tender mushrooms. Drizzle with hummus and sprinkle with basil or other herbs on a tray. You can briefly put the portobellos back in the air fryer to warm the hummus if you want. Remove the mushrooms and top each with equal amounts of zucchini, peppers, and olives and sprinkle with dried basil, salt, and pepper. Returning 3 minutes to the Air Fryer. Check and rearrange the mushrooms if using a rack. Switch to the Air Fryer for another 3 minutes, or until tender mushrooms. Drizzle with hummus and sprinkle with basil or other herbs on a plate. You may briefly place the portobellos back in the air fryer to cook the hummus if you want.

NUTRITIONAL INFORMATION

Amount Per Serving (1 mushroom pizza)

Calories 70Calories from Fat 14 % Daily Value Fat 1.56g 2% Sodium 167mg 7% Carbohydrates 11g 4% Fiber 3.46g 14% Sugar 3.79g 4% Protein 4.34g 9%

329. SHRIMP SCAMPI

INGREDIENTS

- 4 tablespoons Butter
- 1 tablespoon lemon juice
- 1 tablespoon Minced Garlic
- 2 teaspoons Red Pepper Flakes
- 1 tablespoon chopped chives, or 1 teaspoon dried chives
- 1 tablespoon chopped fresh basil, or 1 teaspoon dried basil
- 2 tablespoons Chicken Stock, (or white wine)
- 1 lb (453.59 g) defrosted shrimp, (21-25 count)

INSTRUCTIONS

Turn the air fryer up to 330F. Place a 6x 3 metal pan inside and allow it to start heating while collecting ingredients.

In the hot6-inch pan place the butter, garlic, and red pepper flakes.

Allow it to cook until the butter has melted for 2 minutes, stirring once. Don't miss this step. This is what infuses butter with garlic, which is what makes every taste so good.

Open the air fryer, add all ingredients to the pan, stirring gently, in the order specified.

Allow shrimp to cook, stirring once, for 5 minutes. The butter should be well-melted and liquid at this stage, soaking in spiced goodness on the shrimp. Mix well, cover the6-inch saucepan with silicone mitts and let it rest on the counter for 1 minute. You do this so that you let the shrimp cook in the residual heat instead of allowing it to overcook and get rubbery by accident.

Stir in at minute's end. At this stage the shrimps should be well cooked.

Sprinkle fresh basil leaves on top and enjoy.

330. JUICY BEEF KEBABS

INGREDIENTS

- 1 lb beef chuck ribs cut in 1 inch pieces or any other tender cut meat- think nice steak, stew meat
- 1/3 cup low fat sour cream
- 2 tbsp soy sauce
- 8 6 inch skewers
- 1 bell peppers
- 1/2 onion

INSTRUCTIONS

Mix the sour cream in a medium bowl with soy sauce. Place the chunks of beef in the bowl and marinate in 1 "pieces for at least 30 minutes, better overnight. Thread beef, onions and bell peppers onto skewers for about 10 minutes, soak wooden skewers in water. Add some black pepper which is freshly gound. Cook for 10 minutes in preheated to 400F Air fryer, turning half way.

NUTRITIONAL INFORMATION

Calories: 250kcal , Carbohydrates: 4g , Protein: 23g , Fat: 15g , Saturated Fat: 6g , Cholesterol: 84mg , Sodium: 609mg , Potassium: 519mg , Sugar: 2g , Vitamin A: 1010IU , Vitamin C: 39mg , Calcium: 49mg , Iron: 2.7mg

331. SHRIMP EGGROLLS

INGREDIENTS

- 1 teaspoon toasted sesame oil
- 1 teaspoon fresh ground ginger
- 3 garlic cloves, minced
- 1 cup chopped carrots
- 1/2 cup sliced green onion
- 2 tablespoons soy sauce
- 1/2 tablespoon sugar
- 1/4 cup chicken or vegetable broth
- 3 cups coleslaw mix or shredded cabbage
- 10 large cooked shrimp, cut into small pieces
- 10 egg roll wrappers
- 1 egg, beaten

INSTRUCTIONS

Heat up oil over medium heat in a large skillet. Cook for 30 seconds, add the garlic and ginger.

Stir in carrots and green onion, and sauté for 2 minutes.

Alternatively, whisk the soy sauce, sugar and broth together.

Mix in a mixture of soy sauce, coleslaw mixture/cabbage, and shrimp into the vegetable pan and cook for 5 minutes.

Remove the pan from heat and allow it to cool in a strainer for about 15 minutes.

Preheat the air fryer to 390 ° F, as the coleslaw or vegetable mixture is cooling.

Place the wrappers of egg rolls on a work surface. Top each mixture with 3 spoonfuls of veggie or shrimp.

Brush some egg onto the wrapper's bottom. Roll up the wrappers, fold over the sides so that they hold the filling. Brush the egg on the outside of the roll of the egg right before you add it to the air fryer. When you brush it on and let the egg roll sit down, it gets soft and it can rip.

Sprinkle with a cooking spray on the air fryer basket. Carefully add 3-4 rolls of eggs to the basket of the air-fryer. Brush egg rolls to the tops with egg.

Air fry for 8-9 minutes, or until the outside is crispy and crunchy.

Serve straight away

NUTRITIONAL INFORMATION

Air Fryer Shrimp Egg Rolls, Amount Per Serving (2 egg rolls) Calories 240Calories from Fat 18 % Daily Value Fat 2g3% Cholesterol 80mg27% Sodium 913mg40% Carbohydrates 39g13% Fiber 2g8% Sugar 4g4% Protein 12g24%

332. STEAK WITH HERB BUTTER

INGREDIENTS

- 2 8 oz Ribeye steak
- salt
- freshly cracked black pepper
- olive oil
- Garlic Butter
- 1 stick unsalted butter softened
- 2 Tbsp fresh parsley chopped
- 2 tsp garlic minced
- 1 tsp Worcestershire Sauce
- 1/2 tsp salt

INSTRUCTIONS

Prepare Garlic Butter until thoroughly combined by mixing butter, parsley garlic, Worcestershire sauce, and salt.

Place the paper into the parchment and roll it into a sheet. Chill until ready to use.

Remove steak from the refrigerator and allow it to sit for 20 minutes at room temperature. Rub both sides of the steak with a little bit of olive oil and season with salt and freshly cracked black pepper.

Grease your basket with Air Fryer by rubbing a bit of oil on the basket. Air Fryer preheat to 400 degrees Fahrenheit. Place steaks in air fryer once preheated, and cook for 12 minutes, flipping through halfway through. Remove from the air fryer and allow 5 minutes to rest. Fill with butter over garlic.

333. HONEY ROASTED CARROTS

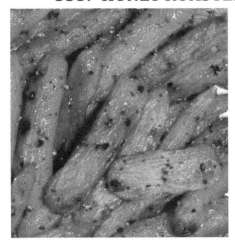

INGREDIENTS

- 3 cups of baby carrots or carrots cut into large chunks
- 1 tbsp Olive oil
- 1 tbsp Honey
- Salt and pepper to taste

INSTRUCTIONS

Blend the carrots and the honey and the olive oil in a bowl.

Make sure that the carrots are well covered.

Mix with pepper and salt.

Cook for 12 minutes on 200 degrees in the Airfryer.

Serve warm.

334. VEGAN SUSHI BURRITO WITH TOFU

INGREDIENTS

- 1/4 block extra firm tofu pressed and sliced
- 1 tablespoon low-sodium soy sauce
- 1/4 teaspoon ground ginger
- 1/4 teaspoon garlic powder
- sriracha sauce to taste
- 2 cups Pressure Cooker Sushi Rice cooked and cooled (use 1 cup dry white rice, 1 cup water, follow everything else the same.)
- 2 sheets nori
- Filling Ingredients
- the tofu that you just made
- 1/4 a Haas avocado sliced into thin pieces
- 3 tablespoons sliced mango
- 1 green onion green parts only
- 2 tablespoons pickled ginger (optional)
- 2 tablespoons panko breadcrumbs

INSTRUCTIONS

Make the Air Fryer Tofu In a shallow bowl, whisk the soy, ginger, garlic and sriracha sauce together. Add the tofu, coat it gently in the marinade. Set some 10 minutes aside.

Move the tofu to your air fryer bowl, and cook at 370F for 15 minutes, shaking 8 minutes later.

Make The Sushi Burrito Lay out one piece of the nori and cover the entire sheet in a sushi rice coat, leaving you around a 1/2? Uncovered piece of nori along one edge. If you need a visual for this move see the video at the top. Humid fingertips allow this by avoiding sticking.

About 1/2 Arrange half of each of the filling ingredients from the coated edge of the nori sheet, except for the rice panko, as in the video. Sprinkle 1 spoonful of breadcrumbs over the entire filling.

Ever so gently, roll the sushi burrito once over, and use the nori's exposed part to seal it off. Sealed side down, let the roll stand for 5 minutes before serving.

Repeat the steps of the Sushi Burrito with the other nori sheet and filling ingredients left over.

335. TOFU AND VEGETABLES

INGREDIENTS

- Tofu
- 1 block (14oz /400 g) extra-firm tofu , pressed and cut into cubes
- 1 tablespoon sesame oil
- 1 tablespoon soy sauce
- 3 tablespoons cornstarch (or tapioca starch)
- Sauce (Footnote 1)
- 2 tablespoons orange zest
- 1/2 cup orange juice
- 3 tablespoons rice vinegar (or distilled white vinegar)
- 1 tablespoon light soy sauce (or soy sauce, or tamari for gluten free)
- 1 tablespoon Shaoxing wine (or dry sherry, or chicken stock)
- 2 tablespoons sugar
- 2 teaspoons cornstarch
- 1/4 teaspoon fine sea salt
- 2 cloves garlic , minced
- Stir fry
- 2 carrots , sliced
- 1 head broccoli , chopped to bite size

INSTRUCTIONS

Tofu

Attach the sesame oil and soy sauce to the pressed tofu and blend well. Sprinkle over tofu and toss half the cornstarch. Repeat, and ensure that the tofu is uniformly coated.

Preheat your air fryer to 390 degrees F (199 C), unless it's required by your model. Attach the coated tofu to your air-fryer basket once it's dry. Set timer to cook for 5 minutes. Just shake or stir the tofu when the time is up. Cook for another 5 minutes, then again.

Stir fry Combine the ingredients of the fry sauce together in a small bowl.

When the tofu is almost ready, heat 1/4 cup water over medium to high heat in a large non-stick skillet until it boils. Stir in the carrots and broccoli. Cover and cook for 1 to 2 minutes, until the veggies turn tender. Cook and stir the veggies without the cover to allow the water to evaporate completely if there is any water left in the pan.

Again mix the sauce to dissolve the cornstarch completely, then pour it into the skillet. Rapidly stir a few times until the sauce becomes thick. Stir in tofu. Stir in a few more times to bring it all together. Turn onto a plate immediately.

Serve hot over steamed rice as your main.

NUTRITIONAL INFORMATION

Serving: 1of the 3 servings , Calories: 298kcal , Carbohydrates: 32.4g , Protein: 16g , Fat: 12.6g , Sodium: 517mg , Potassium: 609mg , Fiber: 3.8g , Sugar: 15.3g , Calcium: 220mg , Iron: 3.8mg

336. ORANGE TOFU

INGREDIENTS

- 1 pound extra-firm tofu, drained and pressed (or use super-firm tofu)
- 1 Tablespoon tamari
- 1 Tablespoon cornstarch, (or arrowroot powder)
- For the sauce:
- 1 teaspoon orange zest
- 1/3 cup orange juice
- 1/2 cup water
- 2 teaspoons cornstarch, (or arrowroot powder)
- 1/4 teaspoon crushed red pepper flakes
- 1 teaspoon fresh ginger, minced
- 1 teaspoon fresh garlic, minced
- 1 Tablespoon pure maple syrup

INSTRUCTIONS

Cut the cubed tofu.

Place the cubes of tofu in a plastic quarter size storage bag. Place the tamari in and seal the jar. Shake the bag until the tamari is all filled with tofu.

Add the cornstarch spoonful to the bag. Again shake until coated with tofu. Place the tofu aside to marinate for 15 minutes or more.

In the meantime add all the ingredients in the sauce to a small bowl and mix with a spoon. Deposit aside. Place the tofu into a single layer in the air fryer. This is probably going to have to be done in two batches.

Cook the tofu for 10 minutes at 390 degrees, and shake after 5 minutes.

Once the tofu batches have been prepared, add them all to a skillet over medium-high heat. Give a stir to the sauce, and pour over the tofu. Remove tofu and sauce until the sauce has thickened, and heat the tofu through.

Serve with rice and steamed vegetables immediately, if you so wish.

NUTRITIONAL INFORMATION

Calories: 102kcal , Carbohydrates: 11g , Protein: 9g , Fat: 2g , Saturated Fat: 1g , Sodium: 328mg , Potassium: 237mg , Fiber: 1g , Sugar: 6g , Vitamin A: 78IU , Vitamin C: 11mg , Calcium: 41mg , Iron: 1mg

337. CAULIFLOWER ARANCHINI BALLS

INGREDIENTS

- 1 Italian chicken sausage link, casing removed (2 3/4 oz)
- 2 1/4 cups riced cauliflower, frozen works great
- 1/4 teaspoon kosher salt
- 2 tablespoons homemade marinara, plus optional more for serving
- 1/2 cup part skim shredded mozzarella
- 1 large egg, beaten
- 1/4 cup bread crumbs, or gluten-free crumbs
- 1 tablespoon grated Pecorino Romano or parmesan
- cooking spray

INSTRUCTIONS

Heat a medium-high skillet over medium heat. Add the sausage and cook for about 4 to 5 minutes, breaking up the meat with a spoon as it cooks as small as possible.

Add the cauliflower, salt, and marinara and cook over medium heat for 6 minutes, stirring until tender and cooked through.

Remove the skillet from heat and add the mozzarella cheese and stir well to blend. Let it cool for 3 to 4 minutes, until the handling is quick.

Spray a 1/4 cup measuring cup with a cooking spray and fill with a mixture of cauliflower to level the rim. Use a tiny spoon to scoop your palm out and shape it into a cup. Set aside on a platter.

Repeat with the remaining cauliflower, 6 balls should be on.

Put the egg in one dish, and the chopped bread in another.

Stir in the crumbs with the parmesan and blend.

Dip the ball into the egg, then into the crumbs and transfer to a baking sheet. Spray cooking spray on top.

Bake 425F in the oven for 25 minutes, until golden. Bake 400F for 9 minutes, turning halfway until golden when making in an air fryer.

For dipping, serve with marinara sauce.

NUTRITIONAL INFORMATION

Serving: 3balls, Calories: 257kcal, Carbohydrates: 15.6g, Protein: 21.5g, Fat: 11.5g, Saturated Fat: 5g, Cholesterol: 95.5mg, Sodium: 644mg, Fiber: 3g, Sugar: 2.

338. BABA GANOUSH

INGREDIENTS

- 1 medium-sized eggplant around 13 ounces
- 2 teaspoons organic canola oil
- 3 Tablespoons tahini
- 1 Tablespoon lemon juice
- 1 clove garlic minced
- 1/8 teaspoon cumin
- 1/4 teaspoon smoked salt
- 1/8 teaspoon regular salt
- Drizzle extra virgin olive oil optional garnish

INSTRUCTIONS

Cut the stem off the end of the Aubergine. Slice the eggplant lengthwise down the center. Place one teaspoon of canola oil on each half of the eggplant and rub it uniformly over the entire eggplant including the cut side and peel. Prick with a fork into several holes in the eggplant peel.

Place halves of the eggplant cut side down in the bucket of the air fryer. Air for 20 minutes, cook at 400 degrees. (If you don't have an air fryer, then roast the eggplant in the oven. Preheat the oven to 400 degrees and place the eggplant halves cut-side-down on the baking sheet lined with parchment paper. Roast for 45 minutes. Test for doneness at about 35 minutes because cooking times can vary.) The cut side is crispy and toasty, and the peel is wrinkled. Take the half of the eggplant from the air fryer bowl, push it onto a plate and allow it to cool.

Once the eggplant half is cool enough to touch, scoop out the soft eggplant from its peel and place the eggplant in a food processor. You will be able to scoop out all the soft white eggplant with ease. You can have the peel discarded.

To the food processor add the tahini, lemon juice, garlic, cumin, smoked salt, and standard salt. Food processor pulse 4 or 5 times. Baba ganoush is best when there's still a bit of body to it, as opposed to being absolutely smooth. The baba ganoush can be served at once, but it is best if the flavors have an opportunity to meld for at least a few hours. (It's even better if you can make it the day before you want to serve it.) Move it into a covered container and place it in the fridge until you're ready to serve it.

Serve the baba ganoush for a dipping with pita bread and/or sliced vegetables. Before serving, pour a little extra virgin olive oil over the baba ganoush, if you like.

NUTRITIONAL INFORMATION

Calories: 115kcal , Carbohydrates: 9g , Protein: 3g , Fat: 8g , Saturated Fat: 1g , Sodium: 151mg , Potassium: 313mg , Fiber: 3g , Sugar: 4g , Vitamin A: 25IU , Vitamin C: 4.7mg , Calcium: 26mg , Iron: 0.8mg

339. PEANUT BUTTER AND JELLY DONUTS

INGREDIENTS

Doughnuts:

- 1 1/4 Cups all-purpose flour
- 1/3 Cup sugar
- 1/2 Teaspoon baking powder
- 1/2 Teaspoon baking soda
- 3/4 Teaspoon salt
- 1 Egg
- 1/2 Cup buttermilk
- 1 Teaspoon vanilla
- 2 Tablespoons unsalted butter, melted and cooled
- 1 Tablespoon melted butter for brushing the tops

Filling:

- 1/2 Cup Blueberry or strawberry jelly (not preserves)

Glaze:

- 1/2 Cup powdered sugar

- 2 Tablespoons milk
- 2 Tablespoons peanut butter
- Pinch of sea salt

INSTRUCTIONS

Air fried doughnuts with peanut butter glaze Whisk together the flour, sugar, baking powder, baking soda and salt in a large bowl.

The egg, melted butter, buttermilk, and vanilla beat together in a separate bowl.

Create a well in dry ingredient center and pour it in the water. Use a fork to mix, then finish stirring with a large spoon, until the flour is added.

Turn the dough out onto a surface well-floured. Note that, at first, it will be very sticky. Work the dough very slightly before they come together and then pat it out to a thickness of 3/4 Cut out dough rounds and brush them with melted butter using a 3 1/2 "cutter. Cut off 2 pieces of baking paper (doesn't have to be precise) and place each dough round on paper, then inside the air fryer. Work in lots according to how many will fit in your fryer.

Fry for 11 minutes, at 350 degrees. Use a squeeze bottle or pastry sac to fill each doughnut with jelly.

Whisk the ingredients of the glaze together, then slice over each doughnut.

340. COCONUT FRENCH TOAST

INGREDIENTS

- 2 Slices of Gluten-Free Bread (use your favorite)
- 1/2 Cup Lite Culinary Coconut Milk
- 1 Tsp Baking Powder
- 1/2 Cup Unsweetened Shredded Coconut

INSTRUCTIONS

Mix the coconut milk and baking powder together in a large, rimmed dish.

Spread the coconut sliced onto a platter.

Take each slice of bread and soak in the coconut milk mixture for the first time, and a few seconds before transfer to the shredded coconut plate and coat the slice in the coconut completely.

Space both the coated bread slices in your air fryer, close them and set the temperature to 350 ° F and 4 minutes.

Remove and top with maple syrup, or your favorite French toast toppings until finishe

341. CASHEWS BACON BIT

INGREDIENTS

- 3 cups raw cashews
- 2 teaspoons salt
- 3 tablespoons liquid smoke
- 2 tablespoons blackstrap molasses

INSTRUCTIONS

Toss all the ingredients together in a large bowl, ensuring the cashews are coated really well . Pour the cashews into your air fryer tub, and cook for 8-10 minutes at 350F, shaking every 2 minutes to ensure that they cook evenly and test for doneness. You will shake/test every minute over the last 2 minutes to avoid fire. With this recipe, the line between done and burnt can be thin.

Let them cool down to room temperature-about 10-15 minutes-and move to an airtight storage container

342. VEGETARIAN SOUTHWEST EGGROLLS

INGREDIENTS

- 1/4 red onion chopped
- 2-3 garlic cloves chopped
- 16 egg roll wrappers
- 1/2 red pepper chopped
- 1/2 yellow pepper chopped
- 1/2 orange pepper chopped
- 1/4 cup shredded cheese I used sharp cheddar
- 8 oz low-sodium black beans (drained)
- 1 can diced tomatoes and chilis (drained) I used Rotel
- 1 cup frozen kernel corn
- 2 teaspoons cilantro chopped
- 1/2 lime juice of
- 1/4 packet Taco Seasoning I used Trader Joe's
- cooking oil
- cup of water
- Avocado Ranch Dip
- 8 oz sour cream I used fat-free
- 1 avocado
- 1/2 packet Hidden Valley Ranch Dip Seasoning

INSTRUCTIONS

Heat your skillet over medium-high heat. Stir in the garlic and onions. Cook until fragrant, for 2-3 minutes.

Drop all the peppers into the skillet. Blend well. Add the black beans, peas, onions, and cheese for 1-2 minutes. Cook for another 2-3 minutes.

Drizzle all over the fresh lime juice. Attach the seasoning with cilantro and taco. Cut.

Lay the wrappers off an egg roll on a flat surface. Dip a brush in water to cook. Glaze each of the egg roll wrappers along the edges with a wet brush. This will soften the crust, and make rolling easier.

Use 2 rolls of eggs to each. I decided to double roll the rolls of the eggs so they would not leak. If your purchased brand of egg roll wrappers is pretty thick, you may need only one wrapper and no need to double up.

Load the mixture into every single wrapper.

Fold the wrappers to close diagonally. With the filling press firmly on the field, cup it to lock it in place. Fold as triangles on both the left and right sides. Fold the final layer to close over top. To wet the area using the cooking brush and lock it in place. Spray cooking oil on each egg roll.

Load the rolling eggs into the Air Fryer pan. Sprinkle with cooking oil.

Cook it at 380 degrees for 8 minutes. Flip rolls into the egg. Cook for another 4 minutes. Before serving, Nice. Avocado Ranch Dip Peel the avocado and get the pit removed. Avocado Mash in a bowl. I like using a masher on potatoes.

Apply the ranch seasoning and sour cream. Combine well. Stir well.

343. SWEET POTATO CAULIFLOWER PATTIES

INGREDIENTS

- 1 medium to large sweet potato, peeled
- 2 cup cauliflower florets
- 1 green onion, chopped.
- 1 tsp minced garlic
- 2 tbsp organic ranch seasoning mix or dairy seasoning mix of choice
- 1 cup packed cilantro (fresh)
- 1/2 tsp chili powder
- 1/4 tsp cumin
- 2 tbsp arrowroot starch or gluten free flour of choice
- 1/4 cup ground flaxseed
- 1/4 cup sunflower seeds (or pumpkin seeds)
- 1/4 tsp Kosher Salt and pepper (or to taste)
- Dipping sauce of choice

INSTRUCTIONS

Oven preheats to 400F. Line a sheet of baking (or oil), and set aside.

Slice your skinned sweet potato into smaller pieces next. Place and pulse in a food processor or blender until the larger pieces are broken off.

Attach the cauliflower, onion, garlic and start over again.

Add seeds of sunflower, flaxseed, arrowroot (or flour), cilantro, and other seasonings in you. Pulse or place on medium until forming a thick batter. Put batter in a bigger tub. Scoop 1/4 cup of the batter out at a time and shape about 1.5 inches thick into patties. Place on a sheet to bake.

Repeat until around 7-10 patties are on.

Chill for 10 minutes in freeze to allow the patties to set. Place patties in the oven, flipping halfway, for 20 minutes once set. They could take nearer to 25 minutes if you made your patties extra thick.

See notes for the choice to cook an Air Fryer.

NUTRITIONAL INFORMATION

Serving Size: 1 patty Calories: 85Sugar: 1.7 gSodium: 200 mgFat: 2.9 gSaturated Fat: 1.3 gramsUnsaturated Fat: 0Trans Fat: 0Carbohydrates: 9 gFiber: 3.5gProtein: 2.7 gCholesterol: 0 mg

344. SWEET POTATO HASH BROWNS

INGREDIENTS

- 4 sweet potatoes peeled
- 2 garlic cloves minced
- 1 teaspoon cinnamon
- 1 teaspoon paprika
- salt and pepper to taste
- 2 teaspoons olive oil

INSTRUCTIONS

Grate the sweet potatoes using a cheese grater's larger holes.

Place the sweet potatoes in a cold bowl of water. Allow the sweet potatoes 20-25 minutes to soak. Soaking the sweet potatoes in cold water will help the potatoes absorb the starch. This renders them crunchy.

Drain the water from the potatoes and use a paper towel to completely dry them.

Place the potatoes in a dry saucepan. Add extra virgin olive oil, ginger, paprika, salt, and pepper. Stir in the ingredients to mix.

The potatoes are added to the air fryer.

Cook on 400 degrees for 10 minutes.

Open the fryer of air, and shake the potatoes. Cook for yet another ten minutes.

Before serving, Cool.

345. POTATO SKINS

INGREDIENTS

- Peels from 2 pounds of Russet potatoes about 4 medium-sized potatoes
- Spritz oil
- Pinch salt
- Optional toppings: Sauteed minced garlic, seitan bacon, grated non-dairy cheese, non-dairy cream cheese, green onions, and/or ketchup

INSTRUCTIONS

Place the potato peels inside the basket of the air fryer. Sprinkle with butter, and sprinkle with a pinch of salt. Air fry for 6 to 8 minutes at 400 degrees. Stop around halfway through once to shake the basket and provide another spritz of oil to the peels. Check them over the last couple of minutes of cooking to make sure they get brown and crisp but not burnt.

Serve with any of the available toppings immediately, if desired.

Notes When they are cooking the peels shrink. So watch out not to salt them over.

The air fryer functions best when it is not overcrowded. So if you have considerably more peels than needed in this recycling, for best results, air fry in batches. Once the air fryer is hot, however, the peels will probably cook faster too.

NUTRITIONAL INFORMATION

Calories: 60kcal , Carbohydrates: 13g , Protein: 2g , Sodium: 10mg , Potassium: 433mg , Fiber: 2g , Vitamin C: 12mg , Calcium: 31mg , Iron: 3.4mg

346. SOUTHERN YELLOW SQUASH

INGREDIENTS

- 3-4 Yellow Summer Squash (Zucchini would work also)
- 2 Eggs
- 2 tbs Buttermilk
- 1/4 c Cornmeal
- 1/2 c Bread Crumbs, plain (or Panko)
- 1 tsp Salt
- 1/4 tsp Ground Black Pepper
- 1/2 tsp Onion Powder
- 1/4 tsp Garlic Powder
- 1/2 tsp Paprika

INSTRUCTIONS

Slice the squash into bits between 1/4 to 1/2 inch thick. (Optional: season the squash parts with a little salt and pepper before breading for extra flavor) In a cup, mix the egg with buttermilk.

Combine the cornmeal, bread crumbs, and seasonings into a separate bowl.

Dredge the squash slices in the mixture of the eggs, then coat in the mixture of seasoned bread crumbs and arrange cooking racks on the air fryer.

Air fry for 20 minutes at 400 ° F, or until slightly brown.

Serve warm.

347. MEDITERRANEAN VEGETABLES

INGREDIENTS

- Philips Airfryer
- 50 g Cherry Tomatoes
- 1 Large Courgette
- 1 Green Pepper
- 1 Large Parsnip
- 1 Medium Carrot
- 1 Tsp Mixed Herbs
- 2 Tbsp Honey
- 1 Tsp Mustard
- 2 Tsp Garlic Puree
- 6 Tbsp Olive Oil
- Salt & Pepper
- Metric - Imperial

INSTRUCTIONS

Slice the courgette and green pepper up into the bottom of your Airfryer (chopping as you go). Peel and dice the parsnip and carrot and add whole cherry tomatoes for extra flavor while still on the vine.

Drizzle with three tablespoons of olive oil and cook at 180c for 15 minutes. Meanwhile, mix the remaining ingredients in a healthy baking dish from the air fryer.

When the vegetables are cooked, move them to the baking dish from the bottom of the Airfryer and shake well so that all the vegetables are coated in the marinade.

Sprinkle with salt and pepper, and cook on 200c for 5 minutes.

Station. Notes For what you have in, you can change your vegetables, but avoid cauliflower and courgette in the same dish as they both carry a lot of water and ruin the platter. One of my favorite alternatives is adding sweet potatoes as this tastes incredibly honey.

NUTRITIONAL INFORMATION

Calories: 280kcal , Carbohydrates: 21g , Protein: 2g , Fat: 21g , Saturated Fat: 3g , Cholesterol: 0mg , Sodium: 36mg , Potassium: 420mg , Fiber: 3g , Sugar: 13g , Vitamin A: 2815IU , Vitamin C: 43.8mg , Calcium: 38mg , Iron: 0.9mg

348. ZUCCHINI, YELLOW SQUASH, AND CARROTS

INGREDIENTS

- 1 pound broccoli - 2 small heads of broccoli
- 1/4 cup ground flax
- 1/2 cup almond flour
- 1 tsp salt
- 1/2 tsp garlic powder

INSTRUCTIONS

Cook the broccoli for 3 minutes or microwave for 3 minutes Add the steamed broccoli to the mixing bowl Process the broccoli until it resembles rice Add the riced broccoli to a large bowl containing the ground flax, almond flour, salt, and garlic powder.

add the broccoli with the rest of the ingredients, and allow to sit for 1-2 minutes.

Shape 18-20 tots of broccoli by pushing the mixture into one hand's palm then forming tots using the other hand's thumb and pointer finger. Press the blend well together.

Bake for 20 minutes in a 375F oven, turning over with 5 minutes left so that both sides can tan.

INSTRUCTIONS

Form the tots of broccoli in steps 1–7 above.

Position the broccoli tots carefully in a single layer in the air fryer, ensuring they don't overlap.

Set the fryer on air to 375 and cook for 12 minutes.

349. CAULIFLOWER WINGS

INGREDIENTS

- 1 head of cauliflower florets
- 1/2 cup milk we used soy milk
- 1/2 cup water
- 3/4 cup all-purpose flour we used Bob's Red Mill gluten-free baking 1-to-1
- 2 tsp. garlic powder
- 1 tsp. onion powder
- 1 tsp. smoked paprika
- 1/2 tsp. salt
- 1/4 tsp. ground black pepper
- 1 cup frank's red hot sauce
- 2 Tbsp. butter we used earth balance buttery spread
- 1/4 cup molasses

INSTRUCTIONS

Combine all dry ingredients in a mixing bowl (flour, garlic powder, onion powder, smoked paprika, salt, black pepper) and whisk in water and milk until batter has no lumps.

To batter add fresh cauliflower florets and mix well to coat evenly with batter. Remove florets one at a time and pass them to a separate dish to allow excess batter to run away.

Place pounded florets into a single layer of air fryer bowl. Also, try to keep them (if possible) from touching, so that all sides can get direct heat.

Cook for 15 minutes, at 350 degrees. Meanwhile, bring hot sauce, butter, and molasses to a low simmer in a small pot (or microwave)-mix well to combine. Then the heat strip.

When cooking is over, pass the cauliflower to a bowl. Fill with sauce when ready to serve then toss to coat.

serve immediately with your favorite dipping sauce, or none at all. Enjoy it!

350. AVOCADO FRIES WITH LIME DIPPING SAUCE

INGREDIENTS

- 8 ounces 2 small avocados, peeled, pitted and cut into 16 wedges
- large egg, lightly beaten
- 3/4 cup panko breadcrumbs, I used gluten-free
- 1 1/4 teaspoons lime chili seasoning salt, such as Tajin Classic
- For the lime dipping sauce:
- 1/4 cup 0% Greek Yogurt
- tablespoons light mayonnaise
- teaspoons fresh lime juice
- 1/2 teaspoon lime chili seasoning salt, such as Tajin Classic
- 1/8 teaspoon kosher salt

INSTRUCTIONS

Preheat 390F degrees for air-fryer.

Put the egg into a shallow bowl. Combine panko with 1 Teaspoon Tajin on another plate.

Avocado season wedges with 1/4 Tajin Teaspoon. Dip each piece into the egg first, then the panko afterward.

Sprinkle with oil on both sides then move to the air fryer and cook for 7 to 8 minutes cutting in half. Serve hot with sauce to take a dip.

351. BEEF KABOBS

INGREDIENTS

- 1 lb beef chuck ribs cut in 1 inch pieces or any other tender cut meat- think nice steak, stew meat
- 1/3 cup low fat sour cream
- 2 tbsp soy sauce
- 8 6 inch skewers
- 1 bell peppers
- 1/2 onion

INSTRUCTIONS

Mix the sour cream in a medium bowl with soy sauce. Place the chunks of beef in the bowl and marinate in 1 "pieces for at least 30 minutes, better overnight. Thread beef, onions and bell peppers onto skewers for about 10 minutes, soak wooden skewers in water. Add some black pepper which is freshly gound.

Cook for 10 minutes in preheated to 400F Air fryer, turning half way.

NUTRITIONAL INFORMATION

Calories: 250kcal , Carbohydrates: 4g , Protein: 23g , Fat: 15g , Saturated Fat: 6g , Cholesterol: 84mg , Sodium: 609mg , Potassium: 519mg , Sugar: 2g , Vitamin A: 1010IU , Vitamin C: 39mg , Calcium: 49mg , Iron: 2.7mg

352. CAJUN SHRIMP DINNER

INGREDIENTS

- 1 tablespoon Cajun or Creole seasoning
- 24 (1 pound) cleaned and peeled extra jumbo shrimp
- 6 ounces fully cooked Turkey/Chicken Andouille sausage or kielbasa, sliced
- 1 medium zucchini, 8 ounces, sliced into 1/4-inch thick half moons
- 1 medium yellow squash, 8 ounces, sliced into 1/4-inch thick half moons
- 1 large red bell pepper, seeded and cut into thin 1-inch pieces
- 1/4 teaspoon kosher salt
- 2 tablespoons olive oil

INSTRUCTIONS

Combine the Cajun seasoning and the shrimp in a large bowl, toss to coat.

Stir in the sausage, courgettes, squash, bell peppers, and salt and toss with oil.

Preheat 400F Air Fryer.

Transfer the shrimp and vegetables to the air fryer basket in 2 lots (for smaller baskets), and cook for 8 minutes, shaking the basket 2 to 3 times.

Repeat with remaining shrimp and veggies and set aside.

Return the first batch to the air fryer once both batches are cooked, and cook for 1 minute.

353. MAPLE SOY GLAZED SALMON

INGREDIENTS

- 3 tbsp pure maple syrup
- 3 tbsp reduced sodium soy sauce, or gluten-free soy sauce
- 1 tbsp sriracha hot sauce
- 1 clove garlic, smashed
- 4 wild salmon fillets, skinless (6 oz each)

INSTRUCTIONS

In a small bowl, combine maple syrup, soy sauce, sriracha, and garlic, pour into a gallon-sized resealable bag and add the salmon.

Marinate for 20 to 30 minutes, turning over occasionally.

Air fryer preheats to 400F. Spark the basket lightly with a nonstick spray.

Remove the fish from the marinade, with paper towels to reserve and pat dry.

Place the fish in the air fryer, fry air in batches for 7 to 8 minutes, or longer depending on salmon thickness.

In the meantime, pour the marinade into a small saucepan and bring it to a simmer over medium-low heat and reduce to 1 to 2 minutes until it thickens into a glaze. Just before eating, spoon the salmon over.

NUTRITIONAL INFORMATION

Serving: 1g, Calories: 292kcal, Carbohydrates: 12g, Protein: 35g, Fat: 11g, Saturated Fat: 1.5g, Cholesterol: 94mg, Sodium: 797mg, Fiber: 0.5g, Sugar: 10g

354. FISH FINGER SANDWICHES

INGREDIENTS

- 4 small cod fillets (skin removed)
- salt and pepper
- 2 tbsp flour
- 40g dried breadcrumbs
- spray oil
- 250g frozen peas
- 1 tbsp creme fraiche or greek yogurt
- 10–12 capers
- squeeze of lemon juice
- 4 bread rolls or 8 small slices of bread

INSTRUCTIONS

Preheat Air Fryer with Optimum HealthyFry.

Take each filet of cod, season with salt and pepper and dust lightly in the flour. Then roll up in the breadcrumbs quickly. The idea is to have a light breadcrumbs coating on the fish, rather than a thick layer. Repeat for each fillet of cod.

Add a couple of oil spray sprays to the base of the fryer basket. Place the cod filets on top and cook for 15 minutes at a fish setting (200c).

While the fish is cooking, on the hob or in the microwave, cook the peas in boiling water for a few minutes. Drain and then add the cream fraiche, capers, and lemon juice to a blender to taste. Blitz until merged. Remove it from the HealthyFry Air Fryer once the fish has cooked, and start layering your sandwich with the bread, fish and pea puree. You can also add lettuce, tartar sauce and any other favorite toppings of your choice!

355. KETO JICAMA FRIES

INGREDIENTS

- Jicama Fries
- 8 cups Jicama (peeled, chopped into thin matchsticks, 1/4 inch thick and 3 inches long)
- 2 tbsp Olive oil
- 1/2 tsp Garlic powder
- 1 tsp Cumin
- 1 tsp Sea salt
- 1/4 tsp Black pepper
- Keto Chili Topping
- 1 tbsp Olive oil
- 1/2 lb Ground beef
- 7.5 oz Diced tomatoes with green chilies (about 3/4 of a 10-oz can with liquid, no salt added)
- 1/2 tbsp Chili powder (more optional - see instructions)
- 1/2 tbsp Cumin
- 1 tsp Dried oregano
- 1/2 tsp Garlic powder
- 1/2 tsp Sea salt
- Toppings

- 1/2 cup Cheddar cheese (shredded)
- 1/4 cup Green onions (chopped)

INSTRUCTIONS

For an air fryer oven:

Move the fries in a single layer to two racks for air fryer oven. Place the two racks inside the air fryer. Bake within 10 minutes. Move the top rack to the bottom and the bottom to the top, then bake for another 10 to 15 minutes, until the fries are brown in gold.

For a basket air fryer: You may need to do 2 loads. Arrange the fries in the basket in a single layer, and bake for 20-25 minutes. Repeat with batch 2.

Remove the racks or basket from the air fryer when fries are done, and set the temperature to 400 again.

Keto Chili Topping Meanwhile, chili the beef. Heat the olive oil in a large saucepan or small pot over medium heat.

Stir in the ground beef. Increase heat to moderately high. Cook for about 10 minutes, with a spatula breaking apart until browned.

Add the remaining ingredients of chili into the pan/pot and stir. Cook, taste for 5 minutes and adjust the chili powder to taste.

Cook, stirring periodically, for another 5 to 10 minutes or until flavors grow to your taste for as long as you wish.

Assembly

Transfer the fries to an 8x8 baking dish, or any small oven-safe dish or plate that fits inside the fryer oven.

Spoon the fries over the chili. Sprinkle over with shredded cheese.

In the middle of the air fryer oven (or just in the center of a regular air fryer) place the dish or plate on the rack for about 2 to 3 minutes until the cheese melts. For serving, sprinkle with chopped green onions.

356. RASPBERRY BALSAMIC SMOKED PORK CHOPS

INGREDIENTS

- Cooking spray
- 2 large eggs
- 1/4 cup 2% milk
- 1 cup panko (Japanese) bread crumbs
- 1 cup finely chopped pecans
- 4 smoked bone-in pork chops (7-1/2 ounces each)
- 1/4 cup all-purpose flour
- 1/3 cup balsamic vinegar
- 2 tablespoons brown sugar
- 2 tablespoons seedless raspberry jam
- 1 tablespoon thawed frozen orange juice concentrate

INSTRUCTIONS

Preheat the fryer by air to 400 °. Spritz basket with spray for cooking fryer. Whisk the eggs and milk together in a shallow bowl or container. Toss the bread crumbs in another shallow bowl with pecans.

Coat with flour on the pork chops; shake off excess. Dip in a mixture of eggs and then in a mixture of crumbs, patting to help adhere. Working in batches as needed, place chops in the air-fryer basket in a single layer; spritz with spray for cooking.

Cook for 12-15 minutes until golden brown, turning halfway through cooking and spritzing with additional cooking spray. Remove, and stay warm. Repeat with chops leftover. In the meantime, put the remaining ingredients in a small casserole; bring to a boil. Cook and stir for 6-8 minutes, until lightly thickened. And serve with chops

NUTRITIONAL INFORMATION

1 pork chop with 1 tablespoon glaze: 579 calories, 36g fat (10g saturated fat), 106mg cholesterol, 1374mg sodium, 36g carbohydrate (22g sugars, 3g fiber), 32g protein.

357. HAM AND CHEESE TURNOVERS

INGREDIENTS

- 1 tube (13.80 ounces) refrigerated pizza crust
- 1/4 pound thinly sliced black forest deli ham
- 1 medium pear, thinly sliced and divided
- 1/4 cup chopped walnuts, toasted
- 2 tablespoons crumbled blue cheese

INSTRUCTIONS

Preheat the fryer by air to 400 °. Unroll the pizza crust into a 12-in on a lightly floured surface. Total square. Cut into four quadrangles. Layer ham, half slices of pear, walnuts, and blue cheese diagonally over half of each square to within 1/2 in. Of rims. Fold one corner to the opposite corner over filling, forming a triangle; press the edges to seal with a fork.

In batches, arrange turnovers in a greased air-fryer basket in a single layer; spritz with spray for cooking. Cook it for four to six minutes on each side, until it turns golden brown. Garnish with any slices leftover.

NUTRITIONAL INFORMATION

1 turnover: 357 calories, 10g fat (2g saturated fat), 16mg cholesterol, 885mg sodium, 55g carbohydrate (11g sugars, 3g fiber), 15g protein.

358. WASABI CRAB CAKES

INGREDIENTS

- 1 medium sweet red pepper, finely chopped
- 1 celery rib, finely chopped
- 3 green onions, finely chopped
- 2 large egg whites
- 3 tablespoons reduced-fat mayonnaise
- 1/4 teaspoon prepared wasabi
- 1/4 teaspoon salt
- 1/3 cup plus 1/2 cup dry bread crumbs, divided
- 1-1/2 cups lump crabmeat, drained
- Cooking spray

SAUCE:

- 1 celery rib, chopped
- 1/3 cup reduced-fat mayonnaise
- 1 green onion, chopped
- 1 tablespoon sweet pickle relish
- 1/2 teaspoon prepared wasabi
- 1/4 teaspoon celery salt

INSTRUCTIONS

Air fryer preheats to 375 °. Spritz basket with spray for cooking fryer. Combine the first 7 ingredients; substitute crumbs for 1/3 cup of bread. Fold softly in crab.

Place the remaining crumbs of the bread in a shallow bowl. Drop-in crumbs to heap tablespoonfuls of crab mixture. Coat and form gently into 3/4-in.-thick patties. Working in batches as required, place crab cakes in a basket in a single layer. Spritz crab cakes with spray to cook. Cook for 8-12 minutes, until golden brown, turning carefully halfway through cooking and spritzing with additional spray. Replace, and stay warm. Repeat with leftover crab cakes. In the meantime, place sauce ingredients in a food processor; pulse to blend 2 or 3 times or until the desired consistency is achieved. Serve the crab cakes with a sauce to dip immediately.

NUTRITIONAL INFORMATION

1 crab cake with 1 teaspoon sauce: 49 calories, 2g fat (0 saturated fat), 13mg cholesterol, 179mg sodium, 4g carbohydrate (1g sugars, 0 fiber), 3g protein.

359. SWEET AND SOUR PINEAPPLE PORK

INGREDIENTS

- 1 can (8 ounces) unsweetened crushed pineapple, undrained
- 1 cup cider vinegar
- 1/2 cup sugar
- 1/2 cup packed dark brown sugar
- 1/2 cup ketchup
- 2 tablespoons reduced-sodium soy sauce
- 1 tablespoon Dijon mustard
- 1 teaspoon garlic powder
- 2 pork tenderloins (3/4 pound each), halved
- 1/4 teaspoon salt
- 1/4 teaspoon pepper
- Sliced green onions, optional

INSTRUCTIONS

Combine the first eight ingredients into a large saucepan. Bring to a boil; bring down the heat. Simmer, uncovered, for 15-20 minutes, stirring occasionally until thickened.

Preheat the fryer by air to 350 °. Sprinkle with salt and pepper over the pork. Place pork in greased air-fryer basket; spritz with spray for cooking. Cook for 7-8 minutes, until pork, begins to brown around the edges. Turn; pour 1/4 tablespoon sauce over pork. Cook until at least 145 ° reads a thermometer inserted into the pork, 10-12 minutes longer. Let the pork stand five minutes before being sliced. Serve with leftover sauce. To top with sliced green onions if desired.

NUTRITIONAL INFORMATION

5 ounces cooked pork with 1/2 cup sauce: 489 calories, 6g fat (2g saturated fat), 95mg cholesterol, 985mg sodium, 71g carbohydrate (68g sugars, 1g fiber), 35g protein.

360. BOURBON BACON CINNAMON ROLLS

INGREDIENTS

- 8 bacon strips
- 3/4 cup bourbon
- 1 tube (12.4 ounces) refrigerated cinnamon rolls with icing
- 1/2 cup chopped pecans
- 2 tablespoons maple syrup
- 1 teaspoon minced fresh gingerroot

INSTRUCTIONS

Place bacon on a shallow platter; add bourbon. Seal, and cool overnight. Remove bacon and pat dry; throw away bourbon.

Cook bacon over medium heat in a large skillet, until almost crisp but still pliable. Remove to drain to paper towels. Discard all drippings of except 1 teaspoon.

Preheat the fryer by air to 350 °. Separate dough into 8 rolls, with icing packet reserved. Unrolling spiral rolls into long strips; pat dough to 6x1-in shape. Strips and stripes. Place 1 stripe of bacon on each dough strip, trim bacon as needed; reroll, forming a spiral. Pinch to seal ends. Repeat with leftover dough. Transfer 4 rolls to basket with air-fryer; cook for 5 minutes. Turn the rolls over, and cook for about 4 minutes until golden brown.

Meanwhile, pecans and maple syrup are combined. In another bowl, stir ginger along with icing packet contents. Heat remaining bacon drippings in the same skillet over medium heat. Add the pecan mixture; cook for 2-3 minutes, stirring frequently, until lightly toasted.

Drizzle half the icing over moist rolls of cinnamon; cover with half of the pecans. Repeat to produce a second batch.

NUTRITIONAL INFORMATION

1 roll: 267 calories, 14g fat (3g saturated fat), 9mg cholesterol, 490mg sodium, 28g carbohydrate (13g sugars, 1g fiber), 5g protein.

361. FIESTA CHICKEN FINGERS

INGREDIENTS

- 3/4 pound boneless skinless chicken breasts
- 1/2 cup buttermilk
- 1/4 teaspoon pepper
- 1 cup all-purpose flour
- 3 cups corn chips, crushed
- 1 envelope taco seasoning
- Sour cream ranch dip or salsa

INSTRUCTIONS

Preheat the fryer by air to 400 °. Pound chicken breasts up to 1/2-in with a meat mallet. Heavy duty. Cut to one-in. Strips wide.

Then whisk buttermilk and pepper in a shallow bowl. Place the flour in an individual, shallow bowl. In a third bowl, combine the corn chips and taco seasoning. Dip the chicken to coat both sides in flour; shake off excess. Dip in a mixture of buttermilk and then in a mixture of corn chips, patting to help adhere to the coating.

In packets, place chicken in the greased air-fryer basket in a single layer; spritz with spray to cook. Cook, 7-8 minutes on each side, until the coating, is golden brown and the chicken is no longer pink. Repeat with chicken leftover. Serve with salsa or ranch dip.

NUTRITIONAL INFORMATION

1 serving: 676 calories, 36g fat (6g saturated fat), 47mg cholesterol, 1431mg sodium, 60g carbohydrate (4g sugars, 3g fiber), 24g protein.

362. CHOCOLATE CHIP OATMEAL COOKIES

INGREDIENTS

- 1 cup butter, softened
- 3/4 cup sugar
- 3/4 cup packed brown sugar
- 2 large eggs
- 1 teaspoon vanilla extract
- 3 cups quick-cooking oats
- 1-1/2 cups all-purpose flour
- 1 package (3.4 ounces) instant vanilla pudding mix
- 1 teaspoon baking soda
- 1 teaspoon salt
- 2 cups (12 ounces) semisweet chocolate chips
- 1 cup chopped nuts

INSTRUCTIONS

Air fryer preheats to 325 °. In a large bowl, cream butter and sugars, until light and fluffy.. Beat in Vanilla and Eggs. Whisk oats, flour, dry pudding mixture, baking soda and salt in another bowl; gradually beat them into creamed mixture. Stir in nuts and chocolate chips.

Drop the dough onto baking sheets by tablespoonfuls; flatten slightly. Place 1 in on batches. Apart from it in a greased basket of air-fryer. Cook for 8-10 minutes, until lightly browned. To cool off, remove to wire racks.

NUTRITIONAL INFORMATION

1 cookie: 102 calories, 5g fat (3g saturated fat), 12mg cholesterol, 82mg sodium, 13g carbohydrate (8g sugars, 1g fiber), 2g protein.

363. GREEN TOMATO

INGREDIENTS

- 2 medium green tomatoes (about 10 ounces)
- 1/2 teaspoon salt
- 1/4 teaspoon pepper
- 1 large egg, beaten
- 1/4 cup all-purpose flour
- 1 cup panko bread crumbs
- Cooking spray
- 1/2 cup reduced-fat mayonnaise
- 2 green onions, finely chopped
- 1 teaspoon snipped fresh dill or 1/4 teaspoon dill weed
- 8 slices whole wheat bread, toasted
- 8 cooked center-cut bacon strips
- 4 Bibb or Boston lettuce leaves

INSTRUCTIONS

Air fryer preheats to 325 °. In a large bowl, cream butter and sugars, until light and fluffy.. Beat in Vanilla and Eggs. Whisk oats, flour, drPreheat the fryer by air to 350 °. Cut the tomato into 8 slices, around one quarter in. Each one thick. Sprinkle salt and pepper on tomato slices. In separate, shallow bowls, place the eggs, flour and bread crumbs. Dip the slices of tomatoes in the flour, shake off the excess, then dip into the egg and finally into the mixture of bread crumbs, patting to help them adhere.

In batches, place tomato slices in the greased air-fryer basket in a single layer; spritz with cooking spray. Cook for 8-12 minutes until golden brown, turning halfway and spritzing with an extra cooking spray. Remove, and stay warm.

Meanwhile, mix the mayonnaise, dill and green onions. Layer 4 slices of bread each with 2 strips of bacon, 1 leaf of lettuce and 2 slices of tomato.y pudding mixture, baking soda and salt in another bowl; gradually beat them into creamed mixture. Stir in nuts and chocolate chips.

Drop the dough onto baking sheets by tablespoonfuls; flatten slightly. Place 1 in on batches. Apart from it in a greased basket of air-fryer. Cook for 8-10 minutes, until lightly browned. To cool off, remove to wire racks. Spread the mayonnaise mixture over remaining bread slices; place it over top. Serve straight away.

NUTRITIONAL INFORMATION

1 sandwich: 390 calories, 17g fat (3g saturated fat), 45mg cholesterol, 1006mg sodium, 45g carbohydrate (7g sugars, 5g fiber), 16g protein.

364. REUBEN CALZONES

INGREDIENTS

- 1 tube (13.8 ounces) refrigerated pizza crust
- 4 slices Swiss cheese
- 1 cup sauerkraut, rinsed and well drained
- 1/2 pound sliced cooked corned beef
- Thousand Island salad dressing

INSTRUCTIONS

Preheat the fryer by air to 400 °. Spritz basket with air-fryer cooking spray. Unroll the pizza crust dough on a lightly floured surface and pat it into a 12-in. Full square. Cut to four squares. Layer 1 slice of cheese and a fourth diagonally over half of each square of sauerkraut and corned beef up to within 1/2 in. For rims. Fold 1 corner to the opposite corner over filling, forming a triangle; press the edges to seal with a fork. Place 2 calzones in greased fryer basket in a single layer.

Cook for 8-12 minutes until the calzones are golden brown, flipping halfway through cooking. Repeat with remaining calzones. Remove and keep warm; Serve with dressing for salads.

NUTRITIONAL INFORMATION

1 calzone: 430 calories, 17g fat (6g saturated fat), 66mg cholesterol, 1471mg sodium, 49g carbohydrate (7g sugars, 2g fiber), 21g protein.

365. LEMON SLICE SUGAR COOKIES

INGREDIENTS

- 1/2 cup unsalted butter, softened
- 1 package (3.4 ounces) instant lemon pudding mix
- 1/2 cup sugar
- 1 large egg, room temperature
- 2 tablespoons 2% milk
- 1-1/2 cups all-purpose flour
- 1 teaspoon baking powder
- 1/4 teaspoon salt
- ICING:
- 2/3 cup confectioners' sugar
- 2 to 4 teaspoons lemon juice

INSTRUCTIONS

Cream butter, pudding mixture and sugar in a large bowl, until light and fluffy. Beat in milk and egg. Whisk the flour, baking powder and salt in another bowl; beat gradually into creamed mixture.

Divide the batter into half. Forme each into a 6-in.-long roll on a lightly floured surface. Wrap it and allow it to chill for 3 hours, or until firm.

Air fryer preheats to 325 °. Cross-section dough unwraps and cuts into 1/2 in. Sliced slices. Place the slices in a foil-lined fryer basket in a single layer. Cook for 8-12 minutes, until edges, are light brown. Cool down for 2 minutes in a basket. Remove to wire racks to fully cool down. Repeat with leftover dough. Mix sugar from the confectioners and enough lemon juice in a small bowl to achieve drizzling consistency. Drizzle cookies over. Let stand till set.

To Make Ahead: Dough can be done 2 days beforehand. Put in a resealable container and wrap it in. Store it in the fridge.

Freeze option: Place wrapped logs and freeze in a resealable container. Unwrap frozen logs to use, and cut them into slices. Cook as directed, adding 1-2 minutes more time.

NUTRITIONAL INFORMATION

1 cookie: 110 calories, 4g fat (2g saturated fat), 18mg cholesterol, 99mg sodium, 17g carbohydrate (11g sugars, 0 fiber), 1g protein.

366. PEPPERMINT LAVA CAKES

INGREDIENTS

- 2/3 cup semisweet chocolate chips
- 1/2 cup butter, cubed
- 1 cup confectioners' sugar
- 2 large eggs
- 2 large egg yolks
- 1 teaspoon peppermint extract
- 6 tablespoons all-purpose flour
- 2 tablespoons finely crushed peppermint candies, optional

INSTRUCTIONS

Air fryer preheats to 375 °. Melt the chocolate chips and butter in a microwave-safe bowl for 30 seconds; mix until smooth. Whisk the sugar, eggs, egg yolks in the confectioners and extract until mixed. Fold it down in flour.

Four 4-oz generously grease and flour. Ramekins; pour the ramekins into the batter. Don't overfill them. Place ramekins in fryer basket; cook until 160 ° is read by a thermometer, and set the edges of cakes for 10-12 minutes. Don't overcook them.

Remove it from the oven and let stand for 5 minutes. Carefully run a knife several times around the sides of the ramekins to loosen the cake; invert it to dessert plates. Sprinkle on crushed dumplings. Serve straight away.

NUTRITIONAL INFORMATION

1 serving: 563 calories, 36g fat (21g saturated fat), 246mg cholesterol, 226mg sodium, 57g carbohydrate (45g sugars, 2g fiber), 7g protein.

367. QUENTIN'S PEACH-BOURBON WINGS

INGREDIENTS

- 1/2 cup peach preserves
- 1 tablespoon brown sugar
- 1 garlic cloves, minced
- 1/4 teaspoon salt
- 2 tablespoons white vinegar
- 2 tablespoons bourbon
- 1 teaspoon cornstarch
- 1-1/2 teaspoons water
- 2 pounds chicken wings

INSTRUCTIONS

Preheat the fryer by air to 400 °. In a food processor put preserves, brown sugar, garlic, and salt; process until blended. Transfer to a saucepan. Remove bourbon and vinegar, and bring it to a boil. Reduce heat; simmer, uncovered, for 4-6 minutes until slightly thickened.

Mix the cornstarch and water in a small bowl until smooth; stir in preserve mixture. Return to a boil, constantly stirring; cook and stir for 1-2 minutes, or until thick. Apply 1/4 cup sauce to drink.

Using a sharp knife, cut each chicken wing through the two joints; discard tips on the wing. Spray basket with cooking spray to the air fryer. Working in batches as needed, place wing pieces in the air fryer basket in a single layer. 6 Minutes to cook; Turn over and clean the mixture with preserve. Return to air fryer and cook for 6-8 minutes, until browned and juices run free. Remove, and stay warm. Repeat on remaining pieces of a wing. Serve wings with reserved sauce, immediately.

368. CORN NUTS

INGREDIENTS

- 14 ounces giant white corn (such as Goya)
- 3 tablespoons vegetable oil
- 1 1/2 teaspoons salt

INSTRUCTIONS

Place the corn in a large bowl, cover with water and let sit for 8 hours to re-hydrate overnight.

Drain the corn and spread it over a large baking sheet in an even layer. Pat dry with towels made from paper. Dry air for 20 minutes.

Air fryer preheats to 400 degrees F (200 degrees C).

Put the corn in a bowl. Season with oil and salt. Remove until the coating is even.

Place the corn in batches in an even layer in the air fryer basket. Cook for a further 10 minutes. Shake basket and continue cooking for another 10 minutes. Shake basket and cook for another 5 minutes, and transfer to a towel-lined sheet of paper. Repeat with leftover corn. Let the corn nuts cool down, about 20 minutes, until crisp.

369. SMOKY CHICKPEAS

INGREDIENTS

- 1 15 oz can chickpeas , rinsed and drained well
- 1 tablespoon sunflower oil (or preferred oil)
- 2 tablespoons lemon juice
- 3/4 teaspoon smoked paprika
- 1/2 teaspoon ground cumin
- 1/2 teaspoon granulated garlic
- 1/4 teaspoon granulated onion
- 1/2 teaspoon sea salt , more to taste
- 1/8 teaspoon cayenne pepper (optional)

INSTRUCTIONS

Put the Air Fryer up to 390 ° F.

Place the rinsed chickpeas in the basket, then fry until dry for 15 minutes. At midway mark shake basket once.

You can prepare the seasoning whilst they cook. Place the butter, lemon and any seasonings in a medium bowl. Whisk well to combine.

The fried chickpeas are carefully added to the seasoning bowl. Stir well to combine.

Return the experienced chickpeas to your air fryer basket and set to 360 ° F. Now fry for 2-3 minutes until it reaches desired crispiness. At midway mark shake basket once.

Seasoning taste, and add if necessary. Enjoy immediately, or store for 3-5 days in an airtight container. Let it cool completely before storing it.

370. NUTTY FRENCH TOAST

INGREDIENTS

- 1 cup (99g) rolled oats
- 1 cup (113g) pecans, or nut of your choice
- 2 tablespoons (12g) ground flax seed
- 1 teaspoon (2g) ground cinnamon
- 8 pieces of whole grain vegan bread, regular or cinnamon raisin (use gluten-free bread)
- ¾ cup nondairy milk (plain or vanilla)
- maple syrup, for serving

INSTRUCTIONS

Build the topping by combining your food processor with the oats, nuts, flaxseed and cinnamon and pulse until it looks similar to bread crumbs. Don't over mingle. Pour into a shallow pan that is wide enough to dip the slices of your bread in.

In a second container add the nondairy milk, then soak one or two pieces of bread for about 15 seconds, turn and soak the other side. You don't want to let it go long enough to get mushy.

Place the amount that fits in your basket of air fryer at once, without overlapping. Cook for 3 minutes at 350 degrees, then flip over the bread and cook for 3 more minutes.

Repeat until all of the cooked bread is coated.

Serve with maple syrup on top.

371. BAKED APPLE WITH WALNUTS

INGREDIENTS:

- 1 medium apple or pear
- 2 Tbsp. chopped walnuts
- 2 Tbsp. raisins
- 1 ½ tsp. light margarine, melted
- ¼ tsp. cinnamon
- ¼ tsp. nutmeg
- ¼ cup water

INSTRUCTIONS:

Air fryer preheats to 350 ° F.

Cut the apple or pear around the middle in half, and spoon some flesh out.

Place the apple or pear in the frying pan (which the air fryer may provide) or on the bottom of the air fryer (after removing the accessory).

Combine margarine, cinnamon, nutmeg, walnut, and raisins into a small bowl.

Spoon this mixture into apple/pear halve centers.

Pour water into the saucepan.

Bake for another 20 minutes.

372. VEGGIE WONTONS

INGREDIENTS

- 30 Wonton Wrappers
- 3/4 cup Grated Cabbage
- 1/2 cup Grated White Onion
- 1/2 cup Grated Carrot
- 1/2 cup Finely Chopped Mushrooms
- 3/4 cup Finely Chopped Red Pepper
- 1 tablespoons Chili Sauce
- 1 teaspoon Garlic Powder
- 1/2 teaspoon White Pepper
- Pinch of Salt
- 1/4 cup Water (for sealing wontons)
- Spray Olive Oil

INSTRUCTIONS

In a hot skillet or medium-heat wok throw all your vegetables in. Cook until all the mushroom and onion moisture has released and cooked out of the saucepan.

Remove from heat and add salt, garlic powder, white pepper and chili sauce. Let the mixture cool before having your wontons assembled.

Remove from basket place once cooked and let cool before consuming. Serve alongside with duck sauce or soy!

Place a wonton wrapper onto your work surface. Add 1 spoonful of your veggie mixture to the wonton wrapper center.

Dip your finger in 1/4 cup of water and run your finger along the square wrapper's exposed top half to wet it.

Push the bottom half carefully up and over the mixture making the corners rest offset.

Spray your palm again, and spray the wonton's lower corners. Fold gently over the wonton's bottom corners so that one sits on top of the other and exerts slight pressure to seal it. Make sure the seals along your wonton are not open. Do another 29 times.

Remove from basket place once cooked and let cool before consuming. Serve alongside with duck sauce or soy!

Preheat your air-fryer for 3 minutes to 320 degrees. While spritzing your wontons with a little olive oil preheats them.

Extract from basket place once cooked and let cool before consuming. Serve side by side with Duck Sauce, or Soy Sauce!

373. BACON WRAPPED FILET MIGNON

INGREDIENTS

- 2 filet mignon steaks
- 2 slices of bacon
- 2 to othpicks
- 1 teaspoon freshly cracked peppercorns we use a variety of peppercorns
- 1/2 teaspoon kosher salt
- avocado oil

INSTRUCTIONS

Wrap the bacon around the mignon filet and secure it with a toothpick by pressing the toothpick through the bacon and into the filet, then to the bacon on the other end of the toothpick from the filet.

Season the steak with the salt and pepper or the seasonings you prefer.

Place the mignon filet wrapped with bacon on the air fryer rack.

Sprinkle a small amount of avocado oil on the steak.

How long to cook bacon-wrapped filet mignon Air fry the steak at 375 degrees F for about 10 minutes, and then flip as one side is nice and seared while the other is not.

Fry air for another 5 minutes, or until the desired doneness is reached. We are pursuing a medium.

NUTRITIONAL INFORMATION

Calories: 557kcal , Protein: 29g , Fat: 26g , Saturated Fat: 9g , Cholesterol: 115mg , Sodium: 783mg , Potassium: 560mg , Calcium: 12mg , Iron: 4mg

374. SALTY PISTACHIO SMALL BATCH BROWNIES

INGREDIENTS

- ¼ cup (60ml) nondairy milk
- ¼ cup (60ml) aquafaba
- ½ teaspoon vanilla extract
- ½ cup (48g) whole wheat pastry flour (use gluten-free baking blend)
- ½ cup (99g) vegan sugar (or sweetener of choice, to taste)
- ¼ cup (21g) cocoa powder
- 1 tablespoon (6g) ground flax seeds
- ¼ teaspoon salt
- mix ins: ¼ cup of any one or a combination of the following: chopped walnuts, hazelnuts, pecans, mini vegan chocolate chips, shredded coconut

INSTRUCTIONS

In a bowl, combine the dry ingredients together.

The wet ingredients are then mixed in a large measuring cup. Stir the wet into the dry and blend well.

Add your choice of mix-in(s), and mix again.

Preheat your air fryer to 350 ° F (or as close as it gets to the air fryer).

To keep it completely oil-free, either spray some oil on a 5-inch cake or pie round pan (or a loaf pan that fits into your air fryer), or line it with parchment paper.

Place the pan into the basket for the fryer. Cook for around 20 minutes. If the middle is not well set or when stuck in the middle cook for 5 minutes more a knife does not come out clean and repeat as required. Depending on the size pan and your particular air-fryer, the time may vary.

375. PLANTAIN CHIPS

INGREDIENTS

- 1 each green plantain
- 1 tsp canola oil or canola cooking spray
- 1/2 tsp sea salt or to taste
- Plantain Chips in the Airfryer

INSTRUCTIONS

Peel and cut the plantains in half and slice them into very thin coins or strips. NOTE: If you want consistent, ultra-fine slices, use a mandolin slicer.

Coat the basket fryer with 1/2 tsp of canola oil and lay the slices of the plantain along the bottom. Blend the remaining canola oil over the slices. Season with to taste sea salt.

Depending on the thickness of the slices, air fry your plantain chips at 350 ° F for 15-20 minutes. During the air frying process, be sure to shake your basket once or twice to make sure they are evenly cooked. After about 10 minutes watching them closely to prevent burning. If you have unevenly cut them, you may need to take some out each time you check-in. NOTE: If your plantains start sticking to the bottom, just lift them off with a pair of tongs and put a good shake on the basket.

Nosh the plantain chips on your air fryer right out of the fryer, or serve with your favorite condiment. Enjoy it!

376. PALEO SALMON CAKES

INGREDIENTS

- 1 lb ALDI Fresh Atlantic Salmon Side (half a side)
- 1/4 Cup Avocado, mashed
- 1/4 Cup Cilantro, diced + additional for garnish
- 1 1/2 tsp Yellow curry powder
- 1/2 tsp Stonemill Sea Salt Grinder
- 1/4 Cup + 4 tsp Tapioca Starch, divided (40g) *Read notes for lower carb version
- 2 SimplyNature Organic Cage Free Brown Eggs
- 1/2 Cup SimplyNature Organic Coconut Flakes (30g)
- SimplyNature Organic Coconut Oil, melted (for brushing)

For the greens:

- 2 tsp SimplyNature Organic Coconut Oil, melted
- 6 Cups SimplyNature Organic Arugula & Spinach Mix, tightly packed
- Pinch of Stonemill Sea Salt Grinder

INSTRUCTIONS

Remove the salmon skin, dice the flesh and place in a large bowl.

Add the avocado, coriander, curry powder, marine salt and stir until well mixed. Then, stir the tapioca starch in 4 tsp until well incorporated.

Line a parchment-papered baking sheet. Form the salmon into 8, 1/4 cup-sized patties, slightly thicker than 1/2 inch, and place them on the pan. Freeze for 20 minutes so that they can work easier.

While the patties freeze, preheat your Air Fryer 10 minutes to 400 degrees and rub the basket with coconut oil. Whisk the eggs in addition, and place them in a shallow plate. Dip one into the tapioca starch once the patties have chilled, ensuring it is fully covered. Then dip it into the egg, completely cover it and gently brush off any excess. Finally, just press the cake's top and sides into the coconut flakes and place it in the air fryer, coconut flake-side up. Repeat with all those cakes. Brush the tops gently with a bit of melted coconut oil (optional but recommended) and cook until golden brown and crispy on the outside, and the inside is juicy and tender about 15 minutes. Note: The patties will stick a little bit to the basked Air Fryer, so use a sharp-edged spatula to remove them.

Heat the coconut oil up in a large pan over medium heat when the cakes have about 5 minutes left to cook. Add a pinch of salt and cook in the Arugula and Spinach Mix, stirring constantly until the greens start to wilt, just 30 seconds-1 minute.

Divide the greens onto 4 plates, then the salmon cakes. Garnish with DEVOUR and extra cilantro!

If you want to bake in the oven: Preheat your oven to 400 degrees and line a parchment paper baking sheet, putting a cooling rack on top of the pan. Rub the rack with coconut oil to cool.

Place the patties, coconut-side up, onto the cooling rack and bake until crispy for 15-17 minutes.

377. TUNA PATTIES

INGREDIENTS

- 2 cans tuna packed in water
- 1 and 1/2 tablespoon almond flour
- 1 and 1/2 tablespoons mayo
- 1 teaspoon dried dill
- 1 teaspoon garlic powder
- 1/2 teaspoon onion powder
- Pinch of salt and pepper
- Juice of 1/2 lemon

INSTRUCTIONS

Mix all the ingredients in a bowl and combine it well. For Air Fryer: Heat up to 400 degrees F, Tuna should still be wet but able to form into patties add an additional tablespoon of almond flour if it is not dry enough to form Form into 4 patties.

Place patties in the basket in a single layer, and cook for 10 minutes. Add an extra 3 minutes if you want them crisper

378. PALEO PARSNIP FRENCH FRIES

INGREDIENTS

- 6 parsnips
- 1/4 cup almond flour
- 1/4 cup water
- salt
- 1/4 cup olive oil

INSTRUCTIONS

Peel and slice the parsnips to 1/2"x 3" Mix the almond flour, water, olive oil and salt in a large bowl and put the parsnips in the mixture and stir until coated.

3 Minutes to preheat the Philips Airfryer to 390F.

Add those parsnips.

Cook for about 12-14 minutes. I cooked mine for 14 minutes and it was perfect.

Take the Airfryer off and enjoy it.

NUTRITIONAL INFORMATION

yield: 4 serving size: 1

amount per serving: calories: 264 total fat: 17g saturated fat: 2g trans fat: 0g unsaturated fat: 15g cholesterol: 0mg sodium: 161mg carbohydrates: 27g fiber: 6g sugar: 7g protein: 3g

379. PALEO CAULIFLOWER TATER TOTS

INGREDIENTS

- 1 large head of cauliflower separated into large florets
- 2 large eggs
- 1/4 cup coconut flour
- 1 tsp garlic powder
- 1 tsp onion powder
- coconut oil spray or mist
- 1 tsp dried parsley
- salt and pepper to taste

INSTRUCTIONS

Set the cauliflower apart into large florets.

Add the florets and 2 tablespoons of water in a large microwaveable bowl. Depending on the power of your microwave, cover with a plastic wrap and microwave for 3 to 5 minutes. The floret is meant to be tender but not mushy. Microwave for 3 minutes initially. If underdone, take another minute or two to microwave. Drain good.

Combine the florets and process them in a chopper or food processor, until they imitate rice grains. Pour it into a saucepan.

Add the beaten eggs, salt, and pepper, coconut flour, garlic powder, onion powder, dried parsley. Blend well.

Take a small quantity of the mix, and shape it like tots. Chill 30 minutes on the cauliflower tots.

380. FLOURLESS CHOCOLATE ALMOND CUPCAKES

INGREDIENTS

- 3 tbls. butter
- 2 tbls. real maple syrup
- 1/2 cup almond flour
- 1/8 tsp. salt
- 1/3 cup chocolate chips
- 1 egg beaten
- 1/2 tsp. vanilla

INSTRUCTIONS

Preheat oven to 350 ° C. Places the liners in the cupcake pan.

For Air Fryer: Preheat at 320oC. Use cupcake liners with silicone.

Add the chocolate chips, butter, and honey in a glass or stainless steel bowl and heat over a double boiler for a few seconds only until the chocolate begins to melt. When the chocolate begins to melt, remove the bowl and start stirring until the butter, honey, and chocolate are well blended. Let it cool off (about 5-8 min.).

In the cooled melted chocolate add the remaining ingredients and stir well with a wooden spoon. Scoop the batter into the cupcake pan that was packed.

Bake for about 15-18 minutes or until a toothpick inserted comes out clean. Bake for 8-12 minutes

If toothpick does not come out clean, then continue cooking at intervals of 3-4 minutes.

Top with slivered almonds and unflavored shredded coconut. Sprinkle on and serve with powdered sugar.

381. GLUTEN-FREE EASY COCONUT PIE

INGREDIENTS

- 2 eggs
- 1 1/2 cups milk (you can use coconut milk or almond milk)
- 1/4 cup butter
- 1 1/2 tsp. vanilla extract
- 1 cup shredded coconut (I used sweetened)
- 1/2 cup granulated Monk Fruit (or your preferred sugar)
- 1/2 cup coconut flour

INSTRUCTIONS

AIR FRYER RECIPE

Coat A Six Non-stick spray pie plate and fill with batter. Continue to follow the instructions set out above.

Cook on the Air Fryer for 10 to 12 minutes at 350 degrees. Check the pie halfway through the cooking time to make sure it isn't burning, give a turn to the plate, use a toothpick to check for doneness. Continue cooking accordingly. Cooking time for an air fryer can vary from one manufacturer to another.

382. CHEESECAKE BITES

INGREDIENTS:

- 8 ounces cream cheese
- 1/2 cup erythritol
- 4 Tablespoons heavy cream, divided
- 1/2 teaspoon vanilla extract
- 1/2 cup almond flour
- 2 Tablespoons erythritol

INSTRUCTIONS

Allow the cream cheese to sit on the counter and soften for 20 minutes.

Fits a paddle attachment stand mixer.

Mix the softened cream cheese, 1/2 cup Erythritol, vanilla and 2 Heavy cream spoonfuls until smooth.

Lined with parchment paper, scoop onto a baking sheet.

Freeze for approximately 30 minutes, until strong.

In a small mixing bowl, combine the almond flour with the 2 Tablespoons erythritol.

Dip the bites from the frozen cheesecake into 2 Tablespoons of cream, then roll into the almond flour mix. Set at 300, place in an air fryer for 2 minutes.

383. PALEO APPLE CIDER VINEGAR DONUTS

INGREDIENTS

- For the Muffins
- 4 large eggs
- 4 tbsp coconut oil melted
- 3 tbsp honey
- 2/3 cup apple cider vinegar
- 1 cup coconut flour
- 1 tsp cinnamon
- 1 tsp baking soda
- pinch salt
- For the Drizzle:
- Turmeric Pumpkin Spice Coffee Syrup

INSTRUCTIONS

Oven preheats to 350 F. Prepare a donut baking pan by spraying liberally with cooking spray or using coconut oil to grease well.

Wish the eggs, salt, honey, apple cider vinegar, and melted coconut oil together in a small bowl.

Sift cinnamon, baking soda, and coconut flour together in a separate bowl, to disperse the dry ingredients well.

Attach the dry ingredients to the wet ingredients until mixed thoroughly. The batter is going to be a bit humid. Transfer the batter to the baking pan for the donut and scoop the batter into the cavities. Use your fingers to evenly spread the batter inside the cavity.

Bake for 10 minutes at 350 F, until golden around the edges.

Remove from the oven and cool in baking for 5-10 minutes before flipping onto a removable wire rack. It's very important that these are cool before you remove them otherwise they're going to fall apart. They need to be a little tough! Drizzle with devour coffee syrup and turmeric pumpkin spice!

384. COCONUT-ENCRUSTED CINNAMON BANANAS

INGREDIENTS

- 4 ripe but firm bananas cut into thirds
- 1/2 cup tapioca flour
- 2 large eggs
- 1 cup shredded coconut flakes
- 1 tsp ground cinnamon
- coconut spray

INSTRUCTIONS

Cut each banana into thirds Make an assembly line-Pour in a shallow dish the tapioca flour in.

Crack the eggs and whisk lightly into another shallow bowl.

In the third shallow dish mix the shredded coconut with the ground cinnamon. Blend well.

Dredge the tapioca flour into the bananas and shake off the excess.

Dip the beaten eggs into it. Make sure egg wash is fully coated.

To coat it fully, roll the bananas in the cinnamon–coconut flakes. Press it firmly to ensure the bananas adhere to the coconut flakes. Keep them in a flat dresser.

Sprinkle the air fryer basket with coconut oil, liberally.

Arrange the bits of coconut-crusted bananas in the bowl for the fryer. Sprinkle with more spray on coconut.

Air fry for 12 minutes at 270F with soil cinnamon and serve warm or at room temperature with a low-carb ice cream scoop (optional).

385. JUICY TURKEY BURGERS WITH ZUCCHINI

INGREDIENTS

- 6 oz grated zucchini, when squeezed 4.25 oz
- 1 lb 93% lean ground turkey
- 1/4 cup seasoned whole wheat or gluten-free breadcrumbs
- 1 clove garlic, grated
- 1 tbsp grated red onion
- 1 tsp kosher salt and fresh pepper
- oil spray

INSTRUCTIONS

Squeeze ALL of the zucchini moisture with paper towels. Combine the ground turkey, zucchini, breadcrumbs, garlic, onions, salt and pepper in a large bowl. Make 5 equal patties, every 4 ounces, not too thick to cook in the center.

Air Fryer Instructions: Use paper towels to squeeze out all moisture well from the zucchini.

Combine the ground turkey, zucchini, breadcrumbs, garlic, onion, pepper and salt in a large bowl. Make 5 patties of equal size, 4 ounces each, 1/2 "thick.

Preheat the fryer by air to 370F.

Cook 10 minutes in a single layer in two lots, turning halfway until browned and cooked through in the middle.

386. CRISPY CHEESY VEGAN QUESARITO

INGREDIENTS

- 2 large gluten free tortillas
- 4 tablespoons Vegan Queso, divided
- 2-3 tablespoons grated cheese (this cheese used here)
- 3 tablespoons Meaty Crumbles
- 3-4 tablespoons Simple Spanish Rice
- 1-2 tablespoons Spicy Almond Sauce
- 1 tablespoon cashew cream or dairy free sour cream / yogurt
- add ins: fresh baby spinach, fresh bell peppers or roasted red peppers

INSTRUCTIONS

Lay flat on the prep surface for the first tortilla.

Cut about an inch from around the whole edge of the second tortilla carefully using a knife, making one smaller tortilla. Deposit aside.

The vegan queso spread around the center of the tortilla on the first tortilla, in a circle the size of the smaller tortilla. Add 3 spoons of grated cheese to the top of the cheese, in an even layer across the small circle, reserving 1 spoonful of grated cheese. Top the cheese/cheese circle with the tinier second tortilla, slightly press down.

Spoon a line of meaty crumbles onto the middle of the second smaller tortilla. Spoon a meaty line crumbles. Spoon the Spanish rice on top of the meaty crumbles, followed by the tangy cream sauce and a cashew/sour cream.

Following the instructions found in the above video, tightly fold and roll a burrito. Secure the edge with 1 tablespoon of grated cheese reserved. This cheese will melt and remain packed on the burrito.

Place sealed side-down burrito cheese in the air fryer basket.

Crisp in the air fryer at 370 ° F for 6-7 minutes, or until lightly golden and crisp.

Instructions for baking an oven: The same steps for assembly as above. Place the quesarito onto a baking sheet. Bake for 12-15 minutes at 350 ° F, or till golden and crisp.

Instructions for Skillet: Make quesadilla layer as above. Fry over medium-low heat in a dry skillet, watch carefully and turn to each side for a golden brown crisp.

Remove from skillet, transfer to the surface for preparation. Apply ingredients in the order above into the middle of a quesadilla. Fold in and roll carefully into a tight burrito. Back to the skillet to warm up, turning every minute or so on each side. Alternatively, Bake for 6-7 minutes in a 350 ° F oven.

NUTRITIONAL INFORMATION

Amount Per Serving: Calories: 514 Total Fat: 18g Saturated Fat: 11g Trans Fat: 1g Unsaturated Fat: 4g Sodium: 230mg Carbohydrates: 13g Fiber: 10g Sugar: 6g Protein: 22g

387. CHIPOTLE QUESADILLAS WITH MINTY MANGO SALSA

INGREDIENTS:

- 8 gluten free tortillas
- 1 avocado, pitted and peeled
- 1 (8 ounce) package Organic Chipotle Tofu Baked
- 4 ounces dairy free cheese, grated
- dairy free butter, for cooking
- Minty Mango Salsa

INSTRUCTIONS

Scoop peeling an avocado. Layout four tortillas, mash one-fourth of each tortilla with avocado.

Crumble a two-ounce TofuBaked piece onto each tortilla, in an even layer above avocado.

Sprinkle over each tortilla one ounce of grated cheese, and over TofuBaked in one even layer.

Fill each one with one of the four remaining tortillas and click together.

Air fryer instructions: Secure quesadilla with toothpicks to keep from ' flying around. Cook the Taco Crunch Wrap at 370 ° F for 7 minutes, rotating over halfway.

Flip carefully to the other side, then add more butter as needed. Cover and cook until golden brown, crisp on both sides, fill is heated and cheese is melted.

Repeat the cooking process, with three quesadillas remaining. Cut into equal pieces in four to six, top with Minty Mango Salsa. Serving warm.

388. WHISKEY GARLIC TOFU OVER VEGETABLE QUINOA

INGREDIENTS:

- 1/4 cup whiskey
- 1/4 cup vegan sugar (coconut, maple)
- 2 garlic cloves, peeled and minced
- 1 tablespoon apple cider vinegar
- 1 teaspoon onion powder
- sea salt and black pepper
- 1 block extra firm tofu, pressed

INSTRUCTIONS

When using an air fryer, line basket with round parchment.

Preheat the oven to 350 ° F if used. Line parchment baking sheet.

Slice into half-inch slabs once the tofu is pressed–with a regular tofu block, on the short side I cut into three segments, then slice each segment in half in a lengthwise direction.

Combine whiskey, sugar, garlic, onion powder and vinegar in a saucepan. Continually stir, bring to a boil and then reduce to simmer. Simmer for 10 minutes, and stir frequently. Remove from heat and allow slightly to cool.

Coat all slices of tofu, put them on the prepared baking sheets.

Fry in the air fryer at 370 for 7 minutes. Turn/flip, cook another three to four minutes.

Bake for 25 minutes at 350 ° F, and turn after 12 minutes. Serve over salad or Great Mashed Potatoes, or quinoa vegetables.

389. VEGAN GOAT CHEESE BACON WRAPPED DATES

INGREDIENTS:

- 8 Medjool dates, pitted
- 3+ tablespoons Vegan Goat Cheese (or your favorite vegan soft cheese)
- Smoky Rich Double Layer Rice Paper Bacon

INSTRUCTIONS

Preheat oven to 350 degrees F. Line a parchment-filled baking sheet.

Slice the date lengthwise (if you have already pitted your dates, look for the slice already made). Fill every date with goat cheese (approximately one teaspoon in each).

Make bacon strips by recipe. Wrap uncooked bacon around the date they are filled. Repeat on all dates.

Bake for 15-18 minutes, at 350 ° F. Serving warm.

390. BLACK BEAN TOTCHOS WITH GARLIC LEMON SAUCE

INGREDIENTS

- 1 1/4 cups tater tots
- 1 cup black beans
- salsa
- sour cream (dairy free / vegan)
- garlic lemon sauce (recipe follows)

INSTRUCTIONS

Use air fryer to prepare. Set temperatures to 400 ° F, cook tater tots for seven minutes. Remove, shake, add edamame, to turn the tot's tater. Return to air fryer and cook for another 5 minutes, until the tots are fully cooked and the edamame is hot.

If using an oven, preheat oven to 425 ° F. Line parchment baking sheet.

Arrange tater tots into a single layer on a lined (parchment) baking sheet. Bake for 15 minutes, remove temperature from oven to 375 ° F. Move to one side of the baking sheet using a spatula, flip tater tots and keep in a single layer.

Prepare the garlic lemon sauce, slice the green onion and prep toppings while the tater tots bake.

Assemble touches: pile tots on two plates, black beans, salsa, sour cream and lemon sauce with garlic. Top with green onion and serve straight away.

391. BEETROOT CHIPS

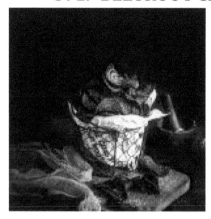

INGREDIENTS

- 2 Medium Sized Beetroot
- 1/2 Tsp Oil
- Salt to taste
- Pepper Optional

INSTRUCTIONS

Wash the Beetroot, peel the skin, then set aside the skin. Slice them thinly using a mandoline slicer. Better slice them evenly thin with your knife if you don't have a slicer.

Use the skin to dye your prop if you want it in your food waste, or dump it.

Spread the slices of beetroot on the paper and place another paper over it. Keep that 10 minutes aside. This process will allow the beetroot thins to absorb any extra moisture.

Throw the sliced beetroot into oil and sprinkle on the beetroot with the salt required. Preheat the Airfryer for 4 minutes until 150 C. Pull the basket out of the air fryer and put the chips inside. Slide the fryer back into the air and fry for 15 minutes. After every 5 minutes make sure to remove in between, and give it a good shake. Once the chips on the outer edges are slightly crisp and tender in the middle, let them cool down for some time.

Slide back the basket with the chips, and heat for another 3 minutes at 180 C. Overall, the chips will be really crisp and perfect to much at once.

Season with salt from the sea and freshly ground pepper if you like it or just mash it as it is. Anyway, we love it.

392. COCONUT SHRIMP WITH SPICY MARMALADE SAUCE

INGREDIENTS

- 8 large shrimp shelled and deveined
- 8 ounces coconut milk
- 1/2 cup shredded sweetened coconut
- 1/2 cup panko bread
- 1/2 teaspoon cayenner pepper
- 1/4 teaspoon kosher salt
- 1/4 teaspoon fresh ground pepper
- 1/2 cup orange marmalade
- 1 tablespoon honey
- 1 teaspoon mustard
- 1/4 teaspoon hot sauce

INSTRUCTIONS

Clean, and set aside the shrimp.

Whisk the coconut milk in a small bowl, and season with salt and pepper. Deposit aside. Whisk the coconut, panko, cayenne pepper, salt, and pepper together in a separate, small bowl.

Dip the shrimp one at a time into the coconut milk, the panko, then place them in the fryer's basket. Repeat until it coats all the shrimps. Cook the shrimp at 350 degrees in the fryer for 20 minutes, or until the shrimp is cooked through.

While the shrimp cook, whisk the marmalade, honey, mustard, and hot sauce together.

Serve the shrimp straight away with the sauce.

393. EGGLESS CHOCOLATE CHIP MUFFINS

INGREDIENTS

- 1/2 cup self raising flour
- 1/2 cup all purpose flour baking powder salt or use half tsp pinch
- 1 tbsp cocoa Nesquik or powder
- 1/4 tsp baking soda
- 1/4 cup sugar
- 1 tbsp honey
- 2 tbsps yogurt
- 4 tbsps milk
- 2 tbsps vegetable oil
- 1/2 tsp vanilla extract
- 1 tsp apple cider vinegar (or regular vinegar)
- 2 tbsps chocolate chips

INSTRUCTIONS

Airfryer preheats to 200xb0C.

Remove 1 tbsp of flour from the 1/2 cup flour and add 1 tbsp of cocoa or Nesquick powder. This is to ensure that the dry component total is 1/2 cup. Attach the baking powder and salt, if you use plain flour and do not collect flour on your own.

Stir in baking soda and sugar and combine it with a fork.

Whisk together milk, yogurt, oil, and vanilla extract in a measuring jug or small bowl, until combined.

Make the dry ingredients well, and add the wet ingredients. Stir in vinegar.

Stir to merge. Do not over-mix, at this stage a few lumps of flour are ok. Blend into chocolate chips. Spoon the mixture into 6 silicone cupcake/muffin molds Position 4 at a time in the preheated air fryer wire rack.

Set timer at 8 minutes, after which a skewer/tester can be inserted to see if it comes out cleanly. At this point, you can keep the second batch for baking.

Remove for 5 minutes, then cool. Remove from molds, and cover or place in refrigerator airtight containers.

You can store that in an airtight box for 4-5 days in the refrigerator.

394. KETO RADISH CHIPS

INGREDIENTS

- One bag of radish slices
- Avocado oil or olive oil in a spritzer
- salt
- pepper
- garlic powder
- onion powder

INSTRUCTIONS

Wash and pat off-dry slices of radish. Place the radishes and spread evenly in the air fryer basket. Spritz with oil, 3-4 times. Sprinkle with the salt, pepper, ground garlic, and onion powder.

Cook in the air fryer at 370 ° for 5 minutes. Stir them up a little and continue cooking for another five minutes.

After 10 minutes, spritz 3-4 more times with oil and sprinkle with a little extra salt, pepper, garlic powder, and onion powder.

Cook for another 5 minutes, and stir them up again. Cook another 3 minutes to keep a close eye that they are not getting too crispy.

395. CHERRY PIE

INGREDIENTS

- 2 rolls refrigerated pie crust
- All-purpose flour for dusting
- 1 can cherry pie filling 12.5-ounce
- 1 egg beaten
- 1 tablespoon water
- 1 tablespoon raw sugar

INSTRUCTIONS

Defrost the crust of the refrigerated pie and place it on a flat, floured surface of work.

Roll out the thawed pie crust, and reverse the dough with a shallow air fryer baking pan.

Cut the pan around, making your cut a half-inch wider than the pan itself.

Repeat with the crust of the second pie, only make the cut the same size or slightly smaller than the pan.

Layout the larger crust at the bottom of the baking pan, gently pressing into the dough to conform to the shape of the pan.

Spoon in the filling of a cherry pie. Place the smaller piece of crust over the filling, and pinch each crust edge together.

OR-cut the second piece into 1 "strips and weave in a lattice pattern before placing over the top of the pie. Make a few cuts at the top of the dough. In a small bowl, whisk the egg and water together. Sprinkle the egg gently over the top of the pie. Sprinkle with the raw sugar and place the pan in the air fryer basket. Bake at 320 degrees for 30 minutes, until golden brown and flaky.

396. MOZZARELLA CHEESE STICKS

INGREDIENTS

- 6 mozzarella cheese sticks
- 1/2 cup seasoned Italian breadcrumbs
- 1 egg
- 3 tablespoons milk
- 1/2 cup flour

INSTRUCTIONS

Split sticks of mozzarella cheese into two.

Put the crumbs in a bowl. Place the flour in an individual bowl. Blend together the egg and milk, and put in another dish.

Dip the cheese sticks into the milk, then the egg and then the crumbs of the crust.

Lay cheese sticks on a sheet of cookies and put in a freezer for 1-2 hours or until solid.

Place breaded sticks, without overcrowding, in fry basket.

Optional but delicious: Mist the sticks with some cooking oil so they'll beautifully crisp up.

Set some cooking time at 400 degrees for 10 minutes.

397. CHOCOLATE ZUCCHINI BREAD

INGREDIENTS

- 1/2 cup all-purpose flour
- 1/4 cup cocoa powder
- 1/2 teaspoon baking soda
- 1/4 teaspoon salt
- 1 egg at room temperature
- 6 tablespoons packed light brown sugar
- 2 tablespoons butter melted and slightly cooled
- 2 tablespoons vegetable oil
- 1/2 teaspoon vanilla extract
- ¾ cup packed shredded zucchini
- 1/2 cup semisweet chocolate chips divided

INSTRUCTIONS

The Air Fryer is preheated to 310 degrees.

Grease with shortening to a mini loaf pan. Deposit aside.

Whisk the flour, cocoa powder, baking soda, and salt together in a medium mixing bowl. Deposit aside.

Combine eggs, brown sugar, melted butter, oil, and vanilla in a larger bowl. Whisk smoothly until.

Add the dry ingredients and mix them until just combined.

Fold in the zucchini and most chocolate chips, setting aside some for the top.

Transfer to mini loaf prepared pan.

Sprinkle over remaining chocolate chips.

Bake for 30 to 35 minutes in air fryer at 310 degrees, or until the toothpick test comes out clean.

Remove from the air fryer and cool down on a wire rack until warm.

Then remove from the loaf pan before storing in an airtight container and continue cooling on the wire rack.

398. APPLE PIE

INGREDIENTS

- Air Fryer
- 325 g Small Apple Chunks
- 50 g Caster Sugar
- Pie Pan
- Air Fryer Apple Pie Ingredients:
- 2 Tsp Cinnamon
- ½ Tsp Nutmeg
- 400 g Air Fryer Pie Crust
- 1 Small Lemon zest and juice
- 1 Small Egg for egg wash
- Metric – Imperial

INSTRUCTIONS

Roll out the pie crust, and place it inside the pie pan bottom.

Take your peeled and diced apples and your lemon, cinnamon, and nutmeg in the pie pan and push them down and make sure there are no apple gaps.

Remove the pie crust's second layer, and press over your apples. Stab with a knife in the middle to allow the pie room to breathe, then add a layer of egg wash using a pastry brush.

Put the middle shelf in the air fryer oven, and cook for 30 minutes at 180c/360f.

Serve with milk, custard and ice cream.

399. BLACKBERRY HAND PIES

INGREDIENTS

- 1 package refrigerated pie dough
- 1 egg beaten
- FOR FILLING:
- 12 oz fresh blackberries
- ¼ cup sugar
- 3 tbsp all-purpose flour
- 2 tbsp lemon juice
- ½ tsp cinnamon

FOR ICING:

- 1 cup Powder sugar
- 1/2 lemon

INSTRUCTIONS

In your machine, preheat the Air Fryer by wiping clean and preheat if necessary.

FOR FILLING: Rinse and lay the blackberries on a plate covered with a paper towel.

Set sideways for 1 hour to allow drying of the berries.

Cut in half, and put in a medium tub.

Add the sugar, lemon juice, cinnamon and flour and combine to toss.

Pour over your blackberry mixture into a medium cooked saucepan.

Mash the berries until slightly chunky, with a potato masher.

Turn off the heat, and set sideways.

PIE: Use your countertop or spread flour on top to cover with cutting board.

Lay the pie crusts and roll them gently out to 1/4 "thickness. Use a large circle cookie cutter to cut out 6 circles. Place the dough circles on a baking sheet. Put 1 tbsp of filling in the middle of the pie dough. Blend the edges of the pie dough with the beaten egg. Fold the dough over and press the dough with your fingertips to seal.

ICING: In a small bowl, add iced ingredients.

Mix until well combined with a whisk Let it cool slightly and top with an icing drizzle

NUTRITIONAL INFORMATION

Air Fryer Blackberry Hand Pies

Amount Per Serving

Calories 292Calories from Fat 72% Daily Value, Fat 8g12%, Saturated Fat 2g13%, Cholesterol 27mg9%, Sodium 127mg6%, Potassium 141mg4%, Carbohydrates 51g17%, Fiber 4g17%. Sugar 31g34%, Protein 3g6%, Vitamin A 160IU3%, Vitamin C 18.6mg23%, Calcium 30mg3%, Iron 1.4mg8%

400. CRUSTY ARTISAN BREAD

INGREDIENTS

- 3-4 cups all-purpose flour
- 1 tsp salt
- 1/2 tsp dry active yeast
- 1-1/2 cups lukewarm water 115 degrees is perfect

INSTRUCTIONS

In a medium-size bowl, combine 3 cups of the flour along side the opposite ingredients & mix with a wooden spoon until fully combined

Place wrapping over the highest of the dough (touching the dough- not just covering the highest of the bowl)

Set aside during a warm, dark place to rest a minimum of 8 hours (up to about 24 hours)

Remove dough from bowl & place on a well-floured surface & work into a ball (if it's too wet or sticky you'll work more flour in- but it shouldn't be too firm)

Allow resting approx half-hour

Place forged iron dutch oven with lid in oven & preheat oven to 450 degrees

Carefully remove once preheated & spray rock bottom with cooking spray

Place dough within the pot, slash the highest several times

Cover & bake half-hour

Remove lid & bake a further 10-15 minutes or until golden & brown

(you know it's done if it sounds hollow when tapped together with your fingernail)

Cool slightly before serving

9 781801 156738